The Complete Consumer Car Guide

The Complete Consumer Car Guide

by
Mike Spaniola

McGraw-Hill Book Company

New York   St. Louis   San Francisco   Auckland
Bogotá   Hamburg   Johannesburg   London
Madrid   Mexico   Milan   Montreal   New Delhi
Panama   Paris   São Paulo   Singapore
Sydney   Tokyo   Toronto

1 2 3 4 5 6 7 8 9 D O C D O C 8 7

ISBN 0-07-059806-1

Library of Congress Cataloging-in-Publication Data

Spaniola, Mike.
  The complete consumer car guide.

  Includes bibliographies and index.
  1. Automobiles.   2. Automobiles—Purchasing.
3. Consumer education.   I. Title.
TL162.S63   1987   629.2′222   86-20154
ISBN 0-07-059806-1

Editing Supervisor: Margery Luhrs

Contents

chapter 1

New-Car Shopping: Life in the Slick Lane

"All That Glitters Isn't Chrome"

You know more about new-car buying than you realize. If you had to sum it all up in one sentence, it would probably be: "Do I like the car?" And although you may not be able to readily list certain intangibles, you know your new car should meet the majority of your practical needs, while suiting your self-image and lifestyle as well.

But for many of us, the excitement ends when the wheeling and dealing begin; we feel ill at ease. Understanding the new-car buying game often determines whether you win or lose. And this chapter is dedicated to making you a winner.

Automotive Sales: Personnel and Techniques

In the words of the Council of Better Business Bureaus, "Don't delude yourself into thinking that all dealers handling specific makes are the same."

So, how do you find that sincerest of new-car dealers and sales staff? Well, good dealerships breed good salespeople. Find one, and you're bound to have found the other.

Professional automobile salespeople don't sell you a car; they assist you in *choosing* one. And given that commissions are a large part of their income, professional, customer-oriented automotive salespeople are generally found at dealerships that keep the customer satisfied; in most instances, these dealerships have good service departments. A professional salesperson will not waste time building a clientele only to lose customers to poor after-the-sale service. And should worse come to worst, a good service department means the difference between a car that is a lemon and one that is not. It's all a matter of expertise.

Dealerships *earn* good reputations—not through the use of gimmicky slogans. Dealerships that consistently advertise "Name your own price," "We beat any deal in town," or "We undersell our competition" warrant a caution flag. No business can operate long in such a fashion; it's economically impossible. A business cannot continually "give away the house" and pay the mortgage on it. Customers who do not realize this fact naively foot the bill. "Deep discount" ads may get you in the front door, but the bottom line on the sales contract seldom reflects these claims.

Salespeople ask a lot of questions, so ask a few of your own. "How long have you been selling cars?" (Not toasters or sprinkler systems.) Anyone can sell you a car, but can this person knowledgeably assist you in choosing one? Are there certificates on display indicating that the salesperson attends company-sponsored seminars that promote product knowledge? You are expected to know your job, so why expect less from the salesperson?

Is the salesperson with whom you are dealing willing to show and explain the advantages and disadvantages of different models, to let you test-drive three or four cars? Or is the salesperson simply looking to make a quick deal? Remember, you are *paying* this person to perform a service. Ask yourself, "Why should I buy a car from this salesperson?" Ask the sales representative, "What can you do for *me*?"

Visit the dealership's service department. If possible, have your present car serviced there. Is the service department organized? Service bays strewn with old parts, haphazardly placed tools, and an excess of personal effects all invite lost work orders, parts, and tools—inefficiencies that add up to a bottom line of bigger repair bills and longer, less effective service visits.

Find out how many cars the dealership services on an average day and how many service managers they employ. A good ratio is 1 service manager per 28 service orders. Service managers are your liaison with the mechanics. If a service manager is too busy, that person will have time neither to listen attentively to your problem nor to properly relay the details to the service staff. Some of the more highly praised dealership service departments employ 1 service manager per 16 service orders.

Better dealerships also have a customer relations representative who, after repairs are completed, calls to confirm that all went well. Better dealerships provide new-car buyers with booklets that list competitive repair prices, maintenance schedules, hours of operation, and other pertinent information. Some service departments are open 6 days a week, with hours that rival those of neighborhood convenience stores. The better the service department, the more a dealership values everyone knowing that fact.

Does the service department have rental cars available for its service customers? What is the charge? Under what conditions are loaners (rental cars free of charge) available? Will the service department provide transportation to your home or to work after you have dropped off your car? Do they accept checks and charge cards?

Of course, you would be fortunate to have such a well-managed dealership nearby. But they *are* out there—find one! Too often, service personnel lead the public to believe, "We're doing everything we can to repair your car as quickly as possible." You know better now, so put that knowledge to use in deciding where to buy an expensive asset—your next new car.

Reading Between the Lines: Automotive Advertising

Once you're out in the marketplace, advertising becomes a major factor in influencing your buying decisions. Manufacturers provide general market appeal; dealerships provide specific market deals.

Overall, be wary. Advertising needn't always be moral to be legal; courts have ruled that many forms of advertisement are not offers to sell but merely "invitations to bargain," unless very explicit language is used.

Automakers tend to get the buying public infatuated with select makes and models, knowing that the image of superior models will translate into sales of more practical ones. Chevrolet spends millions promoting the Corvette, a car for which consumer demand has always exceeded production goals. Likewise, manufacturers support professional racing, because it's long been an industry axiom that "what races on Sunday, sells on Monday" (see Figs. 1-1 and 1-2). This automotive sleight of hand can narrow your perception of the automotive marketplace, causing you to overlook cars that may be better suited to your needs. Don't let corporate advertising preprogram you; remain open-minded.

Fig. 1-1   This Ford Motor Co. public relations photograph illustrates more than meets the eye. It encompasses the old automotive marketing adage "What races on Sunday, sells on Monday." (*Courtesy Ford Motor Co.*)

Fig. 1-2 The Corvette. Did it subliminally get you to buy a Chevette? (*Courtesy Chevrolet Motor Division.*)

Dealership ads tug at consumer purse strings. "The deal of a lifetime," "easy credit terms," and supposed "markdowns" may bring in customers, but these "deals" tend to be little more than figments of the dealer's imagination. Some common examples:

"We sell at wholesale!" Of course, all dealers sell at wholesale prices—to one another. This doesn't mean they are going to sell to *you* at wholesale.

"Push it, pull it—$1000 for any used car!" Along with this enticement will be new-car prices. If a model is advertised for "only" $7000, unwary consumers will subtract the $1000 trade-in value, believing the new car sells for $6000. The dealer really wants $8000, though; the "$1000 minimum trade-in value" has already been deducted from the advertised price. Should your trade-in be worth much less than the $1000 the dealer gives you, the new-car price will be increased accordingly; you can count on that.

"All new cars only $99 over our cost! We will show you the factory invoice!" This is a loaded but perfectly legal statement. It does not reflect dealer holdback—a sum periodically paid to dealers by the manufacturer *after* the sale. Holdback amounts are generally 2 to 3 percent of the retail price. Some dealers even *charge* the customer for the holdback and state as much in the sales contract: "plus the holdback cost which is returned to dealer." New-car buyers think this is a legitimate reimbursement and legally, though unwittingly, approve of this double-dipping by signing the contract. Also, dealers receive volume discounts throughout the year. These discounts, like holdbacks, are not reflected on the invoice, because they are tallied after the sale.

"Free sunroof, rustproofing . . . (you name it, etc.)!" Nothing is free. People do, however, develop a psychological block against further bargaining when they are told they are receiving $500 worth of options "free." This cost is almost always reflected in a higher cost for the complete automobile.

"$500 rebate on these models!" or *"Low-interest loans available!"* Check these qualifying terms carefully. Some apply only to certain models, to cars purchased between specified dates, or to cars delivered to the customer within a specified time. These may often be bait-and-switch tactics, with rebates applied only to the undesirable, slower-selling models. If a dealer contribution is required, the cost of your new car is sure to reflect this portion of the rebate, nullifying any potential savings.

When perusing the new-car ads, carefully examine those with asterisks or fine print that call attention to "participating dealers only." If you find an attractive offer—one with special financing or warranty terms—be sure the dealership you visit participates in these programs.

New-Car Sales Techniques

"The customer needs to be *pushed* off the fence—with a good hard close. . . . You will never have a better chance to close than when that customer is at that nervous, doubtful, threatening peak of interest. You must push him into a positive decision."

Passage from a sales manual

After a period of new-car shopping, you will begin thinking, "What am I waiting for? I'll wind up shopping around for weeks. I like this car; I'll buy it." Careful! That really isn't you thinking; it's your salesperson.

Salespeople look for common ground between themselves and their customers—families, friends, occupations, and hobbies are good topics of conversation. While this makes for a fine exchange of pleasantries, once the customer is softened, the selling game begins.

The salesperson monitors the conversation for opportunities to close (finalize) the deal by overcoming the customer's nagging doubts—the fear of making a bad decision. The customer is fighting impulse, hoping to think more carefully later. The salesperson, on the other hand, is encouraging the emotions, hoping the customer will react spontaneously.

A common ploy, sometimes referred to as power selling, puts the customer in a positive frame of mind by the repetition of questions invoking a yes answer: "Nice day, isn't it?" Even the customer's questions may be turned around: "Is this model available with a vinyl top?" The salesperson replies, "Do you *want* a vinyl top?" or the salesperson might say, "I think you'd really enjoy this car, wouldn't you?" The customer might respond, "Sure, but I can't afford it." Now comes the hard sell.

Customer: "The car costs too much."

Seller: "There's no denying that's a lot of money, but let's delete an option. It may be a matter of too much car instead of too much money. And if it still costs too much, let's take off another option (etc., etc., ad nauseam)."

Customer: "I want to discuss it with my spouse."

Seller: "That's a good idea; I'm sure I'd want to do the same thing. But wouldn't it be too bad if your spouse liked this car and we couldn't agree on figures? Let's do this. Let's see if we can arrive at some mutually agreeable figures. We'll put an order together just to show your spouse. That's OK, isn't it?"

In these examples, note that the conversation is never allowed to die. The salesperson continually challenges the buyer to come up with excuse after excuse, hoping the customer will finally break. What a way to buy a car!

Although it might be wise to draw up prices for the bank, do so only because *you* want to and not because you were baited into it. The best way to avoid being baited is to relax and simply restate your intentions—"I'm still shopping," or "I want to discuss it with other parties." Refuse to answer further questions. Use negative body language: fold your arms, rub your eyes, yawn, but don't let a salesperson preempt your common sense. You, after all, have to live with the car and its payments; the salesperson is most concerned with closing a sale.

There is also a showroom technique called the "six-position sell," a minitour around the exterior of a vehicle (see Fig. 1-3). It aids a salesperson in quickly judging the effectiveness of the sales spiel and the receptiveness of the customer. The first spot in which the salesperson and prospective customer stand is at the center front of the car, where the salesperson describes the grille, bumper, and other features within proximity; the second position is at the passenger side of the car; the third position, at the rear of the passenger door; the fourth position, at the rear of the vehicle; and the fifth position, just behind the driver's door. The salesperson then opens the driver's door for the customer. It is said that if a prospective customer opens the door without prompting and sits inside, the salesperson has done a very good job of applying the six-position sell and has an equally good chance of selling the vehicle.

Deciding on the Best Car for Your Needs

The better prepared you are in your search for that new car, the smoother and more rewarding will be the transaction. Here's a list of questions to consider. Give some thought to the answers beforehand; it's better to think things over in familiar surroundings than at the dealership. Seek the

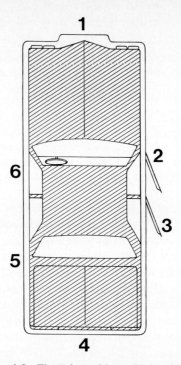

Fig. 1-3 The "six-position sell" is said to help a salesperson quickly size up a customer's intentions. The salesperson tours the vehicle with the customer, stopping briefly at the numbered points. (*Illustration by Art Spaniola*)

input of your family members, and anticipate future needs. New cars are kept by their original owners for an average of 5.2 years.

- What will be the primary use of the car? Is it to be a second car or the only car? Will it be a commuter? Will more than one person be driving the car?

- How well does your present car satisfy your cargo and passenger needs? How often will you be traveling with children, and how many of them are under the age of 12? Do you regularly take pets with you?

- Will the car be used frequently on long business trips? Do you plan to take frequent vacation drives, and will you be pulling a trailer or doing any other such towing?

- Are warranty terms and extended-service coverage plans something you want to consider in selecting your next car?

• Is owner serviceability important? Can routine items such as washer and brake fluids, coolant, and oil levels be checked easily?

• Was the upkeep on your last car too high, and should you consider a model with lower maintenance and operating costs?

• How severe are the winters, and what effect will this have on your driving needs? Will your vehicle be kept in a garage?.

• How much do you have for a down payment, and how much can you afford for a monthly payment?

• Keeping both budget and practicality in mind, list the following in order of their importance to you: economy, luxury, performance, prestige.

Selecting the Correct Model

There are four basic model sizes—subcompact, compact, intermediate, and full size. Models are further defined by body styles. For example, Chevrolet (the *make*) assembles the Caprice (a full-size *model*), which is available as a two-door coupe; a four-door sedan; or a four-door, three-seat station wagon (the *body styles*).

Coupes, whether two-door or four-door, are generally more stylish and have greater window visibility. Sedans, on the other hand, whether two-door or four-door, usually have larger window pillars and appear boxier, but they are roomier and sturdier than coupes (see Fig. 1-4). Hatchbacks are two-door or four-door compacts with a back window that opens up as a trunk lid might. Most also provide for a fold-down mechanism on the back seat. Because of this arrangement of the rear trunk and window, a two-door hatchback may be referred to as a three-door, and a four-door hatchback as a five-door.

Subcompacts make good second cars and are typically used for short jaunts around town. As a primary means of transportation, their stiffer ride and above-average noise level can be annoying, but their economy and maneuverability are certainly assets.

Compacts are excellent cars for commuting, and they combine the best of the intermediate and the subcompact—provided that seating for no more than two adults and one small child is anticipated. The backseat in most compacts serves in a pinch, but most are more cosmetic than functional. Trunk space in compacts needs to be evaluated individually. Overall, compacts offer economy, ease of operation, and versatility of body style—two-door, four-door, hatchback, station wagon—which subcompacts lack (see Fig. 1-5).

Intermediates offer a good compromise between roominess, comfort, and price. These models usually meet the needs of a family of four or five. Intermediates also seem to be available with more options than either

Fig. 1-4 The Ford Thunderbird coupe (*top*) and Ford LTD Crown Victoria sedan (*bottom*) contrast the basic differences between coupe and sedan body styles. (*Courtesy Ford Motor Co.*)

subcompact or compact models. Intermediates can seat four adults comfortably, and five less comfortably. Four-door models offer more backseat space, smaller door size for easier clearance, and greater boarding ease than two-door models (see Fig. 1-6).

Full-size cars offer roomy interiors, are more opulently appointed, and have large trunks. Many full-size cars are sturdy sedans that ride smoother and better accommodate a full line of options; in test collisions, they are safer too. Full-size cars, though, are the most expensive to operate. Their resale value hinges on the highly unpredictable cost of fuel. The attractions of a full-size car are room and comfort with a touch of luxury.

Station wagons, while never in vogue, do offer the most sensible choice for those who need or would like a maximum of both passenger

Fig. 1-5 The Renault Encore is a compact hatchback. The lift-up rear window is sometimes referred to as an extra door, which accounts for model descriptions such as three- and five-door hatchbacks. (*Courtesy American Motors Corp.*)

and cargo space. Station wagons are now available in a wider range of models; you can "have your cake and eat it, too" by ordering a compact or intermediate-sized station wagon. Granted, the cargo and passenger space may be greater with a standard full-size vehicle, but you get a good compromise between room and price with smaller cars. The extra cost of a station wagon, though, is a fickle commodity to try to recoup at resale

Fig. 1-6 Intermediate models offer good all-around versatility. This Mercury Sable is available in a choice of body styles and offers room and style without big-car operating costs. (*Courtesy Ford Motor Co.*)

time. Station wagons, it seems, will never be anyone's idea of a "dream" car (see Fig. 1-6).

Minivans are in vogue, and with good reason: they fill a niche in the van and station wagon market. "If customers are satisfied that the minivan handles like a car," says Jack Madejchick, Chevrolet's marketing director, "then it's probably the station wagon of the future." Minivans boast fuel economy, handling, utility, and style that have been difficult to achieve in vans. Unlike full-size vans, minivans fit easily into home garages and car washes. They can seat more adults in more comfort than station wagons can, and they enable passengers to move about inside

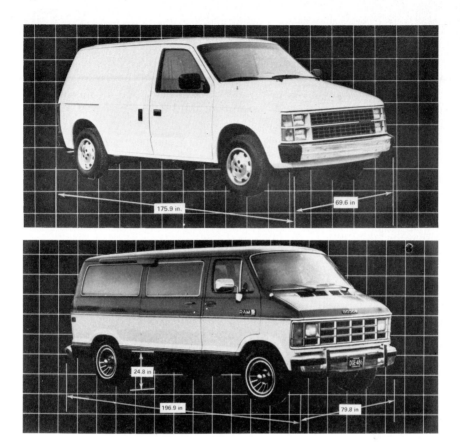

Fig. 1-7 Note the more compact dimensions of the minivan (*top*) as compared with the full-size version (*bottom*). This design allows minivans to fit into most home garages and offers carlike passenger entry, both popular features. (*Courtesy Chrysler Corp.*)

more easily. Some minivans have seats that can be removed for hauling cargo (see Fig. 1-7).

These downsize vans offer carlike interiors and options and, overall, are competitively priced with automobiles. Although minivans are classified as trucks according to some industry sources and the U.S. government, many—especially Chrysler minivans—are sold to the car-buying public.

Full-size vans may be roomier than minivans, but they are usually more expensive to purchase and operate, more awkward to handle, and have limited driver visibility. Additionally, the design of their "step up" to the passenger compartment is not a plus with some buyers. Full-size vans are best left to commercial use. (With station wagons and vans, consider your payload. Too heavy a load means you'll wear out tires, springs, and axles faster. Check with your dealer for particulars.)

While the difference in price between the four basic model sizes has become increasingly blurred, respective differences in operating costs have not varied all that much. A great sales deal on a full-size vehicle with high operating costs is *no* bargain. (Minivans can be placed in the category of intermediate models for operating-cost comparisons.)

At 12,000 miles a year, the difference in first-year operating costs between a subcompact and a compact is more than $1000; between a compact and an intermediate, more than $500; and between a compact and a full-size car, about $1700. (Figures are based on average U.S. automobile operating costs, published annually by the Hertz Corporation, and include depreciation, insurance, licenses, registration, inspection and other fees, plus interest, maintenance, accessories, and repairs, along with gasoline and other service station charges.)

Other Considerations

You may wish to check Chapter 2 for a more complete discussion of manufacturer warranties. What happens if service problems arise with your new vehicle? What recourse is available beyond the dealership and the manufacturer's regional office? Ford and Chrysler operate their own arbitration programs. Some manufacturers use the National Automobile Dealers Association's AUTOCAP program, but this program is not nationwide, and not all eligible dealers participate.

Other manufacturers, such as GM, American Motors, and Nissan, use the Better Business Bureau's Auto Line program. With Auto Line, the consumer has a say in choosing the arbitrator; with other programs, you may never even know who was involved in the decision-making process. No single arbitration program has all the answers, but not all programs are equal, either. Chapter 2 lists arbitration programs by automaker and details the nuances and pitfalls of each.

The National Highway Traffic Safety Administration (NHTSA) operates a toll-free auto safety hotline that provides callers with information regarding auto safety recalls, crash test results, fuel economy ratings, and other consumer information related to operating and maintaining a vehicle. This information may help you decide among the last two or three remaining makes and models on your list. The NHTSA number within the continental United States, the Virgin Islands, and parts of Puerto Rico is (800) 424-9393, and from Washington, D.C., Alaska, or Hawaii, call (202) 426-0123 (a toll call). The hotline is also available to the hearing-impaired through teleprinter receiving and sending facilities found in many libraries and public institutions serving the deaf. The toll-free teleprinter number is (800) 424-9153; in Washington, D.C., 755-8919.

At your local library, you may want to peruse back issues of *Consumer Reports* (April is the new-car buying issue), and *The Car Book* by Jack Gillis. Gillis's book is updated annually to provide the most recent economy and safety results on the latest makes and models.

The best time to shop for car insurance is *before* you buy the car. A vehicle's ease of repair, cost of replacement parts, resistance to damage, theft rate, and personal liability record all determine insurance cost. Cadillacs and Corvettes, for instance, are usually expensive to insure because they are expensive to repair and have high theft rates. But did you know that the Volkswagen Rabbit Convertible placed right between the two in terms of theft one year?

Insurance costs abound with surprises—especially now that expensive-to-repair unibodies are fast becoming an industry standard. A phone call to your agent is all it takes to check. For more on vehicle insurance, consult Chapter 4.

Option Selection

Not all options increase resale value, but all options do increase the sale price and the salesperson's commission. Options that are worthwhile are of value throughout ownership and at resale time as well. Of course, everyone has some personal but not-so-practical option favorites that would be sorely missed even at twice the price; so treat yourself, or suffer a bout of buyer's remorse.

Engine size is defined by volume displacement and number of cylinders, usually four, six, or eight. An L-4 is an in-line, four-cylinder engine—the cylinders are all in one row, or line (see Fig. 1-8). A V-6 is a six-cylinder engine with three cylinders on each side, forming a V arrangement when viewed from the front. An L-6 is an in-line, six-cylinder engine in which all cylinders are in one line. A V-8 has eight cylinders, four to a side. Some engines are better balanced in a V configuration than in-line. Engine balance produces smoother idling and less operating vibration. Certain Chrysler, Mitsubishi, and Porsche in-line engines also incorporate balance shafts to accomplish this (see Fig. 1-9).

Cubic-inch displacement (CID) was once used to describe engine displacement, but now that engines have been downsized and metric measurements adapted, the use of liters (L) has become commonplace. In general terms, displacement relates directly to the power of an engine. The larger the displacement figure, the more powerful the engine; the smaller the figure, the less the power but the better the overall economy.

Fig. 1-8 Cross section of an in-line four-cylinder engine. Displacement is 1.6 liters. (*Courtesy Chrysler Corp.*)

Subcompacts and compacts do well with 2.0-L four-cylinder engines; intermediates with 2.0-L to 4.0-L four- or six-cylinder engines; and full-size vehicles with six- to eight-cylinder engines of at least 3.0 L. (One liter of displacement equals approximately 61.02 cubic inches of displacement: 2.0 L = 122 CID, 2.8 L = 170 CID, 3.5 L = 214 CID, 5.0 L = 305 CID, and 5.7 L = 348 CID.)

Standard engines (those included in the base price) generally suffice for city and some highway driving, but opt for the next size larger if you routinely load a car with passengers or materials or if you plan to pull a

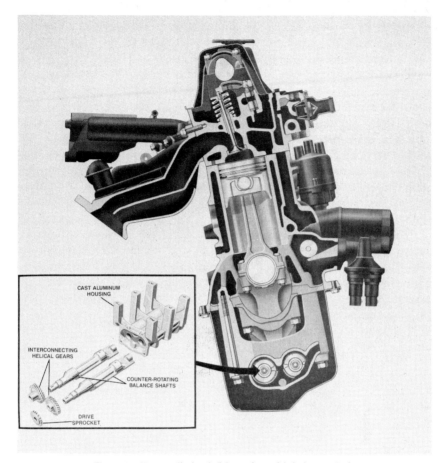

Fig. 1-9   Four-cylinder 2.5-L engine with balance shafts.

trailer or a boat. If you do the majority of your driving at highway speeds, a four-cylinder of less than 2.2 L is not recommended; you would be sending a pony to do a horse's job. Full-size, and some intermediate, models may already be factory-equipped with large six- or eight-cylinder engines that will handle most driving needs.

Fuel-injection systems are better economically and functionally than carbureted engines. Fuel injection provides a more precise means of metering fuel and eliminates many of the mechanical adjustments associated with carburetors. Electronic fuel injection (EFI) is better than throttle-body fuel injection because it is more precise.

Turbocharger units can be added to engines with fuel injection to increase midrange and top-end performance. Turbochargers recirculate exhaust gases to compress combustion air-fuel mixtures and can increase the horsepower of a small engine 35 to 60 percent without raising overall fuel consumption (see Fig. 1-10).

Turbochargers require adherence to special operational procedures and require more frequent oil changes. Turbocharger temperatures can reach 600°F, which can char oil and, if charring is excessive, may require the eventual overhaul of the unit. Although not widely available, inter-cooled turbochargers, which use a water-cooled bearing housing, are best. Intercoolers also increase turbocharger air-intake density by cooling it, which increases horsepower. Some say turbochargers are risky propositions in any form, but Chrysler has been selling three times as many as their nearest competitors and provides a 5-year/50,000-mile warranty as well.

One last point on engine selection: new-car sales personnel may not always recommend a larger-than-standard-size engine even though they would benefit from the price increase. In these days of EPA-enforced fuel-economy standards, a salesperson might be following a company mandate to steer customers away from larger, less fuel-efficient engines. Automakers face millions of dollars in fines if they do not meet yearly fuel-economy standards set by the EPA (Corporate Average Fuel Economy, or CAFE, standards).

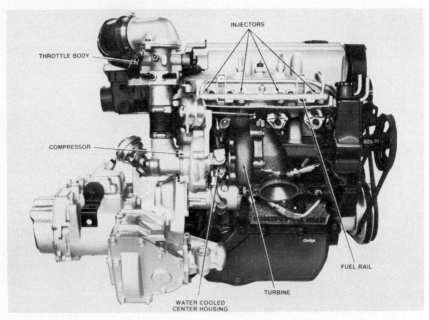

Fig. 1-10   Turbocharged multipoint electronic fuel-injected 2.2-L engine.

Diesel engines.   With their reputation for ruggedness and fuel economy, diesel engines may still tempt a few, but this applies only to the vehicles in which they truly belong: trucks. Under-the-hood space in cars will not accommodate the monster diesels that are worthwhile. As a market reflection of this fact, diesel engines powered 6.6 percent of all new cars in 1981 but dropped to 1.4 percent in 1983.

With a diesel engine, acceleration is sluggish, and starting in cold weather can be troublesome. Because of the extreme susceptibility of the fuel to moisture, diesel engines may stall, bog, and offer just plain temperamental performance. In addition, some people complain of unpleasant diesel fumes. Furthermore, a large part of the initial diesel attraction is gone: the price of diesel fuel now rivals that of unleaded gas, and this shrinking price difference no longer offsets the added cost of a diesel engine.

Front-wheel versus rear-wheel drive.   Because of the forward consolidation of the driving mechanisms, front-wheel-drive (FWD) vehicles have two major advantages: their weight is concentrated above the drive wheels, which makes for better control on slick roads, and they allow for more passenger and storage space than rear-wheel-drive (RWD) vehicles of the same dimensions. RWD vehicles are less expensive to repair than FWDs, which have a transaxle design, and because RWDs better accommodate longer wheelbases and larger load limits, they generally provide for higher towing capacities and a smoother ride.

Transmissions.   The majority of cars now have automatic transmissions, some with fourth-gear overdrive. And with the revival of sporty vehicles, a four-on-the-floor, preferably with overdrive (a fifth-speed), is again popular. To opt for a manual transmission to increase fuel efficiency, though, is no longer as valid as before, because automatic transmissions are being continually redesigned to facilitate better gas mileage.

The trend with many station-wagon and passenger-truck models is toward four-wheel drive (4WD). Most vehicles are either front-wheel *or* rear-wheel drive—that is, two-wheel drive. With a 4WD vehicle, the driver can gear power to all *four* wheels for twice the traction on slippery roads. Once the sole domain of off-road vehicles, many city dwellers now find the added security and safety of 4WD to be a real plus. Vehicles with 4WD, however, do not *stop* any more efficiently on slippery roads than do their two-wheel-drive counterparts, and operation in 4WD does not enhance fuel economy. Still, very little extra maintenance is required with 4WD vehicles unless you do a lot of off-road driving (see Fig. 1-11).

If you are considering 4WD, look for units that can be shifted while the vehicle is in motion and that do not require securing outside wheel adjustments (''locking hubs''). Also, some manufacturers offer 4WD units that switch automatically from two- to four-wheel drive in response

Fig. 1-11   In days of yore, rugged individuals would stand in knee-deep mud and snow, engaging four-wheel-drive locking hubs. Today, four-wheel-drive can be engaged from the driver's seat, one reason for its increasing popularity in both cars and trucks. (*Courtesy Ford Motor Co.*)

to driving conditions. These units are the most convenient, especially if you plan to use 4WD only for inclement weather. This technology is not without its price, and the more sophisticated the unit, the more expensive it is.

Power steering and brakes.   While in motion, subcompacts and compacts may steer well without power-assist steering, but try turning the wheels at a standstill before making your decision. With larger models, if power steering is not standard, order it; it improves parking ease, which may someday save you from scraping the side of your car. New models will soon be converting to electrically assisted power steering, which offers better performance than conventional hydraulic units. As for brakes, nearly all new cars have either two- or four-wheel power-assist disc brakes; yours should too. And if an antilocking braking system (ABS) is available as an option, its computer-activated ability to prevent skids on slick surfaces is a safety feature well worth the extra money.

Sound systems.   Automakers were singing the blues over losing option money to the "aftermarket" in this category. They responded by updating and improving their factory offerings. Although still more expensive than many aftermarket systems, factory systems now offer quality sound and features such as seek-and-scan, cassette auto-reverse and search, and graphic equalizers. A factory radio will generally improve both interior appearance and resale value with the factory neatness they impart to the dashboard area. Less than 2 percent of cars now have AM-only radios, about 15 percent have AM/FM, more than 25 percent have AM/FM stereo cassette-radios, and nearly half are equipped with AM/FM stereos. Resale value is a consideration here.

Air conditioning, tinted windows.   More than 70 percent of passenger cars are now equipped with manually controlled air conditioning, and nearly 90 percent have tinted window glass throughout. A combination of the two does pay off at resale time, and both options have become much appreciated, if not taken for granted, even in northern climates. Order both if you can afford them.

Aftermarket installation is not a viable alternative here. Air conditioning needs to be integrated with the heater and dashboard ductwork to be completely effective, and the factory air option usually includes a larger engine fan and radiator as well. Also, installation of an aftermarket unit has an afterthought appearance that detracts from the looks and legroom of the interior, and therefore, from the resale value.

Cruise control.   Cruise control is a recommended option unless the vehicle will be used primarily for city driving. Today, many people spend more time in freeway traffic than before, and to the many who are accustomed to cruise control, this option has become a necessity. Some units merely maintain a set speed; others allow you to increase or decrease vehicle speed and will automatically reset, all with the touch of a steering-wheel-mounted button or switch. Others allow you to accelerate without disengaging, but the unit must be reset to continue at that speed.

Tilt steering wheel.   If you have long legs or are pregnant often, or both, buy it.

Power door locks and windows.   Much of this equipment is now standard on top-of-the-line models, and is often expected at resale time. Power door locks provide great safety and convenience when traveling with small children or when traversing the less-than-wholesome parts of town. Power windows, on the other hand, are a nuisance when traveling with small children, but if you travel solo a majority of the time, power windows allow you to forgo the acrobatics of manual window operation.

Power seats.   Power seats are a luxury option, especially now that many front seats are designed orthopedically and have a variety of manually adjustable positions. In the past, only two positions were available without power seats: forward and backward. Power seats do offer a height advantage for someone who has problems seeing over the dashboard: power seats move up and down, one thing many fancy manual seats can't do.

Glass-inlaid rear-window defogger.   To clear window fogging, this is a highly recommended safety feature, even in warmer climates. Fan-operated units are less effective; some don't work at all.

Remote-control sideview mirror, intermittent wipers.   If you can afford them (and perhaps you can by judiciously eliminating other options), both offer great convenience and safety. A remote-control mirror is especially handy if two or more people will be driving and readjusting the mirrors of the car.

Vinyl roof, wheel covers. Order these according to your budget and taste. Although some salespeople will swear to the contrary, neither option much influences resale value, except in the case of some top-line models. Even most factory-standard hubcaps look good these days. On the other hand, wire wheel covers are a seldom refused invitation to thieves. Don't let so-called factory "locks" sway you, either; "replacement keys" are often available at auto-parts stores, and if not, thieves do what comes naturally—they steal one.

Exterior color and paint. The trend in exterior colors has been toward reddish brown, red, white, light or dark blue, and silver. Color can affect resale value, and it is usually the garish ones that detract: yellow, orange, and bright reds. Beige is generally a safe bet. Also consider that black shows dirt and scratches easily, and some reds tend to oxidize in sunny climates. Japanese automakers created the demand for pearl metallic paints. The high gloss and depth of these basecoat and clearcoat finishes are very attractive, but they require skilled and expensive refinishing techniques—the higher the metallic content, the more difficult the paint is to match. On the other hand, gloss whites and reds are some of the easiest finishes to match.

Sunroofs. Sunroofs, sometimes called "moon roofs," are more likely to create wind noise and water leaks as the moldings deteriorate with age. You will then get fresh air whether you want it or not. If you insist, the type that can be unlatched and popped open is best; crank-handle operation is best left to more expensive models with more expensive engineering designs. Consider aftermarket installation, too; these appear factory-installed and are less expensive.

Clocks. With computerized cars becoming more common, clocks have become increasingly standard in some shape and location. If your car does not have one, order one—your dashboard will look bare without it, and the clock will still fill space when it quits working in a couple of years.

Fabric sealer for upholstery. Factory-sealed upholstery is a worthwhile option, especially for buyers with small children and pets—or you can buy a commercial spray-on fabric sealer every 6 months and apply it yourself. Better yet, order vinyl seats.

Undercoating. Although it deadens sound, undercoating is not a rust deterrent. Subcompacts and compacts, especially, benefit if the undercoating is properly applied.

Rustproofing. Factory metal treatments and extended rust-through warranties are making rustproofing obsolete. This option dies hard with both customer and salesperson alike, and as long as there's a market, dealers will keep selling it. A $200 rustproofing job is viewed as a mere pittance in safeguarding your $10,000-plus investment. In reality, rustproofing provides peace of mind more than anything else.

Before committing to an option, check to see if any strings are attached. For example, buyers of the 1984 Renault Alliance subcompact could not order an optional $97 five-speed transmission unless they also ordered a $506 interior-exterior package, which, of course, had nothing to do with the transmission. That same year the base-model Pontiac Fiero could not be ordered with either air conditioning or an automatic transmission unless the buyer spent hundreds to upgrade the entire car. These are but two of the many examples that abound with all manufacturers—so look out.

Test Drives

Once you've determined which options you prefer, test-drive a dealer car equipped in a similar fashion. Review your reasons for certain options; if, for example, you ordered power seats to raise the line of vision, do they accomplish this purpose? Most important, be sure you test-drive a vehicle with the same mechanical options: engine, transmission, suspension, and tires—*they are not all the same,* not by a long shot.

Writers at new-model press previews may drive as many as two dozen different models. They do so because there can be great differences in performance and handling. It is unfortunate that new-car buyers cannot personally experience this fact; however, do test-drive! Sure, the salesperson would rather sit around writing up new-car orders all day long, but you're not "imposing" by asking for test drives.

Test drives do not require a technical knowledge of cars. The test drive itself should be 2 to 3 miles long. Acclimate yourself to the vehicle; judge its ride, handling, and performance characteristics by asking yourself: Do I feel comfortable behind the wheel? Am I satisfied with the vehicle's response? Do I like the way the vehicle rides and handles? Take a few corners sharply, accelerate briskly, and experiment with options: Does that optional $700 factory sound system *really* strike a chord in you?

Automotive salespeople generally prefer to warm up the car by driving it first. By all means, though, insist on chauffeuring the salesperson. Driving the vehicle cold should be part of your test drive. Electing to drive first may also spare you further sales bantering. When salespeople drive first, they usually have a preordained spot at which they turn the wheel over to you—but not before they again walk you around the vehicle while further extolling its virtues.

If a sale appears imminent and the distance is practical, you may be urged to drive past your home. This is said to be a sure-fire method of closing a deal; once a prospective new-car buyer sees the car on home turf, emotions run high—especially if the neighbors are watching!

Getting the Best Price

Because many people don't know what a dealer really pays for a car, they are never really convinced that they got a good deal and privately berate themselves for not having bargained more. But pricing information is out there, so guess no longer.

New-Car Pricing Guides

The lowdown on retail ("sticker") versus wholesale price (dealer cost) can be found at your local bookstore or magazine stand. Ask for a copy of either Edmund's or Pace Publication's *New Car Prices*. These guides go for about $3 and contain a wealth of information, including base-model and option availability and their retail and wholesale prices.

Edmund's and Pace frequently publish price updates. Edmund's domestic new-car price editions are published three times a year—in February, June, and November—and cover GM, Ford, Chrysler, and AMC models. The foreign new-car price editions, which cover 21 makes and more than 200 models, are published twice a year, in April and August.

Pace publishes its new-car price guides in February, April, June, October, and December; its *New Truck and Van Prices* in January, March, May, July, and November; and its *New and Used Foreign Car Prices* in March, June, September, and December. The latter lists 21 makes; Pace did not have a figure on the number of models the guide included. These price guides list dealer cost and retail ("sticker") price for both vehicle and options, enabling you to determine your leverage in dealer negotiations.

One guide user wrote Pace Publications: "My husband and I began to shop for a new car about four months ago, and five different salespeople told us five different things about the same car. I found a copy of your *Buyer's Guide Report* and was amazed to find out how uninformed the car-buying public really is. From then on we had the upper hand when visiting a dealership; one salesperson was even downright rude when he found out how well informed we were. The salesperson from whom we purchased our car realized we had our facts and figures on paper, and we got a deal that was fair to both parties."

Both guides list new cars by make and model, available body styles, and standard equipment—including base engine. Destination charges, dealer cost, and list price for all available options are also spelled out. In a way, it's a bit as though you were taking home a group of dealerships to study them in the nonintimidating privacy of your own home. With the aid of a calculator and your list of desirable options, you can find out within half an hour the approximate dealer cost of a new car. You are then ready to shop around for the best deal.

As William Badnow, editor of *Edmund's New Car Prices,* notes, better deals are more likely in urban areas, where there is greater dealer competition, than in rural areas, and on domestic models rather than on foreign ones, especially when import quotas are in effect. Getting the best price on any vehicle Badnow says, "is a matter of shopping around." Approach the salesperson and say, 'This is what I want; what's your best price?' and see who comes the closest to the wholesale figure."

Consumers Union, of *Consumer Reports* fame, operates an "Auto-Price Service" that provides computer printouts of dealer prices. The service costs $9 for one set of new-car prices, $17 for two, and $24 for three. The printouts include a list of options recommended in *Consumer Reports,* along with advice on negotiating your best deal. It's up to you to decide whether these inclusions justify the extra expense. Although Consumers Union's computer can be updated instantaneously, there is no guarantee that prices will remain the same in the time it takes for you to receive the printout and put it to use.

The Best Time of Year to Buy a New Car

Certainly, the best new-car deals are possible any time, but if you can plan your purchase, the winter months present good bargaining opportunities. Winter doldrums, holiday expenses, and winter clothing and fuel bills keep automobile sales to a minimum. The end of the month is better yet, because dealership sales staffs are being pushed to meet monthly sales quotas.

Some might also tell you that August or September, just before the introduction of the new models, is a good time to buy. Realistically, though, the proliferation of this notion is in the best interest of new-car dealers, and not the new-car-buying public. During annual "make-room-for-the-new-models" sales, consumers must select from factory and dealer lot leftovers, and buyers will be hit with radically accelerated depreciation the minute the new models come out, despite the fact that the car was never used during the previous model year. Even accounting for *potentially* lower mileage at resale time, the depreciation factor will not be offset. The bottom line is that often it costs more to buy a car at model year-end clearance time.

September bargain hunters can also be baited to order the more expensive new models with statements such as "Price increases are only 2 percent over last year's on comparably equipped models." The phrase "comparably equipped" is a masterpiece of illogical logistics. If last year's model cost $8000, and this year's model costs $8160, the difference is 2 percent, but only if the phrase "comparably equipped" is used.

What they don't tell you is that last year's $8000 model did not have this year's larger engine, deluxe interior package, or automatic transmission as standard equipment. This year's $8160 model *does*. If you subtract these options from last year's "comparably equipped" model, you would realize that last year's model actually cost only $7040, but when "comparably equipped" with all this year's standard equipment, the car retailed for $8000. The actual price increase? Not 2 percent, but 13.7 percent, because you get last year's options at this year's prices, like it or not.

The worst time to buy, without a doubt, is in springtime; it's a seller's market. Love is in the air, or so they say, and America's love affair with the automobile is in full swing, too. In this high-demand market, dealers have little reason to deal. Even the additional springtime profits from the owner sale of a used car will likely be negated by the higher cost of the replacement vehicle.

Dealer Demonstrator Models

These "new used" cars are sometimes good values—if you don't mind buying a new car with 5000 or so miles on it. Demonstrator models, or "demos" as they are more popularly known, are new cars driven by members of the sales staff.

The maximum number of miles before which a demo is termed a used car varies from state to state, but it is somewhere in the 5000-mile range; some demos may be sold with less mileage than that.

The advantages include an extended warranty that renews full-term coverage when you take possession, manufacturer and dealer credits that reduce sale price, and even low-interest finance in some cases. Generally, though, the discount on demos is not much greater than that which you could get on a new car if you're willing to deal.

Obviously, no one dealer has a large surplus of demonstrator models, so check around if the idea appeals to you.

Arranging Financing

Three-quarters of all new-car buyers finance their purchases. Over 60 percent opt to repay in 48 to 59 months; 20 percent finance for 36 to 47 months. An average of $8500 is financed, with a monthly payment average of $240. Half of the loans are from banks, a third from finance companies, and the remaining 17 percent from credit unions.

Another way to finance without using these commercial resources is to borrow against the cash value of a life insurance policy of sufficient equity. Interest rates are low, or the money can even be deducted from the policy's cash value. (Do not, however, be sold a whole-term life insurance policy on this basis. The rate of interest paid you is so low that this "borrow against" benefit is duly offset.)

Wherever you finance your loan, do so only after comparing interest rates and the accumulated total at maturity. Compare this accrued figure at 30 months versus 36, 36 versus 48, and so on. This can often be revealing. Also, check all ancillary conditions of the loan: credit life insurance, early-repayment provisions, and default options. Whereas some loans require you to pay full-term interest, others cease interest accumulation upon termination of the loan (either upon payoff or repossession).

Credit unions and other financial institutions associated with employment are especially good sources of loans. Some sort of membership criterion is usually required, often church affiliation or place of employment. Although the down payments required may be larger than those for other lending institutions, the interest rates on credit union loans are often three to four percentage points lower than those from major lending institutions, and with the vast majority of new-car loans extending to 48 months and beyond, savings can be substantial.

Credit unions generally include insurance (credit life) free of charge that provides for loan repayment if the loan holder dies. If the credit union is affiliated with your place of employment, you may also have the added convenience of payroll deductions. The maximum amount of money a credit union can lend varies from state to state, and with today's inflated new-car prices, it may not be enough. Even so, consider partial credit union financing.

Dealer finance programs provide the convenience of one-stop shopping, have a vested interest in qualifying you for your loan and, for the most part, offer bank-competitive interest rates. To encourage business, dealer finance programs also offer cut-rate interest from time to time. These "deals," though, are generally blown way out of proportion by the sales staff, who divert the attention of a naive buyer from the higher cost of the vehicle and lower trade-in prices by continually referring back to the low interest rate.

Dealers, however, are in no position to give you that "great deal" on both the car *and* the loan terms. To an extent that few consumers realize, dealerships are very dependent on the profits generated by their company-sponsored loan programs; these rival vehicle sales profits. And be wary of the salesperson who says, "I could get fired for this, but so-and-so down the street can give you much better terms." The salesperson is interested only in receiving a kickback for the recommendation, and not in securing you better loan terms.

Low-interest, dealer-arranged financing often does, however, force banks to lower their new-car loan rates—but check the fine print. Banks are beginning to add creatively titled new-car-loan "processing fees," "filing fees," and "origination fees" that can substantially increase the total cost of the loan. Some banks now offer balloon loans on vehicles, similar to those used in real estate and leasing. Generally, balloon loan down payments are lower, but the interest rate is higher. Balloon loans are calculated on the difference between a vehicle's sale price and its expected resale value at the end of the loan period, which can cut monthly payments by 20 percent or more. At the end of a balloon loan, the expected resale value is due in full, though. For example, if a vehicle costs $9000, and the balloon loan is for 36 months, the bank would figure vehicle resale at the end of that 36-month period, let's say at $4000. Balloon loan payments would then be based on the difference, which in this example is $5000, and not on the total $9000 purchase price. However, at the loan's end, a consumer must come up with the difference, and can either sell the car to the bank, keep the car and pay off the loan in full, sell the car and hope for more than is owed, or refinance the outstanding amount.

Closing the Deal

New-car contracts contain a clause that reads "This order shall not become binding until accepted by dealer or his authorized representative." This legal disclaimer can void negotiating that took place with the salesperson. Generally, if you have selected a reputable dealer, you needn't worry, but *it is advisable to have an "authorized representative" sign the order form before you leave the dealership.*

Also, it is wisest not to sign anything except the final and agreed-upon order form. Do not sign "worksheets" or "appraisal forms." You have no need to do so, and there are court precedents in which buyers signed forms clearly labeled "Worksheet—Not a Purchase Order," but were held liable for the order because a deposit had been left at the salesperson's prompting.

It is also in a consumer's best interests to *never sign an order form that is not completed in full.* A salesperson completing paperwork details after a customer has signed an order form may mean well, but verbal misunderstandings can lead to discrepancies. A dealer who deliberately changed or misrepresented facts on a contract could be charged with deceptive sales practices under state consumer-protection laws, but in the case of an honest error, there is no intent to defraud. It is in the best interest of all parties that the order form be completed in full before you sign.

You should consider certain other clauses that are generally found on the back of the order form:

1. The clause that excuses the dealer from breach of contract if the manufacturer fails to ship the vehicle as ordered
2. The integration, or merger, clause, which disclaims all oral promises regardless of any discussion between the customer and salesperson
3. The clause permitting the dealer to retain the down payment if the buyer refuses delivery
4. The two clauses that deal with the dealer's right to pass on manufacturer price increases to the customer, and to deliver a vehicle the manufacturer has changed since the customer ordered it

Consider the following modifications: For (1) and (4), note that acceptance of the vehicle is dependent upon your approval if substantial design or mechanical changes alter the vehicle's value or use to you, and they set a limit on the price increases. If you reject the vehicle for these reasons, then (3) would not apply and you would be entitled to a full and unconditional refund. As for (2), get everything in writing and review the order form with the salesperson before and after the "authorized representative" has signed the order form. As a practical matter, most dealers will refund new-car deposits unless the vehicle color or options make it a particularly difficult model to resell. As an added assurance, though, a consumer should leave as small a deposit as possible. Also, most order forms say nothing about how long a consumer must wait before taking delivery. If a 2- to 3-month wait is too long, then have it stated that "the buyer may cancel, and the dealer will return the deposit in full if the vehicle cannot be delivered within 30 days of the stated delivery date."

As to trade-in appraisal or sale of your present vehicle, you may wish to consult the section, "Owner Sale of a Used Car," in Chapter 3.

Accepting Delivery

It is estimated that only 5 out of every 100 new cars shipped from the factory reach their destinations unblemished. How's that for a sobering figure? Paint, body, tire, and vandal-related damage often occur in transit.

The problem is such that Ford, for example, is testing the shipping of some of its cars via enclosed tractor-trailers, in which new cars are loaded by hydraulics, in lieu of the open-air rail-and-truck transports commonly used. General Motors has testing equipment to duplicate freight-train movement, allowing analysis of transport stress and strain, which can cause wheel bearings to wear prematurely, antenna masts to snap, and windows and paint to crack; these items were neither designed nor intended to withstand transport motions. Let this lend credence to the importance of physically checking in a new car.

Most new-car deficiencies are corrected during predelivery preparation, but stories are legion of vehicles delivered in poor shape because of the low priority sometimes given to these inspections. A consumer should check for paint and body flaws (other than the incidental factory blemishes that might be found later) and missing parts, such as hubcaps, gas and oil-filler caps, cigarette lighters, and ashtrays. Carefully review your copy of the purchase order with the option list on the car, *then take the car for a test drive. This is your right. Don't be rushed by a salesperson who views new-car deliveries only as an after-sale nuisance.* You have to live with the car; they do not. And this is your best opportunity to reject the vehicle. Before leaving the dealership, check to see that you have the following:

• Title and registration (each properly completed)
• Proof-of-insurance form
• License plates *on* the car
• All door, trunk, and ignition keys
• Inspection stickers (where required)
• All warranty papers (signed and dated by the dealer where indicated)
• Sufficient gasoline

Rejecting Delivery of a Vehicle

The ideal time to reject a vehicle that is unsatisfactory for any reason is just prior to accepting delivery. Once delivery of a vehicle is accepted, returning the vehicle is difficult, and a full refund is virtually impossible. In all cases, working with the dealer in seeking a satisfactory solution is the most desirable route for all parties, but the buyer does have two options in rejecting a vehicle *before* accepting delivery.

The Uniform Commercial Code (UCC) permits a buyer to reject an automobile if it fails to conform to the provisions of the sales contract. This could include wrong options, color, or defective equipment. This UCC regulation is known as the "perfect tender rule." (Louisiana is the only state in which the UCC is not effective.) A buyer may also reject an automobile if there is a serious defect. A serious defect is one that substantially impairs the use and value of the vehicle. In most cases, one major defect or a series of lesser defects constitutes "substantial impairment." Under the law, the dealer must be given a chance to repair the vehicle or make it acceptable to the buyer and to redeliver it. The buyer can then reject the vehicle again, or even reject the repair attempt itself in some cases if the defect is substantial. To cite one such case, a new car burst into flames a short distance from the dealership because of faulty wiring. The owner rejected the dealer's offer of repair, and the court upheld that right. Another court case involved a new car that stalled repeatedly on the drive home, finally quitting altogether. The car was towed back to the dealer, who diagnosed the problem as a bad transmission. Despite this repairable defect, the court ruled that the "buyer's faith" in the vehicle was so "shaken that it reasonably destroyed confidence in the integrity and reliability of the vehicle." The consumer was able to reject both the car and the repair attempt.

Rejection of a vehicle should be given in writing to both the manufacturer and the dealership and must include a detailed summary of the defects for which it was rejected. The written notice should be sent or delivered immediately following the rejection. If the buyer financed through the dealer, it is generally agreed that no payments need be made. If the vehicle was financed elsewhere, payments should be made, because even though the buyer has rejected a vehicle, a finance institution may still repossess or place a lien on the vehicle.

Most states follow the rule that the buyer should not use the rejected vehicle in any way, shape, or form, as continued use can be used as evidence against the buyer's rejection. Instead, drive the vehicle to the dealership and give the keys and ownership documents back to the dealer, owner, or manager (not to the salesperson). The vehicle may be put in storage or otherwise kept out of use, particularly when the dealer makes return of the car difficult. A lawsuit is sometimes necessary to obtain the refund and incidental expenses, such as car rentals. If the rejection does not occur immediately after delivery, a dealer can charge equitable rental for use of the vehicle. The only event in which a vehicle can be returned to the *manufacturer* is if the dealership that delivered the vehicle has gone out of business; otherwise, the contract is strictly between the dealer and the customer, not the manufacturer.

Alternatives to Dealer Purchase

Leasing

Although vehicle leasing is in vogue, statements such as "in the near future, 70 percent of all new cars will be leased" distort consumer perceptions. Many of these cars will be used as corporate fleet vehicles, and in that context leasing is a viable alternative to purchasing. But for those to whom income tax laws do not allow vehicle deductions, leasing is a less feasible option. Over a 3-year period, leasing costs about 15 to 20 percent more than would a loan (based on an annual interest rate of 12 percent). For the average new-car buyer, leasing is a much-overemphasized alternative to purchasing.

New-car dealers, on the other hand, find it is beneficial to advocate leasing, because leasing "moves" cars. Very little cash on hand is needed, and a lease and monthly lease payments are often lower than finance payments, all of which tempts consumers. Leasing eliminates the legalities of repossession if nonpayment occurs. There is also the potential for additional profit from the sale of the car at the expiration of some leases.

There are some generally accepted rules of thumb that determine whether or not you should lease. If you plan to purchase a new car at least every third year, depreciation losses will equal if not surpass leasing losses. If you use the car at least 75 percent of the time for business and your credit rating and finances are in order, leasing will (1) provide an itemized account of your vehicle operating costs at tax time, (2) prevent your having to resell or trade in vehicles, (3) let you invest the down-payment sum elsewhere, in lieu of turning it over with each new car purchase, and (4) allow you to forgo the legwork of new-car purchasing.

Leases are either open- or closed-end. Either type may contain any number of provisions, including the option to purchase. If all provisions of either lease were equal, closed-end leases would generally be the more expensive of the two when *total* costs and not just payments are considered. With an open-end vehicle lease, your total cost depends on the difference between resale value projected when the lease was signed and a vehicle's actual resale value at the end of the lease. If the vehicle sells for more, you can pocket the profit; if it sells for less, you pay the difference.

For example, a leasing company might estimate a vehicle's worth at $2000 after 3 years of normal use. If the car is worth only $1500 when you return it, you owe $500. The law limits closeout payments in an open-end lease to no more than three times the average monthly payment—unless you have agreed to a higher payment or you have put more than average mileage on the vehicle. The law allows for binding third-party estimates in cases of dispute. In a closed-end lease, you are not responsible for the value of the vehicle when you return it and will not have to make a balloon payment. As a result, closed-end leases usually have higher monthly payments than open-end leases.

In an open-end (sometimes referred to as a "finance") vehicle lease, there are about 20 disclosures, or agreements, between the lessor and the lessee. In a closed-end lease, there are about 15. Both contain many of the same provisions, though. Disclosures that deal with fees and taxes, insurance, estimated value at lease end, total lease obligation, standards for wear and use, maintenance, warranties, early termination or default, late payment, and option to purchase should be given close consideration.

If the lessee is required to provide insurance, the contract should state exactly which type to buy and what the liability amounts are. Be aware that the total lease obligation disclosure does not include security deposits or insurance premiums. Vehicle maintenance may be divided between parties or may be the obligation of only one; expressed warranties may be provided for by the manufacturer, the lessor, or both. Also, inquire as to what methods are used in determining charges for early termination of the lease by either party.

If you have questions about the law in connection with a lease transaction from a bank, write to the Board of Governors, the Federal Reserve System, Washington, D.C. 20551. Federal reserve banks are also located in Atlanta, Boston, Chicago, Cleveland, Dallas, Kansas City, Minneapolis, New York, Philadelphia, Richmond, Virginia, San Francisco, and St. Louis.

For information on leasing from sources other than banks, write to the Federal Trade Commission, Consumer Leasing, Washington, D.C. 20580. Regional offices in the following cities can also assist you: Atlanta, Boston, Chicago, Cleveland, Dallas, Denver, Los Angeles, New York, San Francisco, and Seattle. Be sure to include the name and address of the business or institution with which you are dealing. Addresses and phone numbers of these regional offices are listed in Appendix F.

Rentals

Interestingly enough, for those who work in urban areas with good mass-transit systems, renting a vehicle may be a more viable option than either leasing or purchasing. Renting a compact car 45 weekends out of the year, and 2 weeks a year for vacation time, would cost approximately $3000 a year. If that sounds expensive, consider that the yearly (and nonequity) operating cost of the same car is approximately $3441. And if you think you might use a car even less often, you may be in the money by renting your ride.

Auto Brokerage Firms

Auto brokers are independent new-car sales agents who operate free of allegiance to any particular automaker. They will sell you a Ford as soon as they will a Chevy or a Toyota. They take a profit up front and that's that. Auto brokers operate by ordering vehicles in volume through local dealerships the same as corporate fleet administrators. Most auto brokers operate nationwide, which eliminates them from direct competition with the local dealers from whom they buy; in fact, these dealers appreciate the extra business.

Auto brokers spare the consumer from dealer shopping and all the game playing involved in negotiating the best deal. The down side is that vehicle variety impedes detailed knowledge of individual products, bulk-buying practices often make it difficult to obtain a vehicle with the exact options you want, and the paperwork may require extra legwork; this, however, depends in large part on regulations set by the state in which the broker operates. Although these inconveniences may be more tactical than problematic, inquire beforehand. Auto brokers arrange for delivery at a dealership in your locale where trade-in of your old car can also be arranged. Details vary, but this is the basic procedure.

Auto brokers often require you to pay for computer price printouts of the models that you're considering. Fees vary. One national firm was charging $7 for one price quote, $10 for two, and $13 for three. This practice eliminates frivolous "window-shopping" inquiries and covers time spent in putting quotes together; it also maximizes the auto broker's edge—minimal overhead.

If you're interested, check in your local Yellow Pages under "automobile brokers." Check with the Better Business Bureau, too, before conducting anything other than information gathering. Delays in delivery and special-order discrepancies are prevalent problems with some brokers. And, as many of these firms operate within the Detroit area, you may want to check agency reputability with Michigan's Office of Policy and Consumer Affairs, (517) 373-8674. The number of the Detroit Better Business Bureau is (313) 962-7566.

The Gray Market

In 1982, about 2000 "noncomplying imports" entered the United States. By 1985 the number had leaped to 40,000, with Mercedes accounting for 65 percent of that traffic. The number of these cars seized by federal agents, as well as the number of horror stories about service problems, jumped accordingly. If, and when, the value of the U.S. dollar abroad tempts you, be certain you know what's involved. Warranty hassles, certification problems, and government confiscation are all possible scenarios that have cost tens of thousands of dollars.

If you want to know more, both the Department of Transportation

(DOT) and the Environmental Protection Agency (EPA) provide information free of charge. The EPA number is (202) 382-2504; the number of the DOT is (202) 426-1693. A very good book on this topic, the *Handbook of Vehicle Importation,* is available from the Automobile Importers Compliance Association (AICA). To obtain a copy, call the AICA at (703) 352-4519.

chapter 2

Dealing with Manufacturer Warranty and Dealer Service Problems

"The Squeaky Wheel Gets the Grease"

A Detroit-area dealership once hung a red, white, and blue sign above its service desk that read, "Your car has over 14,000 parts, and even if it were 99.9 percent perfect, there would still be 14 things wrong with it."

The sign is gone, but its message remains as an epitaph to the days of fast cars and fast talk. In the modern era of a more worldly automotive consumer, "Let the buyer beware" is today giving way to "Let the seller be fair."

What Can I Do?

When problems arise with new-car warranty repairs, it pays to be both knowledgeable and persistent. Human nature may dictate that we take the course of least resistance, but human beings decide which party first treads the path. Here's a quick rundown of who to see and what you can do in handling warranty problems. All points are discussed within this chapter.

1. The dealership service manager
2. The dealership owner or general manager
3. The manufacturer's regional, district, or zone office
4. The manufacturer's national headquarters
5. Your state consumer council or agency
6. Federal government agencies
7. Consumer agencies
8. Automotive arbitration boards
9. Small-claims court
10. Lemon laws (in most states)
11. Civil lawsuits

Special Considerations

In addition to rejecting an unsatisfactory vehicle at the time of delivery, a vehicle can also be rejected within a short time of delivery. The legal definition of "within a short time" is murky, but it has been variously interpreted from three to 90 days after delivery. The details of rejecting a vehicle are presented at the end of Chapter 1.

These consumer complaint processes also apply to problems with either the federal "defect and design" or "emission performance" warranties, which provide for manufacturer warranty of certain emissions-control items for the lesser of 5 years or 50,000 miles. Chapter 5 contains more details on these warranties.

In areas with inspection and maintenance (I/M) programs, new vehicles can also be voluntarily submitted for emissions testing up to 3 months or 4000 miles. This maneuver may be especially handy for owners of vehicles with ongoing performance problems that the dealer cannot readily solve. A poorly running engine may very well fail an I/M test. The manufacturer would then be responsible for solving the emissions problem. In the process, the cause of the drivability problem may very well be corrected as well.

Usually your problems can be resolved at the dealership or regional level, but you should also be aware that if the dealer is especially surly or uncooperative, you can use third-party arbitration directly. This will eliminate the need to negotiate further with either the dealer or the manufacturer.

Automotive arbitration programs vary, but generally the consumer is free to accept or reject the third-party decision; the company, however, is usually bound by the decision. You may want to skip ahead to the arbitration section in this chapter and read how these procedures apply to your case, because *not all complaints are eligible for arbitration*. The need, though, to pursue arbitration in lieu of more extensive dealer or manufacturer involvement applies to only a small percentage of cases.

Dealing with the Dealership

Many issues can be handled at the dealership level without outside involvement, and this is the most desirable route for all parties. This is best initiated by bringing problems to the attention of the dealership service manager (or body-shop manager for exterior repairs).

Repeated repair attempts are referred to as "comebacks." Service managers should be interested in hearing about comebacks. They should intercede on your behalf with the mechanics. If you feel that they have not done so, ask to speak with the dealership owner or general manager, and remember that it is also helpful to enlist your new-car sales representative as an intermediate.

If you meet resistance, mention that you will contact the regional office of the manufacturer, and that you will also consider arbitration. Should discussion at the dealership level prove futile, contact the regional office directly. But before venturing beyond the realm of the dealership, get your record keeping in order.

Collecting the Necessary Information

In the heat of the moment, venting one's frustrations may seem paramount to mediating a solution to the problem, but without the needed information at hand, you may only increase your feelings of frustration.

For example, the 40- to 60-day maximum for issuance of an arbitration decision can be legally extended if the consumer does not provide complete information. Failure to provide the correct information can be construed as stall tactics, for which the customer may be blamed. Consumers need not add buck-passing ammunition to an already well-stocked arsenal. Make note of the following information:

- Year _____
- Make _____
- Model _____
- Date of purchase _____
- Dealer name and address _____
  _____
- Vehicle identification number (VIN) _____
- Problem specifics _____
  _____
  _____

Keep this information nearby when discussing your case.

The information is easily located; check your payment book, title, or registration. The 13- to 17-digit vehicle identification number is referred to as the VIN number, or simply the VIN. It is stamped on an inlaid metal tag where the dashboard and windshield meet on the driver's side of the vehicle (some are on the driver-side pillar pad). This automotive jargon relays as much to the trained eye as scanner codes do to grocery registers. Be sure that you copy and read the VIN correctly. Double-check the numbers and letters (there are always both), as one can be mistaken for the other (for example, I for 1, O for 0, Z for 7).

Also, the further along you go in rectifying a problem, the more you need copies of service orders. Many an owner justifiably laments not having saved them. Recouping work orders is as simple as asking the dealer for copies; all you should be charged is a copying fee, and perhaps a token processing fee. If your vehicle has been serviced by someone other than the dealer, getting copies will depend on that operation's administrative organization. Getting receipts for routine maintenance can be important in verifying compliance with warranty terms. If you do your own maintenance work, track the date and mileage, and keep receipts for oil, fluids, and parts. In any event, it's always a good idea to organize repair order copies in a notebook for easy future reference.

Dealing with the Manufacturer's Regional Office

Manufacturer regional office locations are generally listed in vehicle owner manuals or can be obtained from the dealer. Also, the addresses and telephone numbers for the national and regional offices of major domestic and foreign automotive manufacturers are listed in Appendixes A and B. If you call the regional office, establish a written record by documenting the conversation with a follow-up letter. Correspondence should be specific and include:

1. A brief history of your case with documentation
2. The vehicle identification number (VIN), year, make, mileage, date of purchase, and dealership name and address
3. Legible photocopies of the original paperwork

Avoid reference to the integrity or honesty of any individual or manufacturer.

Regional offices (also referred to as either zone or district offices) are local branch offices of an automaker's national headquarters. Regional offices generally cover a multistate territory and coordinate dealership sales and parts and service programs; they also assist with customer relations, warranty approvals, and technical problems.

One of the functions of the regional office is to handle consumer complaints that arise from within its network of dealerships. Regional offices are of significance to the consumer, as they are empowered by the company, through factory representatives, to authorize and settle warranty adjustments and disputes. These offices also play a role in dealer distribution of new cars, and consumer complaints can adversely affect apportionment.

Some manufacturers—Ford is one—define dealer networks by districts, and others, such as General Motors, refer to regional offices as zones. Toyota, on the other hand, simply labels them regional offices. General Motors divides their zones by nameplate divisions, having separate offices for Pontiac, Buick, Chevrolet, Oldsmobile, and Cadillac. Ford and Chrysler, on the other hand, do not distinguish between corporate makes and models. Ford districts handle Mercury, Lincoln, and Ford inquiries, and Chrysler zones handle Dodge and Plymouth as well.

To the consumer, regional offices provide an alternate recourse in settling dealer service problems. Consumers should contact the regional office after two unsuccessful attempts by a dealer to repair the same problem. Do so with a letter that follows the suggested format, adding that if the regionally assisted repair attempt fails, you will contact corporate owner relations (at the manufacturer's headquarters), consider arbitration, or both. Don't mistake this for a threat, because it will not intimidate anyone. But in some cases, it helps to indicate that you know the ropes.

Realistically, despite profuse customer relations rhetoric, unless your complaint is of an extreme nature, or was obviously mishandled, contacting the regional office may not yield much. In fact, it may serve only to further confuse and discourage an already trouble-plagued consumer. This can work to the manufacturer's advantage, because consumers sometimes just give up. Clarence Ditlow, head of the Center for Auto Safety in Washington, D.C., an automotive consumer group, said, "Automakers are quite adept at dealing with the 'obnoxious consumer' and solving their complaints, but it's the rest of us, the majority of the population, that gets the runaround."

Regardless of the potential futility, circumventing the regional office may be construed as a lack of owner cooperation; it is always best, then, to contact the regional office before seeking arbitration or the aid of an agency, because in most situations your case will be referred back to these offices anyway.

Should regional office input prove less than satisfactory, the next step is to contact the manufacturer's national offices (Appendixes A and B), using the same method as for contacting the regional office. Send copies of any correspondence to both the dealership and the regional office.

If this step fails to achieve satisfactory results, it is time to add pressure from elsewhere. Next, we'll look at consumer and government agencies, followed by arbitration boards, a state-by-state listing of lemon laws, and, finally, alternate legal recourse.

Government and Consumer Agencies

Federal and state agencies collect and investigate complaints, searching for common denominators that may be of value to the general public. If a federal agency, such as the National Highway Traffic Safety Administration (NHTSA), the Department of Transportation (DOT), or the Environmental Protection Agency (EPA), determines that a safety or emissions defect is prevalent, it will investigate, which may lead to a recall. Granted, all this may be too late for some, but it is never too late to help others. These agencies also often provide informative brochures and pamphlets and alternate information sources. But what they cannot do is to go to bat for you as an individual.

On the other hand, independent consumer agencies do aid individuals, operating within that niche left by government agencies. Some consumer agencies perform a real public service; others may be little more than sounding boards or a common place where disgruntled consumers can shake their heads together in collective disgust. Many of these agencies charge modest fees. Their advice is generally helpful, though.

Dani Liblang, a Detroit-area attorney who has handled a number of product-liability cases, including automotive lemons, states, "There's a lot a consumer can do with a minimum of legal hassle if you know your rights and can articulate them." She refers people to both local consumer and government agencies for information and says, "Once people get pointed in the right direction, they can usually handle the complaint themselves."

Consumer agencies are generally founded and directed by someone who has earned a certificate in "lemonology" through the school of hard knocks, someone who has been through the automotive gauntlet and lived to tell about it, to the benefit of those who wish to listen. A good consumer agency enables you to go the recourse route with a guide.

Unfortunately, since consumer agencies are generally small-budget operations (some made up of only one person), checking their reputability can be difficult, but your Better Business Bureau or state consumer affairs office should have some knowledge of local consumer agency operations. By the nature of their functions, these parties should eventually, if not frequently, cross paths—and exchange opinions as well. Consumer reform advocates may be impatient and highly critical of established systems they feel have failed them. Some may use these tactics to increase their business, too.

When dealing with consumer agencies, be careful that you are not being charged for government brochures and pamphlets that are in the public domain and, therefore, free of charge. Be alert for inferences that their guidance is an essential part of any recourse option, such as arbitration, for which some charge a fee or a percentage of the award. While their advice may be fine, do not look to consumer agency directors to be recognized as your "expert witness" in a court of law. Instead, tap their resources when necessary in locating attorneys who specialize in automotive and product-liability cases. No listing of consumer agencies is presented here, because these agencies come and go. In one listing less than 9 months old, only two of the eight agencies were still in existence. If you wish to seek one out, check the local personal ads, in which some advertise, check with a local media general consumer advocate or organization, or contact the Center for Auto Safety (2001 S Street NW, Washington, D.C. 20009; (202) 328-7700).

The Center for Auto Safety directs its efforts at the broad base of consumers rather than at handling individual complaints. The center was established in 1970 by Ralph Nader and the Consumers Union. It became independent of those founders in 1973, and its staff has increased to include attorneys, researchers, and engineers.

The center has been instrumental in initiating some key recalls, and in promoting and keeping pressure on the government to improve crash protection, fuel economy, tire quality and grading systems, rust protection, air-bag legislation, highway safety, and mobile-home safety standards. The center also initiates legal action. For example, it initiated an administrative lawsuit against General Motors over the ongoing passenger car diesel-engine fiasco; the center also pushed to have the DOT tire grading system reinstated.

Although the Center for Auto Safety and state and federal agencies do not provide direct aid to individuals, do not hesitate to call any or all of them. Collectively, these agencies can bring great pressure to bear if they receive sufficient ammunition. Especially if your problem is safety-related, contact the NHTSA (see "Safety Recalls" in Chapter 7). Keeping consumer dissatisfaction a secret from these agencies only serves the manufacturer involved. Put your experience to work for the benefit of all, and make it a point to send them copies of all correspondence. It's not a bad idea to send copies to your state representative as well.

Appendix F lists the addresses and phone numbers of federal government agencies. State agencies can be located by checking your local telephone directory or directory service under the heading of your state consumer affairs office or consumer protection agency. There may also be an all-purpose information number listed for your state capital building, which may be able to provide you with the number.

Automotive Arbitration

The Better Business Bureau (BBB), which operates Auto Line, the highest-volume arbitration program, is surprised by the large number of people who call them for help without having first contacted the dealership service manager, owner, or factory representative. Automotive arbitration boards were never meant to circumvent established channels of communication, but rather to offer the consumer an alternative to a breakdown, or impasse, in those communications. When necessary, though, arbitration programs can be an effective means of mediating a wide range of issues—from resolving simple repair problems to the buy-back of an automobile. In one instance, a woman whose new station wagon had stalled in the middle of a busy freeway was awarded a new vehicle on the basis that the experience had so traumatized her that she could no longer use the vehicle. Although you should expect much less than this, arbitration is adding a new dimension to the automotive complaint process, one by which a consumer need not be intimidated.

Roger D. Billings, Jr., professor of law at Salmon P. Chase College of Law at Northern Kentucky University, and an authority on automobile warranties, arbitration, and lemon laws, wrote in the January-February 1985 issue of *Case & Comment* that prior to arbitration, "The [consumer's] legal fees often exceeded the money the buyer lost on the car. Dealers' and manufacturers' lawyers were well-aware of this financial handicap when negotiating with the car buyer. Through a remarkable combination of recent laws, and a push among manufacturers for customer satisfaction, a quiet revolution has taken place in automobile warranty law.''

Manufacturers began to experiment with arbitration following the Magnuson-Moss Warranty Act of 1975. The act encouraged the establishment of arbitration boards as a nonlitigious method of settlement; that is, proceedings are held with a minimum of legal counsel, no court costs are assessed, and the cases are settled in a minimum of time. Arbitration programs that conform to Federal Trade Commission (FTC) section 703 guidelines, which most do, must complete hearings within 40 days of the consumer's written request, and within that time span, the arbitrator has 10 days from the close of the hearing to deliver a written decision. An arbitrator can award amounts up to the purchase price of a vehicle. The arbitrator cannot award any monies for personal injury, fraud, or other matters related to breach of contract. Judgments are rendered on whatever seems fair and reasonable within the context of an individual case. Arbitration proceedings are not held to case precedents, as are courts of law.

In six states, local government is involved in automotive arbitration. Connecticut has a three-member arbitration panel that consumers of that state can use if a manufacturer's arbitration program does not conform to FTC guidelines. Vermont provides for a five-member panel that a consumer may use instead of the program sanctioned or operated by a manufacturer regardless of its FTC status, and Texas provides for hearings before its motor vehicle commission. Kentucky has a state-operated arbitration board that is independent of manufacturer arbitration programs. Kentucky's statute is a quasi-lemon law and is discussed in the section on lemon laws. The governments of Florida and Massachusetts oversee arbitration proceedings, and residents of those states are advised to contact their state consumer councils for more information.

There are four major automotive arbitration programs: (1) Auto Line, operated by the Better Business Bureau; (2) the Automotive Consumer Action Program, or AUTOCAP, administered by the National Automobile Dealers Association (NADA) through its dealer network; (3) Ford Motor Company's Consumer Appeals Board (FCAB); and (4) the Chrysler Corporation's Customer Satisfaction Board (see Table 2-1). You can apply for arbitration whether or not your state has repair-or-replace legislation (a lemon law). Arbitration is a prerequisite, however, to pursuit of repair-or-replace laws if the program follows FTC section 703 guidelines.

Arbitration Proceedings

Not all complaints are eligible for arbitration, and guidelines vary greatly from manufacturer to manufacturer, so read the provisions carefully be-

Table 2-1 Arbitration Programs per Automaker*

Manufacturers Using AUTO LINE (BBB Arbitration Program)

American Motors Corporation (Jeep, Renault); Audi; Bentley; General Motors† (Buick, Cadillac, Chevrolet, Pontiac, Oldsmobile, GMC Trucks); Honda‡; Hyundai; Jaguar; Maserati; Nissan (Datsun); Peugeot; Porsche; Rolls-Royce; Saab; Volkswagen; and Volvo.

Manufacturers Using AUTOCAP Arbitration Program

AUTOCAP programs are not nationwide, and not all eligible dealers participate. At this writing, many import manufacturers are changing their arbitration contracts from AUTOCAP to BBB's Auto Line.
Alfa Romeo, BMW, Fiat, Isuzu, Mazda, Mitsubishi, Subaru, and Toyota.

Manufacturer-Administrated Arbitration Programs

Ford Motor Company and Chrysler Corporation.

---

* Mercedes-Benz is the only major automaker that does not provide for an arbitration program.
† Under a unique consent agreement with the FTC, General Motors has agreed to arbitrate through 1991, with very few limitations, the repair of certain alleged defects in about 21 million vehicles made from 1974 to 1983. (Consult the "GM-FTC Arbitration Agreement" section that follows.) Original owners of 1978, 1979, and 1980 GM diesel-engine vehicles may not bring diesel complaints to Auto Line unless they were specially exempt from the class of owners in a 1984 court class action settlement.
‡ Honda is the only manufacturer that does not require the consumer to use arbitration before going to court (*except in California*). This is done to show good faith on their part.

fore filing. Consequential or incidental damages (such as rental cars or towing) may be sought only if both parties agree to them specifically. However, you may still file for such damages in small-claims court. (Small-claims court procedures are discussed in Chapter 5.) Punitive damages can be sought only in a court of law and never through arbitration.

The manufacturer may ask for a 20-day extension on the FTC's 40-day maximum for arbitration proceedings. A manufacturer may request this extension to attempt mediation before going the arbitration route. A consumer can decline a 20-day extension request outright and thus start the clock running on the FTC's 40-day maximum regulation immediately. Consumers who grant such an extension can reverse their decision at any time and start the clock running on the 40-day maximum from that point. This is done by notifying the manufacturer in writing of your intentions.

Although buy-backs are possible, keep in mind that such procedures are complex, deciding issues such as depreciation and a host of "collateral costs of purchase," such as refund of interest payments, sales tax, and license fees. When a major component has failed—an engine or transmission—it may be more sensible to seek extended-warranty coverage if you doubt the durability of the repair. You should seek an interim decision if a repair order is involved; this allows the status of an arbitration case to remain open pending the outcome of repairs. With the BBB's program, for example, all decisions are interim when repairs are ordered.

Never exaggerate your claim or use the strategy of requesting more than you actually seek in the hope of obtaining a lesser, though satisfactory, compromise decision. In either instance, your case will be weakened by lack of substantiation.

Check for any recalls or special policies (service bulletins) issued for your vehicle. Service bulletins list manufacturing and production defects warrantied independent of new-car warranty terms. This information can save you money and support your arbitration case if the defect is associated with your complaint. General Motors and Ford Motor Company are required by the FTC to provide service bulletins to customers who request them. Recalls and special policies are covered in Chapter 7.

In pursuing arbitration, keep the following items organized: purchase contract and finance agreement, including proof of payments and down payments; repair and service records, including routine and warranty-required maintenance; copies of the warranty and service contracts; and all correspondence relating to the case. List these events chronologically, and include the names of persons with whom you spoke.

You may amend information after filing. You also have the right to review materials submitted by the other party if the program operates within FTC section 703, and you should do so in order to respond. And where applicable, familiarize yourself with state lemon laws—the definition of "repair within a reasonable amount of time" and "down time" can substantiate your complaint. (Consult the section "State-by-State Lemon-Law Basics" in this chapter.) If consumers so choose, they may retain an attorney under the provisions of most arbitration programs.

It is your responsibility to assure the appearance of any witnesses or the submission of affidavits (written and notarized testimony). *Ask questions beforehand if you have any apprehensions or misgivings as to the procedures or the validity of your presentation.*

Arbitration programs are not perfect. It should be no surprise that all programs have given rise to complaints about the lack of mediation or contact between the consumer and the manufacturer between the time a complaint is filed and the actual hearing. This is significant, because many cases are routinely settled during this mediation period. There have also been complaints about program refusals to consider consequential damages or repairs. Reports are rife of delays that extend well beyond the FTC-mandated 40- to 60-day limit. Complaints have also been raised of dealers discouraging consumer use of arbitration, and of consumers being told that dealer and regional office involvement is a prerequisite to arbitration, which is not true; it can be suggested only.

These shortcomings should not discourage consumers from seeking arbitration but, instead, should encourage consumers to read the provisions of any arbitration program carefully and to ask questions. Confirm specifics through the information supplied in your owner's manual, or by contacting your dealer, the manufacturer's regional office, or, in the case of GM, the BBB.

Should you feel that the proceedings are not being handled properly, or that you have been given misinformation, contact:

Bureau of Consumer Protection
U.S. Federal Trade Commission
Division of Marketing Practices
Warranties Program, Room 238
6th and Pennsylvania NW
Washington, D.C. 20580
(202) 523-1642

The FTC also maintains regional offices in Atlanta, Boston, Chicago, Cleveland, Dallas, Denver, Los Angeles, New York, San Francisco, and Seattle. The addresses and phone numbers of these offices are listed in Appendix F.

The Auto Line Arbitration Program

General Motors, American Motors, and a dozen or so foreign manufacturers representing about 20 different makes have a contract with the Council of Better Business Bureaus (CBBB), based in Arlington, Virginia, for customer arbitration (see Table 2-1). CBBB is the national headquarters for the approximately 170 local BBB offices throughout the country.

Local BBB offices are set up to administer the Auto Line program at no charge to the consumer in automotive complaint cases. Nationally, Auto Line averages about 250,000 such cases a year; the majority are solved in the 20-day mediation period, which usually precedes arbitration. This mediation period is mandatory, except in the 703 cases that encompass vehicles built in 1984 or later whose manufacturers have written the program into their warranties.

The CBBB states that the mediation period leads to resolution of a full 60 percent of the problems brought to the attention of the BBB and that only about 10 percent of initiated arbitration cases reach the actual hearing phase. The remaining 30 percent of Auto Line contacts are handled through zone office contact, without the need for even the mediation period. Of the cases that do reach arbitration, over half are for vehicles that are 12 to 24 months old; another 40 percent are for vehicles less than 1 year old, and about 10 percent concern vehicles older than 2 years.

Arbitration proceedings are informal, and the case may be presented in person, in writing, or by telephone. The majority of the hearings are presented in person, with the consumer presenting the complaint, and a local employee of the automaker offering a defense. The manufacturer is usually represented by an employee from the local zone, or district, office. The manufacturer's representative may have more arbitration hearing experience than you, so if you have misgivings about the procedure, ask questions beforehand.

Cases are heard by an arbitrator, with a BBB staff member in attendance to advise the arbitrator, if necessary, on procedural matters. The BBB maintains a file of arbitrators—about 15,000 nationwide—all of whom are volunteers; arbitrators are not paid, except for occasional travel expenses. They are taught BBB Auto Line procedures only, and not legal technicalities. Arbitrators hail from all walks of life, and their knowledge of mechanics is about what you might expect to find in a cross section of the general population. It is not unlikely, then, that an arbitrator would not understand what a spun crankshaft bearing is or how it occurs. An arbitrator decides only what is fair to both parties, based on their testimonies (see Fig. 2-1 for a sample BBB automotive case record form).

Selection of the arbitrator is based upon a list of five arbitrators that is given to both the consumer and the manufacturer. The list contains a brief background description of each candidate. Both parties rank the arbitrators according to their preference, and the one representing the highest common ranking is appointed to hear the case. Either party may delete an arbitrator from consideration because of personal, professional, or financial relationships; the other party must then delete that arbitrator as well. In arbitration cases involving the same dealership or manufacturer, arbitrators are limited to hearing no more than two such cases per year, to prevent the company from being too familiar with arbitrators and their voting patterns.

Arbitrator selection usually takes 5 business days. If no candidates are acceptable, the BBB issues new lists; if no selection is received within 5 business days, the BBB appoints an arbitrator from the list. Under oath, the chosen arbitrator vows to make a fair decision, and before hearing the case, he or she must disclose any partisan interests. When an arbitrator is disqualified voluntarily, the BBB may choose the arbitrator representing the second-highest common selection and not necessarily one from a new list.

In certain cases, depending on state law or the nature of the arbitration—for example, buy-back of a defective vehicle—a panel of three arbitrators may hear the case. Selection of the other two arbitrators varies. Sometimes, both first choices are selected, and the next-highest overlapping choice becomes the third arbitrator. In other instances, the two arbitrators given the highest common priority by both parties are selected,

1 **BETTER BUSINESS BUREAU AUTOMOTIVE CASE RECORD** 437708

Date first contact | | | | | | | |
Mo. Day Yr.

(a) Your BBB Code | | | | | | — | | (b) Staff Initials | | | | Contact Name & Tele. _____

(c) Current Vehicle Owner/Lessee (Title, First Name, Middle Initial, Last Name)

(h) Day Phone (| | |)- | | | -| | | |

(d) Address

(i) Night Phone (| | |)- | | | -| | | |

(e) City | | | | | | | | | | | | | (f) State | | | (g) Zip Code | | | | | | | | |

(j) Referred to: Dealer | | | | | | (k) To Mfr. | | | | | (l) Problem Code | | | (m) Code | Program | | | |
(n) Vehicle Model | Mo. Day Yr. | Mo. Day Yr. | (p) Vehicle I.D. #
| | | | | | | | | | | | (o) Year | | | | | | | | | | | | |

(s) Extended Service Contract?
(q) Current Mileage | | | | | | | (r) Date Car Purchased/Delivered | | | | | | Yes | | No | |
Mo. Day Yr.

Purchased New _____ ; Used _____ ; Demo _____ ; Mileage When Purchased _____

Selling Dealer _____
Name   Address   City   State   Zip

Servicing Dealer (if different) _____
Name   Address   City   State   Zip

(t) Brief Description of Problem: _____

(u) Resolution Sought: _____

(v) I have | | have not | | previously contacted the manufacturer's representative about this problem.

INSTRUCTIONS TO THE CONSUMER

This special form for your automotive complaint is sent for two reasons:
1. While you are under no obligation to deal directly with the manufacturer or dealer, our experience has been that this usually resolves a complaint more quickly. **If your problem has been resolved or an adjustment has been promised by the manufacturer or dealer,** please check here | |. Let us know the date when the promised adjustment will be performed | | | | | | and return this form to the Better Business Bureau.   Mo. Day Yr.
2. **If you have been unable to get your complaint resolved,** you should fill out sections "p" through "v" on this form and call or send this information back to us for processing your case further. The make, model, year and VIN (vehicle identification number), together with your brief description of the problem, are critical data and we may not be able to proceed without them. Also, be sure to let us know what you think would be a fair resolution of your problem and include copies of repair bills, cancelled checks and other information necessary to process your complaint.
3. If you decide you do not want the BBB to process this case, please check here | |, and return this form to the BBB.
Note: In order for the BBB to process your case through arbitration, you must own the vehicle in question throughout the entire process.

Please return this form to:

Your Signature _____

Today's Date _____

By the following date: _____   BBB COPY   © Council of Better Business Bureaus, Inc., 1985 All Rights Reserved

Fig. 2-1 BBB automotive case record initiates the Auto Line arbitration program for a consumer with a complaint against an automaker represented by the BBB. (*Courtesy BBB.*)

and they, in turn, choose a third party to chair the panel from the BBB's pool of arbitration volunteers. If both parties have chosen the same arbitrator as their number-one choice, he or she alone may hear the case. In any event, a panel's decision is based on a majority vote.

Dean Determan, vice president of the Council of Better Business Bureaus in Arlington, Virginia, states that 70 percent of all Auto Line cases are heard by a single arbitrator, and that there is rarely a dissenting opinion even when three arbitrators are used.

The arbitrator's decision is binding on the manufacturer only. Although a consumer cannot appeal an arbitrator's decision, a consumer can reject that decision and pursue legal action. The arbitrator's decision may be admissible in court if it involves a warranty problem. The only question that could then be raised would be whether or not the procedure itself was carried out properly, and not the *decision* rendered. Some states, though, find arbitration rulings to be admissible in court whether or not the case was within warranty parameters; yet others consider the rulings hearsay, and therefore inadmissible as evidence. In this regard, it is best to know the legal status in your state beforehand. In any case, if a consumer accepts the results of an arbitration hearing, it is enforceable by a court of law. For example, if a consumer agrees to pay half the repair cost, but later reneges, the manufacturer can take the consumer to court and demand payment.

To proceed with arbitration through the BBB, the consumer must have a tangible loss. For example, a consumer cannot claim loss of resale value because of the poor reputation of a certain make, model, or engine type. Disputed payment may sometimes be held in escrow pending the outcome of the arbitration hearing; in other cases, the hearing may proceed with payments outstanding. Such latitude allows consideration of individual circumstances.

Sometimes residual damages, such as towing or lodging, are allowed to enter into the arbitration process, but this varies from case to case. In general, if you think that you have a legitimate claim, go ahead and ask for its inclusion; you have nothing to lose and everything to gain. However, under no circumstances are losses that extend to personal injury or property damage considered in arbitration hearings.

Before the hearing, the BBB issues an arbitration agreement. This states the issue or issues to be arbitrated and the requested consumer resolution. Both parties have 5 business days in which to sign and return this agreement. Either party may bring expert witnesses. To a consumer, this may entail an independent mechanic who was involved in the repair attempt; a consumer may also retain a lawyer for the proceedings. The only stipulation placed on these witnesses is that the other party involved be notified of their appearance. The same notification requirement holds true if a vehicle inspection is requested by either party. The arbitrator can also subpoena reluctant witnesses. All contact with the arbitrator, though, must be channeled through the BBB.

Statements written under oath and notarized (affidavits), and in some cases, transcripts of questions and answers from supportive parties (depositions), may also be presented. The arbitrator's decision is due no later than 10 days after the hearing is closed. Should additional information be requested by the arbitrator, time will be set aside from the 10-day limit to allow for this. The arbitrator's decision will be sent to both parties via certified mail by the BBB.

Unless the consumer or arbitrator objects, observers may attend arbitration hearings to the extent the BBB determines that reasonable accommodations are available.

Consumers who have gone through the arbitration process receive a questionnaire. In one compilation, of the 40 percent who responded, 35 percent indicated they thought the manufacturer had won, 36 percent thought that they as consumers had won, and 29 percent thought the decision was a compromise. In these split decisions, though, 93 percent of the consumers accepted the arbitrator's decision; that is, if partial reimbursement of a repair was offered, the consumer accepted it. Only 43 percent of the consumers accepted the arbitrator's decisions in favor of the manufacturer.

A state-by-state listing of Better Business Bureau offices is contained in Appendix C.

GM-FTC Arbitration Agreement

The GM-FTC Arbitration Agreement was reached on November 15, 1983, and expanded arbitration of certain alleged defects that could occur in 21 million GM vehicles manufactured between 1974 and April 26, 1983. This unique program is administered through BBB's Auto Line.

Both past and present owners of vehicles affected by this agreement may file for arbitration. Past owners may file for reimbursement of repair costs on eligible components, and current owners may file for repairs or reimbursement of repair costs on eligible components, which are as follows:

1. Turbo Hydramatic 200 automatic transmissions used in a number of rear-wheel-drive vehicles beginning with the 1976 models. These transmissions allegedly have several defects that cause them to wear out prematurely. Repairs run as high as $600.
2. Camshafts and lifters in 305- and 350-CID V-8 gasoline engines produced in plants operated by Chevrolet since 1974. The FTC blames the

premature failure of these components on the fact that some motor oils did not protect against excess wear, and that GM did not disclose in owners' manuals what types of oils were required. Repairs average $400.

3. Fuel-injection pumps or fuel injectors in the 350-CID V-8 diesel engines produced in plants operated by Oldsmobile since 1978. The FTC said that GM did warn buyers of the danger of water contamination, and that in some cases a water filter is needed to prevent corrosion that could cause the fuel-injection pump to fail, necessitating repairs of $300 to $500.

In a separate concession, GM also agreed that owners of vehicles with power-train complaints can seek recourse through GM's arbitration program through November 21, 1991, regardless of mileage, provided that the vehicle is still owned by the person filing. Power-train components are defined as follows:

Cylinder blocks and heads and all internal parts, including camshafts and lifters, manifolds, timing gears, timing-gear chains, or belts and covers, gaskets, water pumps, fuel pumps, and diesel-injection pumps, turbocharger housings and internal parts, turbocharger valves, seals, and gaskets.

Transmission cases and all internal parts, torque converters, vacuum modulators, seals and gaskets, transmission mounts, transfer cases, and all internal parts, seals, and gaskets.

Commercial use of a vehicle, however, is not subject to GM's BBB-administrated arbitration program.

The AUTOCAP Arbitration Program

The Automotive Consumer Action Program (AUTOCAP) is sponsored by the National Automobile Dealers Association (NADA) of McLean, Virginia. Forty-seven dealer associations participate in AUTOCAP. The program is not available in Alabama, Alaska, Arkansas, Delaware, Indiana, Louisiana, Maryland, Minnesota, Mississippi, Missouri, Nebraska, Nevada, New Jersey, and Pennsylvania. Regional coverage only is available in Florida, Michigan, Oklahoma, and Tennessee (see Figs. 2-2 and 2-3). Many import manufacturers are changing their arbitration contracts from AUTOCAP to the BBB's Auto Line; however, for a list of manufacturers currently included, see Table 2-1.

Each state and local dealer association that agrees to participate in AUTOCAP voluntarily commits to finance and administer the program in accordance with NADA standards. The panels meet a minimum of four

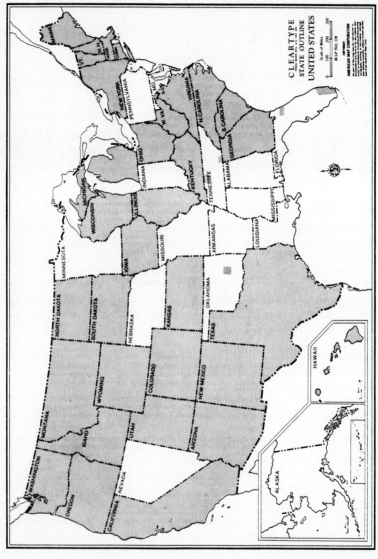

Fig. 2-2 AUTOCAP site map. Shaded areas represent current AUTOCAP locations. (*Courtesy AUTOCAP.*)

CONSUMER
COMPLAINT FORM

AUTOCAP SM
Automotive Consumer Action Program

Case # _____

Local AUTOCAP address:

Tulsa AUTOCAP
525 So. Main, Suite 210
Tulsa, Oklahoma 74103
(918) 592-2291

Staff Person Assigned:

_____

Your Name and Address

_____

_____

_____

Dealer Name and Address

_____

_____

_____

Phone Numbers: Office: _____ Home: _____

Name of person you dealt with: _____

Vehicle Information   Date Purchased: _____

Vehicle make _____ Model _____ Year _____

Purchased: New___ Used___ From _____

Mileage at purchase_____ Present _____

Vehicle Identification No. (VIN)

_____

Manufacturer Name and Address

_____

_____

_____

Name of person you dealt with: _____

DESCRIPTION OF YOUR COMPLAINT

_____

_____

_____

_____

_____

_____

_____

I AM SEEKING THE FOLLOWING REMEDIES OR ADJUSTMENTS:

_____

_____

_____

Please Attach:
Copies of repair orders, receipts, and
other papers relevant to your case

_____
Your Signature

Fig. 2-3 AUTOCAP consumer complaint form used by consumers to initiate an arbitration hearing. (*Courtesy AUTOCAP.*)

times a year; conference calls can be substituted for two in-person panel meetings. Public observers are permitted to attend the in-person meetings.

AUTOCAP arbitration boards are comprised of six members—three consumer and three dealership representatives—all of whom vote. Dealer participation is strictly voluntary. AUTOCAP board decisions are not binding on either dealer or consumer. Because of these exceptions to FTC section 703, the requirement that a consumer arbitrate a case before pursuing repair-or-replace legislation does not apply to AUTOCAP. This is why many AUTOCAP-associated manufacturers are switching, or have switched, to the BBB's Auto Line. Not having a direct tie with the manufacturer, AUTOCAP cannot promise its dealer members the type of national coverage they would need in writing arbitration programs into the manufacturer's warranty.

The consumer should be aware that approximately 20 percent of the dealerships listed as participating in AUTOCAP have yet to sign agreements acknowledging or honoring the program. In these cases, the consumer has no recourse for arbitration. Additionally, AUTOCAP's greatest leverage is with its dealership members and not with the manufacturers. This can dilute not only the magnitude of what a consumer can receive through AUTOCAP but the compliance with AUTOCAP recommendations as well. The AUTOCAP program, then, is to be considered informal, as a go-between for the customer involved in dealer disputes.

AUTOCAP forwards customer complaints to the dealer involved, who is then given the opportunity to settle the problem directly with the customer. The dealer also informs AUTOCAP of any actions taken or offers made. If this mediation period fails, AUTOCAP tries to mediate the situation directly. Should this, too, fail, AUTOCAP then asks both consumer and dealer (and in some cases, the manufacturer) to submit informal written complaints. A local AUTOCAP panel then arbitrates the case, and both customer and dealer receive a written report of the decision.

AUTOCAP declines to become involved in disputes in which litigation has begun, and personal liability, fraud, and claims extending beyond the value of the car are not considered. Regional AUTOCAP addresses and phone numbers can be found in Appendix D.

Ford and Chrysler Arbitration Programs

The Ford Motor Company and the Chrysler Corporation each sponsor an arbitration program. Both programs are separate from one another, but they have many similarities. The Ford Motor Company program is the

Ford Consumer Appeals Board (FCAB), and Chrysler's program is the Customer Satisfaction Board.

FCAB consists of a five-member panel: three consumer representatives, a Ford dealer, and a Lincoln-Mercury dealer. The board decision is binding only on the company and its dealers, but not on the consumer. FCAB hears complaints that arise within 48 months or 50,000 miles, provided the customer still owns the car on which arbitration is sought. (To clarify conflicting reports that consumers may receive from previous FCAB participants, *before February 1985* all complaints were eligible for FCAB arbitration regardless of mileage, time, or warranty parameters, and current ownership was not required.)

Chrysler Corporation's Customer Satisfaction Board consists of five members: a certified auto mechanic, a consumer advocate, a representative of the general public, a dealer, and a representative from Chrysler's zone office. Only the first three are voting members, and the decision they render is binding on the dealer and the corporation but not on the consumer. Chrysler reviews service-related warranty disputes only, and current ownership of the vehicle is a prerequisite to filing (see Fig. 2-4).

Unlike the BBB Auto Line panels, Ford and Chrysler panels most often rely on written instead of oral presentations. Thus, a premium is placed on record-keeping and writing skills (see Figs. 2-4 and 2-5). If written materials are not sufficient, the panel asks for more information. Ford and Chrysler panels review complaints once a month or less often, and the meetings are open to the public upon request.

Ford offers a toll-free number to aid with service information and problems: (800) 241-3673; in Alaska or Hawaii dial (800) 241-3711; and in Georgia dial (800) 282-0959. These numbers are also valuable in learning about special policies (see Chapter 7). Ford's basic response to the consumer is by letter. FCAB has about 20 form letters, beginning with "Response to Telephone Inquiry or Brief Letter" and "Response to Detailed Letter" all the way through to "Response to Customer Dissatisfied with Board Decision."

Although Ford, in 1977, was the first to pioneer arbitration boards, it was not until mid-1983 that FCAB went nationwide. This accounts for Ford's lower annual caseload figure of about 8000, compared to Chrysler's annual caseload of approximately 15,000, despite Chrysler's smaller market share. By comparison, Chrysler's program, begun as a nationwide program in March 1981, experienced a tenfold increase in 3 years. Because of program variables, though, these figures are scarcely indicative of overall customer satisfaction or product quality.

Ford established its own arbitration program after a test program with the BBB's Auto Line in Milwaukee in 1979 and Denver in 1980; as a result the company concluded that it could operate a more cost-effective and

CUSTOMER ARBITRATION BOARD APPLICATION

Did you contact dealership management regarding your complaint?   Yes ☐   No ☐
Did you contact the local Chrysler Zone Office regarding your complaint?   Yes ☐   No ☐
Have you met with the Factory Representative regarding your problem?   Yes ☐   No ☐

Your Name _____ Date _____

Address _____ City _____ State _____ Bus. Phone _____
                                                        Res. Phone _____

Name of Selling Dealer _____ City _____ State _____

Name of Servicing Dealer _____ City _____ State _____

Vehicle: Year _____ Make _____ Model _____

Identification No. _____ Delivery Date _____

Mileage at time of dispute _____ Current Mileage _____

Very Important: Be very specific in describing your current unresolved problems. Include copies of any receipts, service repair orders, complaint letters to the dealer or Zone Representative and any other relevant documents.

Nature of current unresolved problem: * _____
_____
_____
_____

Number and dates of repair attempts (if any):   (1)   (2)   (3)

If more, specify _____

What do you feel should be done to resolve your problem? _____
_____

ARBITRATION AGREEMENT

I understand that I am not bound by the decision of the Board unless I accept it. I also understand, however, that if I accept the Board's decision, the Chrysler Corporation dealer involved and Chrysler Corporation will be bound by the Board's decision. I further understand neither I nor the dealer will attend or be represented by legal counsel at the Board hearing on this dispute. If I am dissatisfied with the Board's decision or the dealer's or Chrysler's eventual performance, I understand that I may pursue other legal remedies, including the use of small claims court. I understand, however, that whether or not I accept the Board's decision, its decision is admissible in any subsequent legal proceeding concerning the dispute. This dispute settlement procedure does not take the place of any state or federal legal remedies available to me.

Signed by _____

*Please use additional sheets of paper as necessary to describe these items.

Fig. 2-4   Chrysler Corp. arbitration agreement form used by consumers to file for an arbitration hearing. (*Courtesy Chrysler Corp.*)

efficient program on its own. Chrysler took the same basic stance after pilot programs in 1979.

Both Chrysler's Customer Satisfaction Board and the FCAB review only service complaints. Cases cannot be for sales problems involving dealers. A consumer requesting reimbursement for a repair may also request reimbursement for consequential expenses, such as lodging or towing, but an arbitration case cannot be opened strictly for reimbursement of consequential expenses only, and neither manufacturer will review a case in which a lawsuit has already been filed against them.

FCAB selects dealers for board members based on a dealer's track record: "those who are or have been profitable with a proven record of customer relations concern and performance as well as high credibility with other dealer associates." Candidates are determined regionally by Ford district offices and must be approved by the company's general office coordinator.

FCAB consumer representatives are selected from candidates screened by an independent source. One of the three FCAB consumer representatives must have automotive expertise, perhaps as an automotive vocational school educator or as a member of the American Automobile Association. The other two are usually affiliated with consumer affairs agencies or may be educators in that field.

Ford sets 18 months as the length of time a board member should serve; this may be as little as 12 months in some cases, especially in situations in which a nearly complete turnover of board members might occur simultaneously; Ford tries to stagger board-member replacement to prevent this. Ford also encourages potential dealer and consumer board candidates to attend meetings. Board meetings are open to anyone who requests permission to attend. If one of the parties involved requests attendance, then the other party (such as the dealership involved) will also be invited to attend.

Chrysler's board selection is very similar to FCAB's, except that Chrysler qualifies and selects its own board members. The consumer-advocate member of the panel may be selected from a state attorney general's office, a state consumer agency, or the BBB, for example. The second consumer member is chosen as a representative of the general public. The third consumer member is a certified mechanic not affiliated with Chrysler. All serve 1-year terms with an option of serving a second. The two nonvoting members of the five-member panel are a Chrysler Corporation dealer and a zone-office representative.

If Chrysler's Customer Satisfaction Board or the FCAB cannot render a decision within the 40- to 60-day limit set by FTC section 703, then the consumer is free to pursue other legal recourse, such as lemon laws or civil suits.

INSTRUCTIONS FOR COMPLETING THE
FORD CONSUMER APPEALS BOARD CUSTOMER STATEMENT

The Ford Consumer Appeals Board is a cost-free, independent, third party dispute settlement mechanism that reviews unresolved service complaints on Ford and Lincoln-Mercury products in the following categories:

Category A. Complaints involving vehicles covered by the new vehicle warranty provided by Ford or by a state vehicle repair/replacement statute.

Category B. Complaints involving vehicles and/or components that are no longer covered by warranty and/or a state repair/replacement statute, but are within 48 months or 50,000 miles of service.

The Board does **not** review service complaints involving:

- A non-Ford product
- A non-Ford dealership
- A Ford Motor Company vehicle in excess of 48 months or 50,000 miles of service except for components covered by a longer term warranty
- A vehicle sales transaction
- A request for reimbursement of consequential expenses unless incidental to a service or product complaint being reviewed
- Alleged personal injury or property damage
- Cases currently in litigation

If you qualify in Category A above, the following five step procedure is suggested, although Steps 1 and 2 are *NOT* **required for Ford Consumer Appeals Board review.**

Step 1. Review your complaint with your dealer or his representative. If the dealer is unable to resolve your complaint to your satisfaction, proceed to Step 2.

Step 2. Contact a District Office of the Ford Parts and Service Division - addresses are listed in the Owner's Guide which is provided with all new Ford Motor Company vehicles.

Step 3. Be sure to complete the information at the top of the statement concerning your name, address, dealer's name and city, and the information about your vehicle.

Step 4. Briefly describe what your unresolved complaint is about and what you want done to resolve your complaint.

Step 5. Attach all documents and maintenance or repair orders which you believe are important to the unresolved complaint(s) and your vehicle's service history. Board decisions are based on this information.

If you qualify in Category B, it is a *REQUIREMENT* **that you follow the five step procedure above. If you have** *NOT* **previously been in contact with Ford Motor Company and you submit this Customer Statement, it will be referred to the appropriate Ford Parts and Service Division District Office for resolution. If you then remain dissatisfied, your complaint may become eligible for Board review.**

WHERE TO SEND:

Mail the original and the second copy of the completed Customer Statement to the Executive Secretary, Ford Consumer Appeals Board, at the address shown on the front of the form. Keep the last copy for your records. An acknowledgment postcard will be mailed to you when your case is opened.

Fig. 2-5 Ford consumer appeals board form used by the consumer to file for an arbitration hearing. (*Courtesy Ford Motor Co.*)

1-85

CUSTOMER'S STATEMENT
FORD CONSUMER APPEALS BOARD

(Date Stamp), for office use only

Case Number _____

Customer Name _____ Home Phone Area Code (_____)_____

Address _____ Bus. Phone Area Code (_____)_____

City _____ State _____ Zip _____ Vehicle I.D. No. _____

Vehicle (Year, Make, Model) _____ Acquired New ☐   Used ☐   Leased ☐

Date Purchased _____ Date of Repair _____ Repair Mileage _____ Current Mileage _____

Selling Dealer _____ City _____

Servicing Dealer _____ City _____

1. Describe your unresolved service complaint:

_____
_____
_____
_____
_____
_____

2. Summary of action you have taken with dealer and Ford Motor Company: (attach copies of any maintenance and repair orders, if available, or additional explanation)

_____
_____
_____
_____
_____
_____

3. If known, name(s) of individuals you contacted: At Dealership _____

   At Ford Motor Company _____

4. Describe exactly what you want done to resolve your complaint:

_____
_____
_____
_____
_____

Signed _____ Date _____

NOTE: The Board's decision is binding on Ford Motor Company and its participating Ford and Lincoln-Mercury dealers; it is not binding on the customer. Therefore, if you are dissatisfied with the Board's decision concerning your case, you are free to pursue other legal remedies.

Retain last copy and forward remaining two copies of completed statement to Executive Secretary, Ford Consumer Appeals Board, P.O. Box 900, Wixom, MI 48096-0900.

Fig. 2-5   (*Continued*)

In independent audits prepared for the FTC in 1984, 60 percent of the Chrysler arbitration participants surveyed said they received at least part of what they wanted; with FCAB, it was 56 percent. With FCAB, 24 percent received all of what they asked for; with Chrysler, the figure was 33 percent.

Over half of all FCAB vehicles were inspected, 73 percent for Chrysler. Most often the consumer, and not the board, made the inspection request, which was usually carried out by a dealership mechanic or a board member. Fifty-seven percent were satisfied with the quality of Chrysler's inspection, 46 percent with Ford's.

Board decisions were considered reasonable by only 34 percent of the FCAB participants surveyed; for Chrysler, 44 percent felt so. The most frequent reason stated for dissatisfaction was that the problem was not completely resolved.

Seventy-five percent of the participants surveyed accepted FCAB rulings; 66 percent accepted Chrysler's board decisions. The participants were evenly split (50:50) as to whether or not they would use either arbitration program again.

The audits also found that the average number of days it took the board to acknowledge the complaint was 19 for FCAB and 18 for Chrysler. The average number of days until the board decision was received was 59 for FCAB and 56 for Chrysler. The average number of days until corrective action was taken was 78 for FCAB and 76 for Chrysler.

Major-Defect Legislation (Lemon Laws)

Three decades after it was first suggested that what was good for General Motors was good for the country, a more worldly U.S. automotive consumer was having inordinate problems with new-car warranty laws. "Lemons-on-wheels" angered enough people that within less than 5 years repair-or-replace legislation, or "lemon laws," had been passed in more than 37 states.

Automotive Lemons: An Overview

Some say lemons are the product of the "Monday/Friday syndrome" of assembly-line sick calls. Others blame it on the domestic industry's rush to remain competitive in the world marketplace. Still others contend that the lemon is a by-product of mass production.

An automobile, though, is no more than an assembled collection of parts. We tend to think of vehicles as being "built" by Ford or Chrysler. These companies and corporations, however, design and assemble parts manufactured in any number of the large and small shops in most industrial areas of the country. These regional suppliers (called *fabricators*), together with assembly plants within their vicinity, are autonomous in a sense. One makes the parts; the other assembles them.

Wide variances can result from this arrangement. Automotive engineers, in fact, design parts and subsystems within acceptable tolerances. An automobile built at one plant with one set of suppliers will vary from the same make and model built at another plant with a different set of suppliers. It's an inevitable consequence of the mass production of interchangeable parts. Also, parts contracts are often given to the lowest bidder, and a shop awarded a contract on the basis of a low bid is not as eager to replace an aging machine used in the manufacturing process.

Machined parts are seldom the same even under ideal conditions; they vary by thousandths of an inch, and tolerances grow as the machines and tools that manufacture the parts begin to wear. Fitting together more than 14,000 parts leaves the door open for a lemon. Add an unmotivated or poorly trained staff, and you've got further trouble yet.

Automakers have begun to combat the lemon recently by requiring more exact specifications, more precise machinery, and more extensively trained personnel. All of this, of course, has contributed to the soaring price of cars, which in turn contributes to consumers' extreme dissatisfaction with the inevitable lemons that still occur.

Lemon-Law History

Shortly after Sally Turner introduced the country's first lemon law into the California State Assembly in 1981, she was visited by a man whom she described as an "ultraslick Washington lobbyist" who warned her in threatening tones against pursuing passage of the bill. Assemblywoman Tanner took great pleasure in booting the man out of her office, and on her second attempt, she saw that the bill passed in the legislature.

California was the first state to *introduce* such legislation, the second to put repair-or-replace legislation into effect. The country's first lemon law was passed in Connecticut in 1982, sponsored by state representative John Woodcock. (New York was the first state to enact repair-or-replace coverage for used cars.)

Lemon laws provide the consumer with a manufacturer ultimatum: either repair it, or replace it. Most state lemon laws state that if a major defect in a new vehicle cannot be repaired within four attempts, or in less than 30 days within the lesser of the first year of operation or 12,000 miles, the manufacturer must either replace the vehicle or provide a refund. A consumer may choose between refund or replacement in Alaska, Washington, D.C., Florida, Maryland, Minnesota, Mississippi, New York,

Pennsylvania, Rhode Island, Vermont, and Wisconsin. In other lemon-law states, this is left to the manufacturer's discretion.

Lemon laws evolved from the Uniform Commercial Code (UCC) and the Magnuson-Moss Warranty Act, both of which lack terminology specific enough to be fairly applied to major vehicle defects—or so thought the residents of the more than 35 states that enacted lemon laws. Although the UCC sets forth warranty obligations and terms, it permits manufacturers to determine the extent to which they will honor a warranty. In other words, manufacturers may exclude complete replacement of a unit containing a defective part if they so choose.

The Magnuson-Moss Warranty Act of 1975 does provide for refund or replacement of a defective product, but only after a "reasonable number of attempts" at repair, which was left undefined; imagine the field day corporate automotive lawyers had with this open-ended provision. The Magnuson-Moss Warranty Act also has another shortcoming when applied to automotive warranties (or, once again, so thought consumers in the 37 lemon-law states). The act set refund-or-replace provisions for full warranties only. The term *limited warranty* is bandied about in commercial descriptions because it acts as a legal disclaimer. Limited warranties need not contain a refund-or-replace provision, and automotive warranties are—you've got it—limited warranties. Lemon laws filled these gaps by holding automakers liable to the refund-or-replace provision of full warranties and by defining a "reasonable number of attempts" at repair as "four attempts, or a total of 30 calendar days during the first year of operation."

State-by-State Lemon-Law Basics

The following provisions are typical of lemon laws.

1. *Major defects* are defined as mechanical defects that *substantially impair the use, market value, or safety of the vehicle.* Continued failure of a transmission or engine within the time parameters provided would probably qualify; continued failure of ancillary items (radio, power windows, water leaks) would probably not.

2. Consumers must first use the manufacturer's arbitration program to resolve the problem, but only if the program is written into the manufacturer's new-car warranty, in which case the owner's manual must also disclose consumer rights under the lemon law.

3. The consumer must give written notice of the defect to the manufacturer during the express warranty period, and the manufacturer must continue to make repairs to correct that defect even after the period ends.

Some states require that the refund include full purchase price, sales tax, license fees, and other charges, all of which are referred to as "collateral costs of purchase." Often an allowance is deducted for the consumer's use of the vehicle; this is generally based on mileage, but *when* this depreciation period ends is often vague. In some cases, it is the point at which arbitration was requested or the point at which the defect first occurred. In yet other cases, vehicles with less than 10,000 miles were assessed free from depreciation.

In *Handling Automobile Warranty and Repossession Cases,* Billings states:

> Many lemon cases will probably turn on the documentary evidence the consumer offers to prove the required number of repair attempts or time in the repair shop for the same defect. If the consumer produces the evidence, the burden shifts to the manufacturer to prove that the alleged defect [is not substantial, or] no longer exists. The consumer should, of course, keep copies of all purchase orders, sales receipts, warranties, repair invoices, letters and other materials concerning the problem. If the vehicle is in the repair shop for more than one day at a time, the repair invoice should show the dates in and out of the shop.

Billings adds that written notice should be sent by certified mail, return receipt requested, to the dealer and the manufacturer before expiration of the new-car warranty. (The national addresses of major automakers are listed in Appendixes A and B.) The letter should include details of the problem, together with the following information:

1. An identification of the defect or defects and which systems of the vehicle are affected
2. The number of times the vehicle has been subject to repairs for the same problem, and the dates of the repairs
3. Copies of the repair invoices
4. The number of business or calendar days (whichever the state law specifies) the vehicle has been out of service for repairs
5. A statement that the defect still exists as of the date of the letter
6. Citation of the law and a statement that the consumer will pursue a replacement or refund claim under the law if the vehicle is not properly repaired
7. A request for information concerning any informal dispute-settlement process the company may have

On the recovery of attorney fees, Billings says, "Some lemon laws provide that the consumer may recover attorney fees and costs if he or she finally prevails in an action. A few provide that the consumer *shall* recover fees and costs. Consumers may also ask for attorney fees under the Magnuson-Moss Act because a lemon law action is a warranty action under state law.''

All states except Kentucky and Texas require that a manufacturer's arbitration program be used before legal action on repair-or-replace legislation can proceed. However, this applies only to arbitration programs that adhere to FTC section 703 guidelines. Therefore, even though a state law may require arbitration before invoking lemon-law litigation, this provision would be waived if the program does not comply with FTC guidelines (such as AUTOCAP). Your state's consumer office can provide you with this information.

Also, most lemon laws do not apply to vehicles such as tractors, farm equipment, any vehicles intended for off-road applications, motorcycles, mopeds, and motor homes excepting the chassis. State-by-state exceptions are noted.

The number of *repair attempts* means the total number of times the vehicle was in for service for the *same major* defect. Most state laws provide for extensions beyond the stated time/mileage parameters if the first occurrence of a major defect is reported to the dealership or manufacturer within the time constraints stated in the lemon law.

Time *in for repairs* applies to the accumulative number of days for which a vehicle was in for service for any and all problems. (This is not limited to major or repeated repairs to the same component.) Repair days are measured by either business or calendar days; calendar days include weekends and legal holidays for which a vehicle was in the custody of a dealership for repairs, while business days do not. Some state laws specify that "acts of God" (floods, storms, etc.) and other conditions beyond the manufacturer's control (civil disorder, power outage, etc.) are not to be counted as repair days.

An asterisk (*) indicates that the law applies only to vehicles purchased on or after the effective date; all other laws apply to the remaining portion of the warranty for any vehicle that was still under warranty on the effective date.

ALASKA: Three repair attempts or 30 business days in for repairs within the lesser of 12 months or the warranty mileage, as provided for under Alaska Stat. section 45.45.300, which went into effect on September 11, 1984.

ARIZONA: Four repair attempts or 30 calendar days in for repairs within the lesser of 12 months or the warranty mileage, as provided for under Ariz. Rev. Stat. Ann. section 44-1261, which went into effect on August 3, 1984, for all vehicles under 10,000 pounds.*

CALIFORNIA: Four repair attempts or 30 calendar days in for repairs within the lesser of 12 months or 12,000 miles, as provided for under Cal. Civ. Code section 1793.2, which went into effect on January 1, 1983.

COLORADO: Four repair attempts or 30 business days in for repair within the lesser of 12 months or the warranty mileage, as provided for under Colo. Rev. Stat. section 42-12-101, which went into effect on July 1, 1984.*

CONNECTICUT: Four repair attempts or 30 calendar days in for repair within the lesser of 24 months or 18,000 miles, as provided for under Conn. Gen. Stat. Ann. section 42-179, which went into effect on September 30, 1984; 12 months or the warranty mileage for the original lemon law effective October 1, 1982.

DELAWARE: Four repair attempts or 30 business days in for repair within the lesser of 12 months or the warranty mileage, as provided for under Del. Code Ann. tit. vi, section 5003, which went into effect with the 1984 model year.

DISTRICT OF COLUMBIA: Four repair attempts or 30 calendar days in for repair within the lesser of 24 months or 18,000 miles as provided for under Act of December 7, 1984, D.C. Act 5-227, which went into effect on that date. (One repair attempt if safety related.)

FLORIDA: Three repair attempts or 15 business days in for repair within the lesser of 12 months or the warranty mileage, as provided for under Fla. Stat. Ann. section 681.104, which went into effect on October 1, 1983. (The first manufacturer-assisted repair attempt is not included.)

HAWAII: Three repair attempts or 30 business days in for repair within the warranty mileage as provided for under Hawaii Rev. Stat. section 437-3.5, which went into effect on May 26, 1984, for all motor vehicles.

ILLINOIS: Four repair attempts or 30 business days in for repair within the lesser of 12 months or 12,000 miles, as provided for under Ill. Rev. Stat. ch. 121 1/2 section 1203, which affects 1985 and later models.

IOWA: Four repair attempts or 30 calendar days in for repair within the lesser of 12 months or the warranty mileage, as provided for under Iowa Code section 322E.1, which went into effect on July 1, 1984.

KENTUCKY: Provides for a state-operated arbitration panel in the settling of automotive disputes for problems that arise within the lesser of 24 months or 25,000 miles. The statute includes a repair-or-replace provision. Ky. Rev. Stat. Ann. section 367.865, effective 1984.

LOUISIANA: Four repair attempts or 30 calendar days in for repair within the lesser of 12 months or the warranty mileage, as provided for under La. Rev. Stat. Ann. section 51:1941, which went into effect on September 3,

1984, for all motor vehicles under 10,000 pounds excepting those in commercial use.

MAINE: Four repair attempts or 30 business days in for repair within the lesser of 12 months or the warranty mileage, as provided for under Me. Rev. Stat. Ann. tit. 10, section 1163, which went into effect on October 1, 1983, for all vehicles excepting those in commercial use weighing more than 8500 pounds.

MARYLAND: Four repair attempts or 30 calendar days in for repair within the lesser of 12 months or 12,000 miles, as provided for under Md. Com. Law Code Ann. section 14-1501, which went into effect on July 1, 1984.* (One repair attempt if safety related.)

MASSACHUSETTS: Three repair attempts or 15 business days in for repair within the lesser of 12 months or 15,000 miles, as provided for under Mass. Ann. Laws ch. 90 section 7N 1/2, which went into effect on January 1, 1984.

MICHIGAN: Four repair attempts or 30 business days in for repair within the lesser of 12 months or the warranty mileage, as provided for under Public Act 87 of 1986, which went into effect on June 25, 1986.*

MINNESOTA: Four repair attempts or 30 business days in for repair within the lesser of 12 months or the warranty mileage, as provided for under Minn. Stat. Ann. section 225 F 665, which went into effect on May 11, 1982.* (One repair attempt if safety related.)

MISSISSIPPI: Three repair attempts or 15 business days in for repair within the lesser of 12 months or the warranty mileage, as provided for under 1985 Miss. Laws Chapter 336.

MISSOURI: Four repair attempts or 30 business days in for repair within the lesser of 12 months or the warranty mileage, as provided for under Mo. Ann. Stat. section 407.560, which went into effect on January 1, 1985.*

MONTANA: Four repair attempts or 30 business days in for repair within the lesser of 12 months or the warranty mileage, as provided for under Mont. Code Ann. section 61-4-503, which went into effect on October 1, 1983, for all vehicles.*

NEBRASKA: Four repair attempts or 30 calendar days in for repair within the lesser of 12 months or the warranty mileage, as provided for under Neb. Rev. Stat. section 60-2703, which went into effect with the 1984 model year.

NEVADA: Four repair attempts or 30 calendar days in for repair within the lesser of 12 months or the warranty mileage, as provided for under Nev. Rev. Stat. section 598-766, which went into effect on July 1, 1983.

NEW HAMPSHIRE: Four repair attempts or 30 business days in for repair within the lesser of 12 months or the warranty mileage, as provided for under N.H. Rev. Stat. Ann. section 357-D-3, which went into effect on July 18, 1983.

NEW JERSEY: Four repair attempts or 30 business days in for repair within the lesser of 12 months or the warranty mileage, as provided for under N.J. Stat. Ann. section 56:12-21, which went into effect on June 20, 1983.*

NEW MEXICO: Four repair attempts or 30 business days in for repair within the lesser of 12 months or the warranty mileage, as provided for under 1985 N.M. Laws Chapter 222, which went into effect on January 1, 1986.

NEW YORK: Four repair attempts or 30 calendar days in for repair within the lesser of 24 months or 18,000 mileage, as provided for under NY Gen. Bus. Law section 198-a, which went into effect on September 1, 1983.

198-b covers used vehicles of a value of $1500 or greater. Up to 36,000 miles, dealers are to issue a 60-day/3,000-mile warranty; more than 36,000 miles, a 30-day/1,000-mile warranty. Consumers are entitled to a refund or replacement vehicle if the dealer fails to correct the same *major* defect after three attempts or if the car is out of service for 15 calendar days. The law went in effect on November 1, 1984, and covers the engine, transmission, drive axle, brakes, radiator, steering, and alternator.

OREGON: Four repair attempts or 30 business days in for repair within the lesser of 12 months or 12,000 miles, as provided for under Or. Rev. Stat. section 646.335, which went into effect on January 1, 1984.*

PENNSYLVANIA: Three repair attempts or 30 calendar days in for repair within the lesser of 12 months, or the greater of 12,000 miles or the warranty mileage, as provided for under Pa. Stat. Ann. tit. 73, section 2001, which went into effect on May 28, 1984.*

RHODE ISLAND: Four repair attempts or 30 calendar days in for repair within the lesser of 12 months or 15,000 miles, as provided for under R.I. Gen. Laws section 31-5.2-1, which went into effect on May 11, 1984.*

TENNESSEE: Four repair attempts or 30 business days in for repair within the lesser of 12 months or the warranty mileage, as provided for under Tenn. Code Ann. section 55-24-103, which went into effect with the 1984 model year.

TEXAS: Four repair attempts or 30 calendar days in for repair within the lesser of 12 months or the warranty mileage, as provided for under Tex. Stat. Ann. art. 4413(36) which went into effect in 1983.

UTAH: Four repair attempts or 30 business days in for repair within the lesser of 12 months or the warranty mileage, as provided for under Utah Code Ann. section 13-21-1 (Supp. 1985).

VERMONT: Three repair attempts or 30 calendar days in for repair within the lesser of 12 months or the warranty mileage, as provided for under Vt. Stat. Ann. tit. ix section 4172, which went into effect with 1985 model year. Trucks over 6000 pounds are exempt.

VIRGINIA: Four repair attempts or 30 calendar days in for repair within the lesser of 12 months or the warranty mileage (12 months on agricultural vehicles) as provided for under Va. Code section 59.1-207.7 (207.9 covers agricultural vehicles), which went into effect on July 1, 1984.

WASHINGTON: Four repair attempts or 30 calendar days in for repair within the lesser of 12 months or the warranty mileage, as provided for under Wash. Rev. Code section 19.118.40, which went into effect on July 4, 1983, for all vehicles. (The 30-calendar-day period does not include repair days during which a dealer provides the consumer with free use of a vehicle of comparable value.)

WEST VIRGINIA: Three repair attempts or 30 calendar days in for repair within the lesser of 12 months or the warranty mileage, as provided for under W. Va. Code section 46A-6A-1, which went into effect on January 1, 1984.* (One repair attempt if safety related.)

WISCONSIN: Four repair attempts or 30 calendar days in for repair within the lesser of 12 months or the warranty mileage, as provided for under Wis. Stat. Ann. section 218.015, which went into effect on November 3, 1983, for all vehicles.*

WYOMING: Four repair attempts or 30 business days in for repair within 12 months, as provided for under Wyo. Stat. section 40-17-101, which went into effect on May 23, 1983, for vehicles weighing less than 10,000 pounds.

Additional Major-Defect Recourse

Common grounds for the filing of a suit stem from breach of contract, breach of warranty, common-law fraud, or state unfair and deceptive acts and practice (UDAP) laws—commonly referred to as consumer protection acts. Each is discussed in the following text, with the exception of rejection of a vehicle, which is outlined at the end of Chapter 1.

Revocation of Acceptance

Revoking acceptance, or revocation, of a vehicle occurs when a substantial defect becomes evident after acceptance of the vehicle by the buyer. The defect must be substantial in that it impairs the use or value of the vehicle, and it must have been present at the time of delivery, though not necessarily discernible until later use of the vehicle. Substantial defects are generally considered as one major defect or as a series of lesser defects.

The largest difference between rejection and revocation is that revocation cannot be claimed for discrepancies in the ordering of the vehicle or for minor defects, as with rejection. Sometimes the dealer must be given an opportunity to make right the defects. In cases of revocation, the failure to repair can also be deemed a breach of warranty. Some courts have ruled that a consumer may revoke a vehicle even though, for example, it may have sustained damage as the result of a collision, provided that the vehicle is returned to its former condition.

Expect a dealer to be well-versed in defending these moves, and for this reason especially, you should consult an attorney to ensure that the revocation of acceptance is properly executed. Dealers commonly try to defend themselves against the action by claiming that the consumer failed to give timely notice of the revocation, or continued using the vehicle after doing so, or by claiming that the vehicle was revoked for minor defects. Order forms specifically exempt the dealer from all warranties and state that the dealer is only an agent of the manufacturer in situations concerning warranty claims, and therefore, is not responsible for the defective vehicle.

When a consumer decides to revoke a vehicle, a written explanation for the action should be sent to the dealer, manufacturer, and finance institution. The vehicle should be returned to the dealer (not the salesperson), the reasons for the action stated, and the title of ownership and keys returned. If the dealer refuses acceptance, the important fact is that the offer was made. A plaintiff witness to this fact is advisable. If refusal occurs, keep the title and keys, but remove your license plates from the vehicle, photograph the vehicle from several angles to verify its condition at the time of revocation, note its odometer reading, and leave the vehicle at the dealership. Often, continued use of the vehicle can seriously impair a buyer's right to revoke acceptance. On the other hand, should odometer mileage increase while the vehicle is with the dealer, this can be used as a sign of the dealer's acceptance of revocation.

Keep organized and in your possession the sales order, bill of sale, and all copies of correspondence, including notes of any phone conversations. Keep all maintenance receipts. It is also a good idea to obtain a written evaluation of the defects from an independent repair shop.

Dealers are generally awarded compensation for the time the vehicle was in use, but sometimes, full purchase price including tax and delivery charges is refunded to the buyer. An attorney can determine amounts due, including incidental and consequential damages (including time lost from work and car rentals) after analysis of a case.

Suing for Damages

The following is intended as an overall summary only of additional actions at law possible under the Magnuson-Moss Warranty Act. This section is intended to allow consumer comparison of individual circumstances to actions that *may* be grounds for legal action. However, judicial interpretation of legal precedents, the knowledge and experience of the attorneys involved, and the presentation of arguments and evidence will always vary the outcome of an individual case.

Usually an attorney will file suit against both the dealer and the manufacturer; the dealer sold the car, but the manufacturer gives the warranty. This covers all bases and doubles the expense of defending a suit, which may lead to an early settlement. As with lemon laws, though, some states stipulate that the manufacturer must have had a chance to repair the defect before bringing the case to court, and often, this is in lieu of, or in spite of, any dealer attempts at repair.

Four counts are generally filed: (1) provisions of the Magnuson-Moss Warranty Act that were violated; (2) a violation of the implied warranty provisions of the UCC; (3) a motion to rescind the dealer sales contract as provided for under the UCC; and (4) an obligation to repurchase the vehicle in states with repair-or-replace legislation. (Louisiana is the only state in which the UCC is not in effect.)

These counts concern breach of warranty and breach of contract. Breach of warranty occurs when the dealer or the manufacturer cannot satisfactorily repair a car in a reasonable amount of time. The vague terms "satisfactorily repair" and "reasonable amount of time" are the legalities upon which a breach of warranty case hinges. These fragile legal parameters have helped the proliferation of state lemon laws.

Nearly all breach of warranty actions require proving that the defect existed at the time of sale and was due to either a flaw in manufacturing or in production. In matters concerning breach of warranty, the statute of limitations is 4 years from the date of sale, but discuss your situation with an attorney, as there are "creative" ways to interpret this statute.

Suits are usually filed in state courts, because district, or federal, courts require a minimum claim of $50,000 under the Magnuson-Moss Warranty Act. Automotive warranty suits seldom approach that figure, unless punitive damages are being sought. State courts, however, do have jurisdiction over out-of-state manufacturers via "long-arm statutes" (hence, the "long arm of the law").

A class action suit may be filed if a number of consumers have a common cause for suit. To file a federal class action suit, a minimum of 100 named plaintiffs is required, and the total claim must be in excess of $50,000. This can be an extremely complex situation, and manufacturers have ways in which to pare down the eligible number of plaintiffs, so as to avoid these suits altogether.

Although the dealership is generally free from breach of warranty suits because of the disclaimer found in new-car contracts, as discussed in Chapter 1, dealer handling of a new-car transaction may have constituted a breach of contract or unfair trade practices. An example of the latter occurred in one case in which a car that had been stolen from the dealer's lot was repaired and sold as a new vehicle. After the buyer experienced problems with the car, he was able to obtain a full refund by proving fraudulent sale.

The following are some of the practices prohibited in the sale of a new car, some of which may be grounds for the filing of a UDAP civil suit: selling a used car as new; selling last year's model as a new model; raising the price after the purchase contract was signed; failing to disclose known defects; promising delivery sooner than was known to be possible; failing to disclose that a new car has been repaired or repainted prior to sale; failing to properly inspect the vehicle before delivery; and intentionally misrepresenting the manufacturer's suggested retail price.

Two good legal references on the subject of warranty disputes are Roger Billings's book *Handling Automobile Warranty and Repossession Cases* and the Center for Auto Safety's *Lemon Law Litigation Manual*.

chapter 3

Traveling in the Dark:
The Used-Car Market

"Look Before You Leap" and
"They Who Hesitate Are Lost"

Buying a used car is more than just the alternative to buying a new car. Used cars can offer value that extends well beyond their purchase price.

A vehicle's most expensive years are its newest ones; during the first years, depreciation can amount to 25 percent of its sales price and larger interest payments compound that loss. Often, the used-car buyer's gain is the new-car buyer's loss.

But don't used cars actually cost more in the long run than new cars because of higher maintenance costs and repair bills? Seldom, if ever. But this is a myth new-car dealers are not quick to dispel.

Take, for example, the extensive and well-respected annual studies compiled and published by The Hertz Corporation on the average operating costs of vehicles in the United States. Year after year, in study after study, Hertz has concluded, "As a car ages, the decline in fixed costs—depreciation, insurance, and interest—traditionally more than offsets the increase in maintenance costs which occur as the vehicle ages."

Buying a new car is seldom a matter of logic, it's a matter of pride in ownership and it carries a high price. If you are undecided as to whether or not you should just keep your present car, then figure the cost to replace it. Very often, the decision to sell your car is more a matter of your ability to purchase another.

Coping with "Used-Car Phobia"

Look for details, but set your sights on the vital few and not the trivial many. It's too easy to become overwhelmed and throw in the towel after a cursory inspection or two. But rather than neglect precautionary measures altogether, narrow them down to a manageable and realistic size; look for those problems associated with given mileage parameters. After all, not even a team of automotive engineers could readily check the dozens of complex systems found in today's automobile.

If it is within your budget, consider buying a one- to three-year old vehicle. These are usually the most trouble-free years and by that point someone else will have taken the largest chunk of the depreciation loss. You will also accrue less in finance charges.

Where Do I Look, and from Whom Should I Buy?

The most common sources of used cars are new-car dealers, used-car dealers, and private owners. Two less common sources are car-rental companies and auctions. There is no single "right" place to buy. A buyer's personality, buying habits, and budget all influence the perceived advantages and disadvantages of each.

New-car dealers.   New-car dealers handle most of the paperwork for the customer and offer immediate financing. This provides for one-stop shopping, a real convenience. New-car dealers also generally offer the largest selection of late-model used vehicles. A dealership's need to maintain good business and community relations often assuages a customer's fears, but that alone is no guarantee that the dealer will satisfy you. New-car dealers are the best able to honor used-car warranties and service contracts, though.

These advantages translate to high overhead and, usually, higher used-car prices. Make and model selection may be limited, too, often to the same ones the dealership offers in new cars. And, although the dealer may not necessarily be at fault, vehicles with odometers that have been rolled back often end up for sale on used-car lots. These illegal rollbacks can be difficult to detect. In addition, both new- and used-car dealers sell the occasional salvage vehicle (see Fig. 3-1). These are collision-damaged vehicles that are sold for salvage by insurance companies. Later, they are purchased by body shops, renovated, and resold. (Salvage vehicles and odometer tampering are discussed more in upcoming sections.)

Used-car dealers.   Used-car dealers generally offer a wide range of prices and selections, because (1) they have less overhead than new-car dealers, (2) they are not affiliated with any one manufacturer, and (3) they sell older vehicles. Besides saving the customer paperwork hassles, used-car lots often have more convenient business hours than do new-car dealerships. And some used-car lot owners and their long-term employees really know *used* cars, whereas their counterparts at new-car dealerships may simply be killing time, hoping to be promoted to new-car sales eventually.

On the other hand, the familiar stereotype of the crooked used-car dealer cannot be readily dismissed. Checking a dealer's reputation before buying can make all the difference afterwards. The handling of warranties and service contracts can be tentative with used-car lots. Also, a customer risks purchasing a vehicle with a rolled-back odometer or a salvage history.

Private owners.   There's no overhead on the homestead, and you might pick up a good deal if you're at all good at bargaining. Dealing directly with the owner on home ground can also give you a good sense of how well or how poorly the vehicle was maintained. The atmosphere is usually more casual than with dealers, too, which may aid in negotiations. In addition, title deficiencies and liberal odometer rollbacks are less likely with private owners.

Coordinating paperwork and bank transactions is a drawback of private-owner transactions, and enforceable warranties or service contracts are practically nonexistent.

Fig. 3-1   Late-model vehicles that have been stolen and stripped are often sold for salvage (*top*), then later reconstructed by body shops and sold as used cars (*bottom*). (*Photo by Mike Spaniola.*)

Used rental cars.   If not the home of the best deal, then certainly rental lots offer the least known of some of the best deals on used cars. Most rental cars are better-maintained throughout the ownership period than the average, privately owned vehicle. A small minority of drivers may treat rental cars as though they were carnival bumper cars, but most of those who rent cars are business people who get no kick out of driving someone else's car; they do it too often.

Between one-third and one-half of all used rental cars are sold to the public every year. Rental cars are often well-equipped and are usually only 1 or 2 years old. Mileage varies with the company, but the average is about 24,000 miles. By this mileage, most lemons have long since been plucked from the fleet—rental-car companies cannot afford to send out limping vehicles. Prices usually run a few hundred dollars less than for cars on dealer lots, because rental companies are more concerned with selling old fleet vehicles than with haggling over a couple hundred bucks. And if all that isn't enough, many companies offer warranties and can arrange financing as well.

Although certain rental companies are allied with certain manufacturers—Avis with GM and Hertz with Ford, for example—most carry a variety of makes and models. Most rental companies offer free pamphlets outlining their rental-car sales procedures. Check with small, local car-rental firms in addition to local offices of national car-rental companies.

Hertz sells about 60,000 cars a year to the public. The cars are 12 to 18 months old and have less than 25,000 miles on them. Sales outlets are available nationwide. Hertz offers warranties, but most outlets do not offer financing. Call a local Hertz office, or dial (800) 848-3424.

Avis sells about 50,000 cars annually at numerous outlets across the country. Most vehicles are slightly over 1 year old, with odometer readings of about 25,000 miles. Avis supplies warranties and can arrange financing. Call either a local Avis office or (516) 222-3575.

National Car Rental sells about 25,000 cars a year to the public; most are about 1 year old, with 22,000 to 24,000 miles on them. National offers one of the best used-car warranties in the business and can arrange for financing. Call a local National office for more information; or call their home office at (612) 830-2121.

Budget Rent-A-Car sells vehicles that are about 1 year old. Financing is available, as are extended service plans (usually through the vehicle manufacturer). For more information, call a local Budget office or (312) 580-5000.

Thrifty Rent-A-Car sells vehicles only from its home office in Tulsa, Oklahoma; the number is (918) 496-2715.

Car-rental firms may use auctions, too, but not all are open to the general public. If you are interested in these, ask each firm about its individual procedures.

Public auctions.   Used-car auctions are often helter-skelter affairs, but that's what makes them fun! Bids are taken on an abandoned rust bucket one minute, a drug dealer's federally confiscated Cadillac the next, and a used, nondescript government vehicle after that. And everyone's there with one goal in mind—to get a good deal, something quite possible, because many auctions sell their cars at wholesale prices. If you have a bit of car sense about you and a suppressed flair for gambling, you may be auction material.

The most frequent source of auction vehicles is the government— local, state, and federal. The U.S. Government Services Administration (GSA) handles the disposition of federal vehicles from 10 regional offices—in Atlanta, Auburn (Washington), Boston, Chicago, Denver, Fort Worth, Kansas City, New York City, Philadelphia, and San Francisco. Each region maintains its own schedule and list of cities in which the vehicles are auctioned. The GSA office in Chicago, for example, auctions vehicles once a week from April through October in Dayton or Columbus, Ohio, or from Cincinnati, Chicago, or Minneapolis.

The GSA sells federal vehicles when they reach the 6-year or 60,000-mile mark; although GSA was experimenting with a cycle half that length, the program has been put on hold. Federal vehicles make up the bulk of vehicles sold, seizure vehicles the remainder. To obtain a list of auction times and places, contact the GSA regional office nearest you.

On the local scene, check with your area police department. In your state's capitol city, check under a listing such as "motor vehicle pool." To enter most large auctions, you need to register ahead of time and to post a security payment, sometimes of $1000 or more, as a show of good faith. It's returnable, of course, if you don't buy.

Before You Shop . . .

All used-car buyers face the dilemma of separating the emotional from the practical; too often, many are wooed by a car's cosmetics. Determine beforehand what car, price, and terms are most practical for you, and then stick with your plan. Do the same when it comes to testing the vehicle for its roadworthiness; don't shortchange yourself.

And be wary of falling for superficial comments. For example, if you question an engine noise, a salesperson or lot owner might reply, "The car isn't used much. Once you start driving it again the oil will get circulated and the noise will go away." If you spot something leaking under the car, the no-problem response might be, "Oh, it's just the transmission gasket, I can fix that before you buy the car."

In the first of these real-life examples, the engine had a sticking valve lifter, a sign of poor maintenance and worse things to come; and in the second instance, the rear housing on the transmission case was cracked. Even though both comments were off-the-mark, both comments still let the sellers off-the-hook. The engine noise will never go away without rebuilding, and replacing the transmission pan gasket would not have stopped the leak, but those were the only commitments the seller made— nothing was mentioned about trying to repair the *real* problem. Be certain you're dealing with facts and not just reassuring words.

Should your state or province require periodic vehicle inspections, have the vehicle inspected *before* you buy it, or make the sale conditional on those grounds. Also, check titles for clues that the car is a salvage vehicle. Most states require words to that effect if a vehicle was originally scrapped as a result of an accident and later resurrected by a repair shop. Such vehicles warrant close scrutiny.

Narrowing the Field

Used-car buying should focus on a car's fair-market value, its repair history, and its mileage. Each point is detailed in this section. Bear in mind that the better your follow-up, the better your odds of getting a satisfactory deal.

Determining Fair-Market Value

Fair-market value is the price for which comparably equipped vehicles of the same model year are selling. This incorporates all of the seasonal fluctuations of the used-car market: springtime usually garners the highest selling prices, the year-end holidays the lowest. The sale price of large, less fuel-efficient cars will vary with the price of gas, and so on.

The classified ads in your local newspaper are the best barometer of current retail prices. You can also check the National Automobile Dealers Association *Official Used Car Guide* or the *Kelley Blue Book,* both of which are usually available at banks, credit unions, insurance agencies, and dealerships.

Another pricing source is the national used-car pricing guides published by Edmund Publications Corporation of West Hempstead, New York, and by Pace Publications, Inc., of Milwaukee, Wisconsin. These

1935 Prototype Beetle

1985 "50th Anniversary" Beetle

Fig. 3-2   The venerable Volkswagen "Bug," one of the most used cars ever made. In 1972, the VW Beetle set a world production record of over 15 million units, surpassing that of the legendary Ford Model T. Today the figure is over 21 million. The VW Bug is still made in Central and South America. (*Courtesy Volkswagen of America.*)

guides, which cost about $3.00 each, list vehicles by year, make, model, body style, original list price, current wholesale price, and average retail price. Both guides are usually available at newsstands and bookstores. Edmund's updates its guide four times yearly—in January, April, July, and October. Pace publishes a new guide each month except in June and September.

Shopping for the best price on a used vehicle can be awkward. It's difficult comparing different makes, models, and years—all with a variety of options, some of which may not be of real value to you but are nonetheless part of the purchase price. Therefore, it helps to decide beforehand which options, models, and body styles you most prefer, and to search out vehicles that best fit those guidelines. You can then narrow down the field by more subjective items such as appearance, color, and styling.

Your budget will finally force you to decide between the few remaining choices. You may be happier in the long run buying a slightly older vehicle that better suits your budget, driving needs, and self-image, than to compromise your needs and wants by purchasing a less desirable vehicle simply because it is newer.

Determining a Vehicle's Track Record

Your tax money is at work in the form of a toll-free number to the National Highway Traffic Safety Administration (NHTSA). By calling their Auto Safety Hotline with the make, model year, and vehicle identification number (VIN) of a particular car, you can find out whether the vehicle was involved in a recall campaign. The Auto Safety Hotline number is (800) 424-9393; in Alaska, Hawaii, and Washington, D.C., call (202) 426-0123. The NHTSA also fields complaints, investigates safety problems, and answers questions concerning federal safety standards and regulations.

Many vehicles have been recalled for minor adjustments or for potential defects. For the most part, the concern of a potential buyer should be whether or not the former owner answered the recall notice. Some owners, though duly notified, never respond.

To confirm whether or not a recall defect was corrected, you can check with an affiliated dealership; or if the dealership cannot supply the answer, contact the manufacturer directly. You must supply the make, model year, and VIN. The addresses and phone numbers for domestic automakers are listed in Appendix A; for foreign manufacturers, they are listed in Appendix B.

Table 3-1 lists some of the best and worst vehicles, compiled from the results of federal tests on safety, fuel economy, preventive maintenance

Table 3-1   How They Rated . . .

Winners

BMW 2002	Chevrolet Caprice/Impala
Chevrolet Celebrity	Datsun 240Z
Dodge Colt or Aries	Ford Escort or Mustang
Honda Accord/Civic	Mercury Lynx/Capri
Oldsmobile Cutlass/Buick Regal	Porsche 911 series
Plymouth Champ or Reliant	Toyota Corolla
Subaru	
Volvo 240 DL	

Losers

AMC Concord or Pacer	Cadillac Seville, 1976–1981
Chevrolet Monza	Dodge Sportsman Wagon
Dodge Aspen	Ford Fairmont
Mercury Zephyr	Jeep CJ5 or CJ7
Pontiac Sunbird	Plymouth Volare
X-Cars*	

Worse Yet

Ford Pintos, 1971–1976
GM 4.3-L and 5.7-L diesel-powered cars, 1978–1981

---

* Buick Skylark, Chevrolet Citation, Oldsmobile Omega, and Pontiac Phoenix.

and repair costs, insurance premium ratings, and available data on frequency of repair. All factors rate equally.

Determining Actual Mileage: Laws and Loopholes

The Department of Transportation estimates that unsuspecting buyers are bilked out of $2 billion a year by dishonest sellers who conceal a vehicle's true mileage by turning back the odometer. If that estimate seems high, consider that many used-car buyers who later develop trouble with their vehicles pass it off simply as having gotten a lemon, not realizing their car has 50,000 extra miles on it.

Vehicles best suited for odometer tampering are those purchased for use in business fleets, as are more than half of all new cars. Odometer rollbacks on these vehicles is profitable because tampering is not easily discerned. Fleet vehicles run up mileage quickly (50,000 to 60,000 in a year or two), and they are traded in while still relatively new in appearance.

The NHTSA has tracked fleet cars that were sold to wholesale buyers at auctions and subsequently resold to a series of dealers, before finally being sold to customers. In a study done for the federal government in 1985 by the Illinois Attorney General's Office, of the 5000 fleet vehicles traced, half had had their odometers rolled back. Although odometer tampering is a federal crime, it's difficult to prove. A "back room" operation often does the dirty work before the vehicle is passed along to a wholesaler or dealer. Of course, if the seller has knowledge of the rollback, the odometer law is violated by conspiracy, but that charge is equally difficult to prove.

A consumer, then, should take some general precautions. If the title to a used car is registered in the dealer's name, be careful. As a general rule, dealers and wholesalers *reassign* titles when selling vehicles between themselves. (When a car is sold to a consumer, the title is *transferred*.) But every time a dealer or wholesaler reassigns a vehicle, a reassignment slip is stapled to the title. And a title with 3 or 4 reassignment slips, each issued in a different state, can put even the most trusting consumer on edge.

So, if a dealer prefers to have the consumer believe a car is a low-mileage local trade-in, the dealer will transfer the title—and not reassign it—to the dealership. And when a title is transferred, the reassignment papers and all their incriminating baggage stay with the old title. The consumer will see only a brand-new title issued in the familiar name of a neighborhood dealer. Also, sometimes dealers or wholesalers register a vehicle in a state in which mileage is not recorded on the title. This enables dealers to reregister the vehicle in their home state, where the altered odometer reading will be recorded as the actual mileage.

Another precaution you should take is to ask to see the written mileage disclosure statement. *All sellers of motor vehicles—private citizens as well as car dealers—are required by federal law to complete an odometer disclosure form at the time of vehicle sale.* The only exceptions are for classic cars and heavy trucks. This federal regulation went into effect on March 9, 1978, and it requires dealers to keep disclosure statements on file for 4 years. If a seller cannot produce a disclosure statement, the vehicle may well have an altered odometer. Also, if a consumer were to research past disclosure statements, a vehicle with an altered odometer would either be missing a statement or would have one indicating higher mileage.

These safeguards are sufficient in the majority of cases; however, even disclosure statements can be falsified, as when a decoy is paid to sign in place of the former owner. Also, on purchase contracts, dealers can claim that the actual mileage is unknown, giving rise to a vicious circle with the consumer caught in the middle. Here are some subjective ways in which to approximate mileage. Don't get lost in the details, but don't neglect precautionary measures, either. Use the suggestions you feel are most applicable to the cars you might be considering buying.

If the title is *not* in the dealer's name, you should verify mileage by contacting the previous owner. Do not let the dealer do it for you, though. A common ploy some dealers use is to call a prearranged contact who poses as the former car owner. Check to see whether the phone directory lists the same name and number supplied by the salesperson, or ask the previous owner questions to which only that person could readily respond—the brand names of accessories or the locations of wear spots or blemishes. (This can also prevent the unwitting purchase of a stolen vehicle, in which case you can lose both the vehicle and the money you have paid on it. A late-model vehicle with fresh paint is one tip-off to a stolen vehicle; not receiving at least one set of the original manufacturer keys is another.)

A good subjective indication of mileage is the degree of wear found on upholstery, door panels, carpeting, and pedal pads. Are the driver side armrest and seat both worn to the same degree, and does this match the approximate wear on the gas, brake, or clutch pedals? Pedal pads are easy to change, and carpet dye can cover a multitude of sins. If the upholstery, carpeting, armrests, and so on seem to be of different vintages, this is grounds for suspicion. Before leaving the interior, look at the individual odometer numbers. Do they read in a straight line, and are there any scrapes or cracks in the plastic? Such signs may indicate tampering.

Check the vehicle's tires. Many factory tires are now rated for up to 40,000 miles. Do the mileage and tires coincide with this? Do all brand names match, or have one or two tires been replaced? If so, it's possible that either hard driving or a suspension problem was the cause. The owner who buys new tires shortly before selling is either a swell person or a wolf in sheep's clothing. Older cars need new tires; low-mileage vehicles do not.

A seller must also inform the buyer if the odometer has been "turned over," that is, if the car has in excess of 99,999 miles. This would seem to be readily apparent, but a renovated business car that has accumulated 135,000 miles in 2 years may go undetected by those with a minimum of mechanical knowledge. If an odometer has been replaced, and the actual mileage cannot be reinstated, federal law requires that a plate or sticker showing the mileage at the time of odometer replacement be placed on the inside doorjamb on the driver's side. It is against federal law to remove this mileage notice.

The federal odometer tampering law, in addition to criminal penalties, allows aggrieved consumers to sue for damages. A consumer has 2 years from the discovery of an altered odometer reading to file suit. To report odometer tampering or for more specifics on odometer tampering laws, you can obtain a free booklet, *Consumer Protection Under the Federal Odometer Law,* from the NHTSA:

Office of Chief Counsel
National Highway Traffic Safety Administration
Department of Transportation
400 7th Street SW, Room 5219
Washington, D.C. 20590
(202) 426-1835

Some top-line computerized cars are programmed to record mileage electronically via microchips. This is a nearly tamperproof method of recording actual vehicle mileage. Should an electronics technician attempt to alter the mileage, a fault code would be activated that could not be removed from the computer circuitry, a permanent testimony to the tampering. Unfortunately, manufacturers plan to use these advanced onboard computers in only the most expensive models.

Purchase from a private owner generally helps to rule out liberal odometer rollbacks, because such vehicles generally wear their true mileage on their sleeves. The glove compartment is a treasure trove of information when you're buying from a private owner. Because it often acts as a catchall from the time of purchase through to the time of sale, a glove compartment may give you a clear picture of the car's history. It may contain roadmaps from 25 states, toll tickets from half a continent away, or perhaps an original title with only a few thousand miles more than the car shows at present. And where do car repair receipts often end up? Besides shedding light on past repairs or maintenance, 90 percent show the car's mileage at the time of service. If you're buying from a dealer, alas, only an owner's manual may be left. But check it, anyway; sometimes incriminating details can be found there.

Evaluating a Vehicle According to Mileage

This list describes common problems by the mileage ranges at which they're most likely to occur. The list also provides additional tip-offs to spotting mileage fraud. To a point, the older a vehicle, the longer you'll need to take to inspect it. However, as age and mileage increase, the value of a thorough inspection decreases. Accordingly, the list concludes at the 60,000-mile mark.

Keep in mind that low mileage is not always a blessing. A car should average about 12,000 miles a year; anything less can be as troublesome as top-heavy mileage. According to David Bowman, Technical Communications Manager for Fram automotive parts, a car that has been driven only for short distances around town may *appear* to be in good shape; but such start-and-stop driving does not give the engine a chance to warm up sufficiently, which can lead to engine problems. In fact, most car manufacturers agree that driving a vehicle for errands totaling less than 8 miles constitutes severe driving conditions. The oil and lubricants simply cannot do their jobs, resulting in the lessening of the engine oil suspension properties that prevent engine grit and sludge buildup.

20,000 Miles or Less

If a seller appears affluent enough to trade in a car with only 20,000 miles on it, the vehicle is probably a solid one to consider. Conversely, the seller may simply be trying to dump a problem vehicle—one damaged in an accident or theft, or one that may be nothing more than a lemon.

Ask to see routine maintenance receipts, a reasonable request. In troublesome vehicles, oil changes are usually performed while the vehicle was *already* in for service. Any repairs not covered by the warranty will be written on the receipt as well. If the owner claims that maintenance work was done locally, check for garage stickers on the inside of the driver's door. (Those who sell "new" used cars seldom have the economic need to do their own oil changes.)

Walk around the vehicle, looking for uneven or wavy body lines, which indicate postaccident repair. Check to see if the exterior paint matches that on the doorjambs, inside the trunk, and under the hood. The doors, trunk, and hood should align properly (approximately a credit card width along the body proper) and should open and close without binding. To check for a bent frame ("dog-tracking"), slowly track the vehicle in a straight line through water onto dry pavement. If the rear tire tracks do not follow in line with the front ones (if the car "dog-tracks"), the car may have a bent frame—a problem you'll want to avoid.

20,000 to 30,000 Miles

By the time a car has 20,000 miles on it, the brakes and tires may be ready for repair or replacement—hardly a reason to rule out an otherwise worthy vehicle. If properly maintained, 2- to 3-year-old vehicles often provide the best used-car value. They have withstood the test of time and have proven themselves to be roadworthy.

Test the brakes by applying firm, even pressure to the brake pedal and holding it for 30 seconds. You should be able to fit the tip of your other shoe between the pedal and the floorboard. If you can't, or if the pedal pressure gradually weakens, have the brakes checked professionally. You should expect tire wear, but it should not be lopsided. Erratic tire wear is often indicative of suspension problems. Any odd wear patterns—such as rippled, lopsided, or bulging sidewalls—warrant a hoist inspection for premature wear of the idler arm, shocks, or tie-rod ends. The presence of these problems may also indicate that the car has been driven roughly.

Check battery strength by disconnecting the ignition coil wire from the distributor, and letting the engine crank for 15 to 30 seconds. This will also reveal starter problems. The engine should be responsive both in starting and in accelerating. If it is not, a tune-up may be in order. Ask the owner or dealer to provide for one as a condition to the terms of the sale. This is for the benefit of all concerned; reluctance on the part of the owner should magnify your reluctance to buy the car.

30,000 to 40,000 Miles

A car that has accumulated 30,000 to 40,000 miles has reached middle age. In addition to the above, suspension problems may occur: wheel bearings, shock absorbers, idler arms, tie-rod ends, or the differential may be affected. Depending on climate, the exhaust system may be hanging on by its last rusty clamp as well.

A road test is a good indicator of potential problems. Let the steering wheel drift of its own accord: Does the car pull to one side? Does the wheel vibrate or shimmy? These are all problems in need of further evaluation. Listen for unusual drivetrain sounds: ticking sounds from the engine or rear-end or transmission whines. Maintain a steady speed through the 25 to 50 mph range for half-minute intervals. Gear noise generally occurs only at certain speeds; for example, between 35 and 40 mph. Not all unusual noises indicate the need for major repairs, but they are indicative of past maintenance, and therefore, of future dependability.

With cars in this mileage bracket, having a front-end alignment done may help you to make up your mind; besides, an alignment would soon be due anyway. And it will reveal much that a visual inspection would not show.

40,000 to 50,000 Miles

The drivetrain should last at least 50,000 miles or 5 years, but, at this mile marker, past and future maintenance is the key to a vehicle's longevity. The transmission fluid and filter, the cooling system, the many filters and emission valves, the universal joints, and the wheel bearings will all need service sooner or later. To that list, add the possible replacement of belts and hoses. Inspect the past maintenance and present condition of as many of these items as possible for use as bargaining chips. Power accessories are risky propositions beyond 50,000 to 60,000 miles. An inoperative clock is at worst what inoperable power windows are at best: an inconvenience.

Accelerate the engine quickly, and watch for either black or blue smoke from the tailpipe upon pedal release. Excessive black smoke can indicate the need for anything from a tune-up to a valve job; blue smoke can indicate anything from the need for new valve seals to an engine overhaul, so have the car checked out. If, and only if, the radiator is cool to the touch, slowly remove the cap, and check the coolant color. At this mileage, the cooling system is especially vulnerable to problems unless it has been properly maintained; a reddish brown color indicates rusty neglect. The problem isn't terminal, but it should be interpreted as a caution flag. About this time, the brakes, tires, and battery will be a definite concern, especially if they are still original equipment. Consider this in direct correlation to the purchase price.

50,000 to 60,000 Miles and Beyond

Some vehicles, like people, grow old gracefully; others struggle to maintain a respectable pace. In addition to the aforementioned items, inspect the car for fluid leaks of all sorts—from the suspension system, brakes, and power train. Also, check all gauges, lights, latches, and switches. Expect exhaust system repairs to be necessary.

Check the wipers, blower fan (for the heater and air conditioner), all engine-monitoring devices (lights, analog, and digital), turn signals, brake lights and, if you're an eternal optimist, the cigarette lighter (if you have a need for it, you are optimistic by nature). To ascertain the extent of interior water leaks, feel for dampness under the floor mats. In severe cases, carpet rot or mildew will already have set in (see Fig. 3-3). Open the trunk and do the same. Should all of these meet with your satisfaction, then pay close attention to the drivetrain items listed earlier. One can never rule out expensive after-purchase repairs with high-mileage vehicles; one can only hope to reduce the odds of such an occurrence through careful prepurchase inspection.

Warranties and the Used Car

If you are not provided with a detailed *written* warranty, a dealer's legal responsibility to you ends the moment you accept the vehicle as-is by driving it off the lot. Although some states require dealers to honor implied warranties in such transactions, many cases wind up in court, where they become time-consuming, expensive propositions. So, if you want after-sale protection against costly repair problems, you will need to receive a *written* warranty.

Fig. 3-3 If you were selling this car, you could spruce up the interior (*top*) with new floor mats. If you were buying, you should check that the mats are not being used as camouflage. The rot and mildew on this carpet (*bottom*) are from a windshield water leak. (*Photo by Mike Spaniola.*)

If you want a warranty, and the dealer is willing to give you one, *the warranty terms must be put in writing. Never rely on oral promises,* even if the dealer promises to take care of a problem after you get home. Many purchase agreements even contain clauses that disavow *written terms* unless an authorized representative—usually the sales manager or an owner—signs the contract. So, to be safe, *always have the authorized representative sign the purchase agreement before leaving the dealer's premises.* This will ensure against unpleasant last-minute surprises at delivery time.

You should never be charged extra for a warranty. Service contracts (discussed in an upcoming section) differ from warranties and cost extra; warranties are included in the purchase price. A written warranty should provide for repair or replacement within a reasonable amount of time, and both of these terms should be defined. What is a reasonable amount of time? What must be repaired or replaced—the entire vehicle or certain components only? And what recourse do you have if repairs cannot be completed within a reasonable amount of time? Coverage will vary with the type of warranty offered.

There are two basic types of written warranties: full and limited. *Full warranties* generally cover parts and labor for the duration of the warranty, such as 90 days or 6 months. Full warranties stipulate that a product be repaired within a reasonable amount of time and in a reasonable number of attempts, or the buyer is entitled to refund or replacement of the product. Buy-back price is generally fair-market replacement value and *not* the original purchase price. The seller is also generally responsible for expenses incurred as a result of a defect covered by the warranty, such as towing, car rental, or lodging.

Limited warranties, unlike full warranties, cover only the cost of repair and do not entitle the buyer to complete replacement of a defective product. (Most new-car warranties are limited warranties, but lemon laws hold new-car manufacturers to the full-warranty obligation of refund or replacement.) Parts *and* labor are not always covered under the terms of a limited warranty, so check this provision carefully.

In Kansas, Maine, Maryland, Massachusetts, Mississippi, West Virginia, and Vermont, implied warranties are still in effect even though no written warranty is made. While this may sound ideal to the used-car buyer, the legal expense of pursuing a claim, as noted earlier, can exceed the cost of the repair.

Implied warranties are not written warranties but instead concern the vague provisions of the Uniform Commercial Code (UCC), which has been interpreted, reinterpreted, and overinterpreted into oblivion. Basically, an implied warranty states that, regardless of the terms of the sale, consumer goods are covered to the extent that they are *merchantable* and *fit for a particular purpose.* These terms also apply to both full and limited warranties.

The implied warranty of merchantability states that any product offered for sale must be in working condition and suitable to the purpose for which it is intended. A defective transmission would most likely be ruled to affect vehicle merchantability; a peeling paint job would probably not.

The implied warranty of fitness for a particular purpose arises when a customer relies on the seller's advice that a product can be used for a particular purpose. For example, if a used-car salesperson states that a vehicle has four-wheel drive, and a consumer buys it for that reason, the consumer has relied on the salesperson's advice about a product's fitness for a particular purpose. The seller may then be responsible to rectify the problem if the vehicle did not have four-wheel drive. A consumer would probably have to go to court to enforce it, though.

These UCC provisions apply only to sales from a dealer, not to those from a private owner, although courts have ruled that private owners who brag about a vehicle's being in "A-1 condition" or "excellent shape" may be held liable for implied warranties, should the vehicle fail to perform; but this is rare. However, if a dealer *or* a private owner knows of a major defect prior to sale, each has an obligation under the law to disclose it. If not, the purchaser may be able to break the contract and sue for any damages resulting from the deception.

In addition to legal recourse under odometer-tampering and warranty laws, other relief is available to the consumer in the purchase of a defective used vehicle. These actions under the law are much the same as those that apply to new vehicles: revocation of acceptance, common-law fraud, and unfair and deceptive acts and practices (UDAP). Also, most dealers are licensed by the city or state in which they operate, which provides consumers with additional recourse. Most states and major cities have either a consumer affairs office or an automotive regulation bureau to which consumers can turn for assistance. These offices can determine whether a dealer has violated a consumer protection act. Recourse is also available if a language barrier between a dealer and consumer can be proven to have caused a misunderstanding. For more information on consumer protection acts, consult the last section in Chapter 2.

The Federal Trade Commission Used-Car Rule

The original FTC used-car rule proposal was patterned after Wisconsin's unique and exemplary used-car law, which has been in effect since October 1974. The final version of the FTC used-car rule, however, deals only with warranty provisions. Wisconsin's law, on the other hand, mandates inspections of used vehicles, disclosure of any defects, and repair of safety-related defects.

Since May 9, 1985, the FTC used-car rule (16 CFR, Part 455) has required the posting of a window sticker called the *buyers guide* (see Fig. 3-4). Its practical implications are that a consumer can more readily determine the warranty status of a vehicle, and used-car dealers can more readily avoid courtroom jostling over express and implied warranties. Buyers guide window stickers must be posted on cars and light trucks of curb weights less than 6000 pounds by establishments that offer six or more vehicles for sale within one year; cars sold in repossession or confiscation cases are exempt.

The sticker must be affixed to the side window of every vehicle offered for sale; it may be removed only for the duration of a test drive. If the sale is conducted in Spanish, the buyers guide must be in Spanish as well. The standard buyers guide window sticker cannot be altered by the dealer, except in states that prohibit as-is sales. Then the "As Is—No Warranty" section should state that, while the dealer does not promise to make repairs, a consumer does have certain rights under state law implied warranties, should serious problems develop.

Information on the final version of the buyers guide must be incorporated into the sales contract. This prevents a salesperson from telling a customer one thing, only to have the sales contract contradict it. If a vehicle is sold with a warranty, the contract must specify whether it is limited or full and must state the buyer/seller percentage distribution of repair costs, the specific systems covered or excluded from the warranty coverage, the duration of the warranty for each of the covered systems, and information about obtaining warranty service. If the vehicle is still covered by the manufacturer's original warranty, the contract will state that the manufacturer's original warranty still applies and will refer the customer to the manufacturer's warranty booklet for details concerning warranty coverage and service location.

The buyers guide also suggests that you ask whether you may have the vehicle inspected and about whether or not you can take the vehicle off the premises to a private mechanic. Some dealers may have good reasons for not permitting the latter, insurance restrictions being a major one. In that case, however, you can bring an independent mechanic to the dealer's lot. The back side of the form lists problems that may occur in components of 14 major systems, an overwhelming list at first glance, but helpful. All major components listed are discussed in this chapter under "Coping with 'Used-Car Phobia'" or in Chapter 5 or 6.

The FTC has free pamphlets that discuss used-car buying and warranties and service contracts that are available to the public. Write: Federal

Trade Commission, Department P, Box 37041, Washington, D.C. 20580. The FTC also operates regional offices, the addresses and phone numbers of which are listed in Appendix F.

New York's Used-Car Repair-or-Replace Law

The first of its kind in the country, this law went in effect on November 1, 1984. New York statute CLS General Business Law section 198-b provides the consumer with a refund, replace, or repair provision in the purchase of a used vehicle from a dealer; private-owner sales are exempt.

The law requires that dealers provide a 60-day or 3000-mile warranty on vehicles with less than 36,000 miles, and a 30-day or 1000-mile warranty on vehicles with 36,000 miles or more. Vehicles that sell for less than $1500 are exempt, as are registered classic cars, motorcycles, motor homes, and off-road vehicles. Dealers are responsible for these warranty terms, even if they do not indicate it in writing. To prevent salespeople from pressuring a consumer to waive this warranty right, the law does not permit its waiver.

The warranty covers the engine, transmission, drive axles, brake system, radiator, steering components, and ignition system. Coverage does not extend to items such as valves or piston rings if normal wear of these items is causing, for example, oil burning or low cylinder compression. Excluded from warranty coverage are vehicles used as rental units and hired vehicles for carrying passengers.

If a vehicle cannot be repaired, and a refund or replacement is due, vehicle wholesale value at the time of the buy-back, *not* the original purchase price, is used. Variables such as accrued mileage and significant physical or mechanical changes—for better or worse—from the time of the sale are taken into account in determining buy-back amount. A consumer can also seek reimbursement of incidental costs and can ask for consequential damages as well.

Service Contracts

Service contracts are not, and should not be referred to as, "extended warranties." Warranties are included in the price of a product; service contracts are sold at an additional cost.

Exercise caution in purchasing a service contract from sources other than the manufacturer or an insurance company. Manufacturers are more likely to have the funds to back the contract, as are insurance companies, which are state-regulated. On the other hand, service contracts administrated through private third-party agreements can leave a consumer without protection if the administrator declares bankruptcy. A case in point is

BUYERS GUIDE

IMPORTANT: Spoken promises are difficult to enforce. Ask the dealer to put all promises in writing. Keep this form.

VEHICLE MAKE   MODEL   YEAR   VIN NUMBER

DEALER STOCK NUMBER (Optional)

WARRANTIES FOR THIS VEHICLE:

☐ AS IS - NO WARRANTY

YOU WILL PAY ALL COSTS FOR ANY REPAIRS. The dealer assumes no responsibility for any repairs regardless of any oral statements about the vehicle.

☐ WARRANTY

☐ **FULL** ☐ **LIMITED WARRANTY. The dealer will pay _____% of the labor and _____% of the parts for the covered systems that fail during the warranty period. Ask the dealer for a copy of the warranty document for a full explanation of warranty coverage, exclusions, and the dealer's repair obligations. Under state law, "implied warranties" may give you even more rights.**

SYSTEMS COVERED: DURATION:

☐ **SERVICE CONTRACT.** A service contract is available at an extra charge on this vehicle. Ask for details as to coverage, deductible, price, and exclusions. If you buy a service contract within 90 days of the time of sale, state law "implied warranties" may give you additional rights.

PRE PURCHASE INSPECTION: ASK THE DEALER IF YOU MAY HAVE THIS VEHICLE INSPECTED BY YOUR MECHANIC EITHER ON OR OFF THE LOT.

SEE THE BACK OF THIS FORM for important additional information, including a list of some major defects that may occur in used motor vehicles.

Fig. 3-4 The Federal Trade Commission (FTC) requires all used-car dealers to place this "Buyers Guide" in the window of each used vehicle offered for sale. The form presents vehicle warranty and inspection information. (*Courtesy FTC Bureau of Consumer Protection.*)

Below is a list of some major defects that may occur in used motor vehicles.

Frame & Body
Frame-cracks, corrective welds, or rusted through
Dogtracks—bent or twisted frame

Engine
Oil leakage, excluding normal seepage
Cracked block or head
Belts missing or inoperable
Knocks or misses related to camshaft lifters and
    push rods
Abnormal exhaust discharge

Transmission & Drive Shaft
Improper fluid level or leakage, excluding normal
    seepage
Cracked or damaged case which is visible
Abnormal noise or vibration caused by faulty
    transmission or drive shaft
Improper shifting or functioning in any gear
Manual clutch slips or chatters

Differential
Improper fluid level or leakage excluding normal
    seepage
Cracked or damaged housing which is visible
Abnormal noise or vibration caused by faulty
    differential

Cooling System
Leakage including radiator
Improperly functioning water pump

Electrical System
Battery leakage
Improperly functioning alternator, generator,
    battery, or starter

Fuel System
Visible leakage

Inoperable Accessories
Gauges or warning devices
Air conditioner
Heater & Defroster

Brake System
Failure warning light broken
Pedal not firm under pressure (DOT spec.)
Not enough pedal reserve (DOT spec.)
Does not stop vehicle in straight line (DOT spec.)
Hoses damaged
Drum or rotor too thin (Mfgr. Specs)
Lining or pad thickness less than 1/32 inch
Power unit not operating or leaking
Structural or mechanical parts damaged

Steering System
Too much free play at steering wheel (DOT specs.)
Free play in linkage more than 1/4 inch
Steering gear binds or jams
Front wheels aligned improperly (DOT specs.)
Power unit belts cracked or slipping
Power unit fluid level improper

Suspension System
Ball joint seals damaged
Structural parts bent or damaged
Stabilizer bar disconnected
Spring broken
Shock absorber mounting loose
Rubber bushings damaged or missing
Radius rod damaged or missing
Shock absorber leaking or functioning improperly

Tires
Tread depth less than 2/32 inch
Sizes mismatched
Visible damage

Wheels
Visible cracks, damage or repairs
Mounting bolts loose or missing

Exhaust System
Leakage

DEALER

ADDRESS

SEE FOR COMPLAINTS

**IMPORTANT: The information on this form is part of any contract to buy this vehicle. Removal of this label
before consumer purchase (except for purpose of test-driving) is a violation of federal law (16 C.F.R. 455).**

Fig. 3-4 (*Continued*)

the North American Dealers Group, which declared bankruptcy in early 1981, leaving 500,000 Carlife service contracts in the lurch. A consumer should ask whether service contracts are available, because the buyers guide will not always indicate whether the state regulates these contracts under insurance laws.

Dealers who sell a vehicle with a service contract cannot disclaim implied warranties (unless the dealer is acting only as an agent for a service contract company). Consumers then retain legal rights provided by the UCC provisions of product merchantability and fitness for a particular purpose that would otherwise be forfeited through as-is sales in most states.

Service contracts may not specify brand names, such as the exclusive use of a specified repair facility for routine maintenance or use of a specific brand of gasoline, unless those goods or services are provided at no charge under the contract. Limitations as to where vehicle repairs covered by the service contract can be performed are legal, though.

Service contract terms vary greatly, but limitations and deductions are common. Generally, a service contract should state the name and address of the company holding legal responsibility for the contract as well as those for the parties servicing the covered components, and the procedure for such. The contract should also fully disclose which components are covered *and* which are not. It should also state whether or not any special maintenance or service is required to keep the contract in effect and should explain how to verify such servicing.

Check on deductibles: do they apply to each repair claim, to the entire repair visit, or to individual parts? Must the owner first pay for repairs and then be reimbursed, or will the holder of the service contract make payment directly to the repair facility? Does the contract cover costs incidental to repair, such as towing, lodging, and car rentals? If repairs are specified only at a certain facility, what becomes of the contract if you move? Any cancellation fees, transfer fees, or method of calculating refunds should be disclosed in the contract.

Owner Sale of a Used Car

You can trade in your used car, sell it yourself, or let a dealer sell it for you. All have their advantages and disadvantages, but selling the car yourself will always be the most profitable alternative. An individual can ask near retail price or perhaps better with none of a dealer's overhead. Even some of the perceived negatives of selling a car yourself can be minimized.

Dealer-Assisted Sales and Trade-ins

Many used-car lots will sell your car on consignment. This requires a flat service fee (usually $1 to $2 a day), a minimum amount of time in which to sell the car (usually 1 month), and a percentage of the sales price (which varies with vehicle worth). This frees the owner from all the hassles associated with selling a car oneself. Some profit will go to the lot owner for his trouble, of course, although for those who haven't the time, inclination, or knowledge to sell a car, consignment usually yields more than a straight dealer trade-in. When selling on consignment, check with the lot owner about insurance arrangements in the case of theft or vandalism to your vehicle, especially with regard to test drives.

Another method, similar to consignment but less profitable for the vehicle owner, is contract selling. With this method, a dealer agrees to pay you a set price for your car (usually wholesale) if and when the dealer can sell it (at retail). This allows dealers to increase their used-car inventories at a minimal cost and to lay claim to the middleman portion of the sale as well. Unlike consignment sales, which allow the seller to share in the profit, contract selling may net you little more than trade-in value.

If you trade in your car, keep cleanup efforts to a minimum. Professional appraisers are little influenced by last-minute cosmetic makeovers. Dealers prep cars, because, on the open market, first impressions are all-important. So, take a lesson from the dealers if you're selling a car yourself: clean it up, because details pay big dividends. But when trading in, forget about trying to beat them at their own game.

For Sale by Owner: Preparing Your Car

The disadvantages to selling a car yourself are often more an annoyance than anything serious: spending weekends by the phone, the odd feeling of letting a stranger test-drive your car, hunting down mutually convenient times to handle paperwork, and perhaps, bearing the cost of advertising.

To maximize your profit, clean the car thoroughly before putting it up for sale. You can either do it yourself or take it to a professional car-cleaning service, as most dealers do. In either case, the extra time and money almost always produce a quicker, more profitable sale.

When doing it yourself, have the following on hand:

• Mild detergent, sponge, paste wax, and wax applicator
• Small bottle of liquid touch-up paint and two small brushes
• Can of silicone spray

- Chrome cleaner and bug and tar remover
- Small tin of polishing compound
- Nonabrasive rags (such as terry cloth) and a chamois cloth

After rinsing off surface dirt, wash the car, leave it wet, and apply the polishing compound and bug and tar remover. If you are unfamiliar with either product, follow the directions closely. Use the polishing compound on surface blemishes, such as those typically found around wheel wells, doors, and trunk locks. It's easy to get carried away with this gritty mixture, and it's similar to wall washing—once you clean a small area, adjoining areas may appear dirtier than before, and you may find yourself going over the entire car. The results will be well worth it, though (see Fig. 3-5).

For vinyl tops and tire sidewalls, use a soft-bristled scrub brush to clean dirt-caked crevices. Then apply chrome cleaner to appropriate surfaces. For deep paint scratches, use touch-up paint. Don't load the brush; instead, use paint sparingly. You should attempt to *fill in* scratches, not paint over them. For best results, use a brush half the width of the scratch.

To remove window decals, use paint thinner, never a razor blade. If these or pieces of a bumper sticker refuse to yield, use a *plastic* pot scrubber on them.

After any touch-up paint has dried, start waxing. Spray-on wax is not recommended for presale use, as oversprays on moldings and vinyl tops will leave a white residue that will detract from the car's appearance.

The interior is next. Pull out the mats, empty storage areas (including the glove compartment and the trunk), and vacuum. A pair of new floor mats is a relatively inexpensive investment that always spruces up a car's interior. Old mats only *appear* acceptable because you're accustomed to them.

Next, apply silicone spray to the door, hood, and trunk hinges, inside lock cylinders, and on any two surfaces where friction produces squeaking. (It also eliminates wind noise when sprayed on window weather stripping.) Before cleaning the windows, use your array of interior cleaners or renewal products. When using a cleaning agent on the interior, first test it in an inconspicuous place; it may need diluting if it cleans *too* well.

One of the most-neglected cleanup areas is one that prospective buyers usually see first when opening the door—the door edges and the doorjamb. Make sure these are wiped clean of all dirt and grit, and polish them as best you can. If the inside of the driver's door has service stickers that display exemplary vehicle maintenance, leave them on; otherwise, remove them.

As to the engine compartment, you can clean it yourself or have it

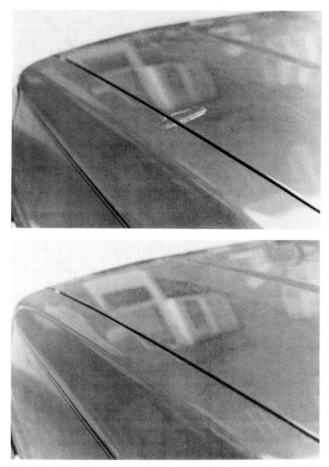

Fig. 3-5 Polishing compound works wonders in removing surface scrapes and scratches. You can apply it by hand to remove road film, oxidation, and a multitude of other paint blemishes that would otherwise detract from resale value. (*Photo by Mike Spaniola.*)

professionally steam-cleaned; either is better than a dirty engine. Commercial engine degreasers are available at most auto-parts stores, but follow directions closely. Rubber parts such as heater hoses can be damaged if degreasers are applied too liberally, and damp electrical connections—which can prevent a car from running if wet—can result if steam or water spray is applied too liberally around the distributor and wire harnesses.

Finally, check all fluid levels, and if a tune-up is in order, have it done. For the money, a tune-up will help to sell the vehicle with an efficiency that few other efforts can duplicate.

Professional Car-Cleaning Services

These facilities are generally found in all but the smallest cities, and, while catering to auto dealerships for their livelihood, most also welcome privately owned vehicles.

Prices vary with the method and thoroughness of the job. A few calls should give you a good idea of what's available in your area. Generally speaking, expect quotes between $75 and $150. For much less, most shops will clean just under the hood, if that's all you specify. Check in the commercial section of the phone directory under automobile washing and polishing or automobile upholstery cleaning.

Most facilities require an appointment, usually made a day in advance, and will need to keep the car for one working day. When inquiring about these services, ask exactly what engine compartment, interior, exterior, and underbody services are performed. You'll note that facilities with lower price quotes will generally not do as thorough a job.

Some places steam-clean under the hood; others use a process called *power washing*. The latter involves chemical sprays that dissolve grease deposits. This prevents soggy electrical system problems and is said to clean plastic parts better than steam. Some shops will even touch up engine paint as well.

Inside, the carpets should be shampooed, dried, and cleaned. One of the better methods is extraction cleaning, in which carpeted areas are cleaned while still wet. Seating areas, trim pads, door panels, the dashboard, and the like should be cleaned *and* sealed with a preservative that will protect and highlight the material used in these areas.

On the exterior, paint should be buffed or rubbed out, small scratches touched up, the surface waxed, and all exterior vinyl reconditioned. Some shops will also recondition tire sidewalls to look like new. Ask if the shop uses camel-hair pinstriping brushes for paint touch-ups; these yield excellent results in the hands of persons skilled in their use. Generally, there is no charge for paint, unless the color is unique and must be ordered specially. In that case, you should receive any leftover portion.

Underbody servicing usually consists of degreasing the entire chassis. This gets rid of drippings that result from accumulated grease and oil. Some shops will even spray paint wheel well openings (called *blacking out*). This adds a finished appearance to the car that is as subtle as it is effective.

Determining Sale Price

On the open market, fair-market value is the only real barometer of a used vehicle's worth. Determining fair-market value, though, need not require an accountant or a computer program.

John P. Finsland, Shell Oil consumer relations representative and author of Shell's *The Car Buying and Selling Book,* advises that prospective sellers check the classified section of the local newspaper to get an idea of how the different makes and models are priced.

Other pricing sources include used-car pricing guides published by Edmund Publications Corporation of West Hempstead, New York, and by Pace Publications, Inc., of Milwaukee, Wisconsin. These are generally available at newsstands and bookstores. The National Automobile Dealers Association *Official Used Car Guide* or the *Kelley Blue Book* are other good sources that are usually available at banks, credit unions, insurance agencies, and dealerships.

Vehicle mileage, condition, and options will further help you to determine the asking price. Carefully word your ad's description of the car to reflect these considerations, because putting the wrong price on the car—either too high or too low—is one of the worst things you can do. Most people check a car's price before calling, so it's best to list one. Allow yourself a 10 percent margin for bargaining, and if you're still unsure what price to list, state that it is negotiable or subject to the best offer. If you won't accept less than the listed price, state that the price is firm.

Announcing the Sale

After all this is said and done, place an ad in the classified section of your local newspaper. This is still the best way to announce a sale. When placing the ad, keep the following in mind.

1. Use a local paper first; if close enough to home, prospective buyers will usually show up, and may even be on time. Local ad rates are cheaper, and paperwork, mechanical inspections, and other pre- and postsale details will be more convenient. In large metro areas, local papers aid in locating buyers with whom the seller has more in common.

2. If no one is available at your home to answer the phone (or if no one is knowledgeable enough to answer questions), list the hours during which buyers should call. For your convenience, don't be afraid to limit calling times, but don't be too restrictive.

3. Use descriptive terms, and play up the positive. For example, if your vehicle has climate control or an AM/FM radio with cassette, list it and not just "A/C" or "radio." Extended warranties are a plus. New muffler or tires? Tell the world, but do not publicize a litany of recent repairs or anything of a serious nature (overhauls) in an ad. It frightens people away.

4. Limit the subjective. Exterior and interior colors need not be mentioned; neither do aftermarket additions, unless you are selling a van.

There is little reason to mention mileage, unless it is to justify a higher asking price.

5. Use the following standard abbreviations to save on the number of classified ad lines you'll need:

A/C (or "air"): air conditioning
alarm: theft-deterrent alarm system
auto: automatic transmission
bst ofr: best offer
cass: cassette player
cruise: cruise control
conv: convertible
cyl: cylinder (4, 6, or 8)
dr: door (2, or 4)
fuel inj: throttle-body or elec-
    tronic fuel-injection system
4- or 5-spd: four- or five-speed
    manual transmission
FWD: front-wheel drive
4WD: four-wheel drive
lo mi: low mileage
mint: showroom-like condition
neg: (price) negotiable
orig mi: original mileage
pass: passenger (2, 4, etc.)

pb: power brakes
pd: power disc brakes
ps: power steering
p seats: power seats
p sunrf: power sunroof
pw: power windows
"power" or "loaded": equipped
    with most available options
radar: police radar detector
r def: rear-window defroster
rstpf: rustproofing
triple (color): interior, exterior,
    and vinyl top all same color
T-tops: removable roof panels
WSW: white sidewall tires
WW (sometimes, "wires"): wire
    wheels or covers
X-cond or exc cond: excellent
    condition

Single words, such as vinyl for vinyl top, wagon for station wagon, manual for standard transmission, warr. or warranty for extended or new-car warranties still in effect, and radials for steel- or glass-belted radial tires, are also acceptable.

6. If the car needs minor repair, such as a muffler, relay this fact to callers but not necessarily in the ad itself; better yet, have it fixed. Avoid generalities such as "runs" or "needs repair."

7. List attributes that justify an asking price above fair-market value (such as low mileage); otherwise a buyer might pass the ad by in favor of less expensive vehicles. Be careful of superlatives, though. Some courts have ruled that private owners may be held liable for implied warranties if they use terms such as "A-1 condition" or "like new." To be on the safe side, be careful about what you say in this regard, and certainly about what you put in print.

Automotive-Gate: Common Cover-ups and Scams

The following is a potpourri of items gathered from veterans of the day-to-day selling of used cars.

An old used-car lot scam is the saving-you-sales-tax routine. A prospective buyer is told that a car costs $4500, but, at the time of contract signing, the buyer notices the amount has been "dropped" $500, to $4000. The salesperson explains that, although the vehicle still does cost $4500, he has dropped the $500 from the contract as a favor to the buyer, to lessen the amount of sales tax owed. In reality, however, the car-lot owner or manager only expects the $4000 listed on the sales contract, which leaves the salesperson free to pocket the extra $500, while an appreciative customer smiles all the way home. The only truth to the salesperson's story is that the money is indeed tax free—for the salesperson, that is.

Car lots curtail this practice by requiring multiple signatures on the final sales contracts, which involves too many people to make such deals worthwhile. But before you sign a sales contract, check to see that it has at least two signatures, one of which is either the sales manager's or the car lot owner's.

Spare tires, batteries, radios, floor mats—you name it—bolted down or otherwise, are notorious for disappearing before actual vehicle possession. *Before* the deal, determine what stays and what goes *after* the papers are signed. A radar detector or a CB radio, for example, could easily be construed as belonging to either the car's owner or the prospective buyer. Confirm that items such as spare tires, floor mats, radios, and sound systems are or are not part of the deal. This will avoid haggling at delivery time.

When leaving a deposit on a vehicle, perform a visual check of the battery, tires, and spare, and in the presence of the owner or salesperson. Make exaggerated notice of their brand names and any other identifying marks. This helps to discourage a seller from swapping the newer battery, for example, with an older one before you take possession of the vehicle.

In the final analysis, getting *any* agreement in writing is *never* a bad idea, because after all is said and done, that ounce of prevention will always be worth a pound of cure.

chapter 4

Insuring Your Vehicle: Placing a Premium on Peace of Mind

"From Policies to Prevention"

It has long been advocated that sometimes you have to spend money to make money. Well, sometimes you have to spend money to *save* money.

Vehicle insurance, however, is seldom viewed in that regard. Most motorists realize the value of insurance, but their reasons for begrudgingly mailing off their premiums once or twice a year are less obvious to them.

Statistically, we can expect to receive substantial monetary benefit from a car insurance policy only once or twice every 20 years. And further putting off some motorists is the fact that vehicle insurance is generally mandatory, if not by state law, then by the lien holder of your vehicle. But an entirely different set of statistics clearly shows why the coverage, and not just the price of the policy, needs serious consideration.

Every year, more than 30 million traffic accidents cause more than 40,000 deaths, 5 million injuries, and more than $60 billion in damages. Those who drive inadequately insured or uninsured vehicles may wind up learning a very costly lesson in economics.

In many states, the owner of a registered vehicle is required to carry vehicle insurance (or in a few cases, to post other forms of security). In every state, a driver involved in an accident may lose the right to drive if unable to provide proof of financial responsibility up to certain dollar amounts. Most of us buy this financial responsibility in the form of car insurance.

Planning and Reviewing Coverage

Vehicle insurance is an ongoing affair. Often it is contracted hastily, as an afterthought to the purchase of a car, and coverage and cost are seldom given a second thought thereafter. Purchasing a different car should not be the only time you think about insurance coverage, and you needn't always change companies to obtain better claim service, coverage, or lower premiums. Review your coverage periodically; don't wait until a rate increase jogs your memory. Insurance coverage should be carefully planned.

Premium charges are based on a vehicle's ease of repair, cost of replacement parts, theft rate, and past record of collision and liability payouts. This is the nonnegotiable portion of the policy. The remaining two-thirds of the premium charge are based on intended vehicle use, the number of persons who drive the vehicle, and the particulars of the principal driver: annual mileage, driving record, and place of residence.

States are divided into rating territories determined by population density, traffic congestion, and other such variables. Local premium charges are affected directly by the number and cost of accidents caused by drivers within the rating territory; the number of thefts affects the cost of comprehensive coverage. Many of these rate-setting factors are collected, analyzed, and determined by the Insurance Services Office, Inc., whose headquarters are in New York City. The information is then disseminated to insurers nationwide. The following factors play a role in determining insurance rates; these guidelines seldom vary to any significant degree from one insurer to the next. The most important factor is how they apply to *you*.

Age and Marital Status

If you've recently turned 25 or 30, you are probably due for a reduction; check around, and you will probably find a company that will offer you one. The same applies if you are under 30 and recently married.

Business Mileage

If you have recently retired, be sure to adjust your business mileage accordingly. The same holds true if you become self-employed and work at your home. If you have moved closer to work or have taken a job that is closer to home, reduce your business driving allowance accordingly. Again, if your present agent tells you it won't make a difference, another agent might tell you it does.

Driving Record

It's not advisable to change insurance companies if you've recently been cited for several moving violations. If you try, you'll risk having your record called up and your premiums raised because of a poor driving record. The same is true if you buy another car and seek insurance. If your present premiums are based on a poor driving record, you may be in for a premium reduction when past offenses are dropped from your record. Your state department of motor vehicles (or secretary of state office) can tell you how long driving offenses remain on your record.

Discount Plans

Discount plans are offered by many insurance companies to persons fitting into any of the following categories: senior citizens (and more recently, drivers over 50), nonsmokers, farmers, women aged 30 to 64 who are the only driver in the household, and good students (3.0+ grade-point average). If you own more than one car, ride or drive in a car pool, have recently completed a defensive driving course, or if you use passive restraints—particularly air bags—you may be eligible for a discount. Check with your agent for details. Once again, if your present insurer is stingy with discounts, try other companies.

Your Deductible

As accident repairs continue to rise in cost, deductibles continue to rise as well. Ten years ago, a $500 deductible would have been unheard of; today they are commonplace. If you still have a $100 or even a $250 deductible, compare your present premium to one with a higher deductible. You will pay more in the event of a claim, but then insurance is a venture in calculated risks.

Above all, *be honest* in relaying facts about your driving record and habits. If a falsehood is uncovered after the fact, you jeopardize your coverage. You also risk being turned down by an insurer who may have otherwise offered you good coverage at a fair price.

Basic Vehicle Insurance Coverage

The Insurance Information Institute, a New York City-based nonprofit clearinghouse for insurance-related information, lists six basic types of auto insurance coverage.

1. *Bodily-injury liability* provides money to pay the cost of your legal defense and any claims against you if your car injures or kills someone.
2. *Property-damage liability* provides money to pay claims and defense costs for vehicular damage to property.
3. *Medical payment insurance* pays medical expenses resulting from accidental injuries, covering you, your family, and other passengers in your car. Medical payment insurance differs from bodily injury coverage in two ways: (1) it covers medical expenses incurred by you, your family members, or passengers, and (2) payment is made regardless of who was at fault.
4. *Uninsured motorist protection* pays for injuries caused by an uninsured or hit-and-run driver, including those that might occur to you as a pedestrian. In most states, it also applies to injuries caused by a motorist whose automobile insurance company has gone out of business.

5. *Collision insurance** pays for damage to your car resulting from a collision.

6. *Comprehensive physical damage insurance* pays for damages when your car is stolen or damaged by fire, flood, hail, or acts of vandalism. Comprehensive insurance covers the vehicle in nonaccident situations.

Liability Coverage

Liability coverage is a very important part of your insurance coverage. It covers you against lawsuits generated from either bodily-injury liability or property-damage liability claims. These two forms of coverage are often referred to as PL (personal liability) and PD (property damage). Deductibles never apply to liability coverage.

Single-limit (as opposed to the split-limit PL and PD coverage) is available from some insurers in some states. These policies set one limit for which it will be responsible, regardless of the specifics. This amount can vary from $50,000 to $1 million. In addition, you may also be able to obtain a separate policy, often referred to as an "umbrella" policy, that will cover you for $1 million more. To obtain an umbrella policy, though, it may be necessary to carry high-limit liability coverage on your primary policy, such as $100,000/$300,000.

You may want to keep the following figures in mind when reviewing bodily-injury liability insurance coverage. In a 1982 study by the Department of Transportation (DOT), the cost *per accident victim* ranged from $1845 for minor collisions (those in which occupants received scrapes, bruises, and cuts) to $51,487 for severe accidents (those in which victims suffered serious head, spinal, and internal injuries) to $334,304 per victim in accidents involving fatalities (results reported in 1984 dollars). Money spent to reasonably increase liability coverage is money well spent. A settlement to an aggrieved party in excess of your coverage could mean the forfeiture of your personal belongings and income to reach parity.

Bodily-Injury Liability

Bodily liability insurance coverage applies to situations in which your car injures or kills pedestrians, persons riding in other cars, or passengers in

---

* If a vehicle is hit while parked, the situation is considered to be an accident, and collision coverage, rather than comprehensive coverage, applies. Finding this out after the fact often angers the vehicle owner, as collision deductibles are higher than those for comprehensive ones, sometimes by twice as much.

your car. Coverage is effective provided that the insured vehicle is driven by you, a member of your family who lives with you, or others who drive your car with your permission. You and all members of your family who live with you are covered even when driving someone else's car, if you have the owner's permission. When claims or lawsuits are brought against you, bodily-injury liability insurance provides protection in the form of legal defense, and if either your insurance company or a court decides that you are legally liable for the injury, the company will pay the damages assessed against you up to the policy limits.

All states and Canadian provinces have compulsory liability minimums. A number of states mandate split-limit coverage of $10,000 in the event of injury or death to one party, and $20,000 for injury or death to two or more people. Alaska has the highest compulsory limit at $50,000/$100,000. Canadian provinces mandate single-limit coverage that varies from $50,000 to $200,000.

Property-Damage Liability

You are liable for property damage when your vehicle damages the property of others. More often than not, the damaged property is another vehicle, but you are also covered for damage to such items as lamp posts, fire hydrants, telephone poles, buildings, and pets.

Property-damage liability insurance applies whenever your car is driven by you, members of your immediate family, or others who drive your car with your permission. You and all members of your family who live with you are covered even while driving someone else's car, if you have the owner's permission. When claims or lawsuits are brought against you, property-damage liability insurance provides protection in the form of legal defense and as payment of damages for which you are legally liable, up to the limits of your policy.

In a number of states, minimum property-damage coverage is $5000; in most others, it is $10,000 to $15,000. In Alaska, Nebraska, and New Hampshire, the minimum is $25,000. Canadian drivers are covered by the single-limit amount.

Shopping for Insurance Coverage

There are two sources of vehicle insurance: public and private insurance companies. Public insurance companies sell stock and operate as any other major corporation, presumably to increase shareholder dividends. Private, or mutual, insurance companies do not sell stock; instead, in theory, every policyholder owns a small part of the company. In very general terms, public insurance companies *may* have larger assets and, therefore, may be more likely to remain solvent and not haggle over minor claim discrepancies. Mutual insurance companies *may* be less expensive, because they pay year-end dividends to policyholders. Independent insurance agents and agencies are not affiliated with any particular company or mutual, yet they may sell policies from one or the other or both. Because of this, independents generally offer the widest choice of plans and prices. However, unless an independent agent writes frequently for one company, the agent may lack the clout to go to bat for a consumer when necessary. There are no hard-and-fast rules, however; exceptions abound, and a consumer should shop around.

All these variables need to be weighed against two things: *coverage* and *claim service*. How efficiently is claim service handled? Will an insurance company adjuster estimate repairs, or do you have to drive around town collecting three estimates? Is the adjuster's repair estimate negotiable if extra repair becomes evident? Do you have your choice of repair shops? The latter is especially important in the case of unibody repair. Most new cars have unibody construction and are expensive to repair properly. Not all body shops have the necessary equipment or the expertise to do the job.

Before you buy insurance, ask two or three local body-shop managers which are the best and worst insurance companies with which they deal. A few quick phone calls is all it takes.

Collision Coverage

Collision coverage applies when your car is damaged as a result of a collision with another vehicle or object—whether the vehicle was parked or in motion. In states with no-fault laws, the damage is paid by your insurance company regardless of who was at fault. Deductibles range from $100 to $1000, with the most common being $250.

Comprehensive Coverage

Comprehensive coverage provides protection against financial loss resulting from fire, theft, larceny, glass breakage, falling objects, missiles, explosions, earthquakes, windstorms, hail, water, floods, vandalism or malicious mischief, riot or civil insurrections, or collision with an animal. However, it does not apply if your car is damaged in a collision with another car or object when your vehicle is parked. This could be anything from another vehicle sideswiping your car in a parking lot to a garbage dumpster or shopping cart errantly pushed into it.

Deductibles for comprehensive insurance are usually $50 to $500, and though expensive, zero-deductible comprehensive is generally available as well.

Other Coverage Considerations

When shopping for insurance, check on exactly what is covered in the event of theft. Does the policy cover nonautomotive items such as personal effects, toolboxes, and cassettes? Losing an uninsured $200 coat *and* your car is adding insult to injury.

If your vehicle is in better-than-average condition, get a notarized appraisal. This can be done by a dealership, a professional appraiser, or through your insurance company; check with your insurance agent. Some companies also offer "stated amount coverage" which provides for an agreed upon replacement value in the event of a total loss. The extra cost may be worth it if an older car is in better-than-average condition. Otherwise, you will be compensated at fair-market value only, which is the going price of a comparably equipped vehicle as determined by local newspaper ads.

When shopping for car insurance, obtain a listing of all coverage options available. Sometimes, for as little as $10 a year, you can be guaranteed a loaner if your vehicle is stolen or is disabled as a result of an accident. This coverage can be especially valuable in the event of theft, for which some insurers require a 30-day waiting period before processing your claim.

Towing is another nominal-fee extra that you may find useful. You should also ask your agent about coverage for lodging and meals, should your vehicle become disabled during an out-of-town trip. This could be a real budget-saver if it is ever needed.

Check on wage-loss and substitute-service coverage. If you are disabled as a result of an accident, will your policy cover lost wages and, if so, how soon will you receive compensation and for how long? Will it provide for the care of your dependents while you are disabled (substitute service)? In states without no-fault insurance, the party at fault is usually required to compensate for such losses, but in states with no-fault insurance laws, such coverage is not always included. It's worth inquiring as to how these provisions are handled under the terms of your present policy.

No-Fault Insurance

With no-fault insurance, each person's financial losses, such as medical and hospital expenses and loss of income, are paid by that individual's insurance company, regardless of who is at fault; however, each state has different limitations and restrictions. No-fault insurance still offers the same six basic forms of coverage, though. All states could be said to have some form of no-fault insurance (such as medical payments insurance), but much of what is discussed here applies only to those states that mandate no-fault coverage for all registered vehicles.

Massachusetts, in 1977, was the first state to enact a no-fault insurance law. Florida, Delaware, Oregon, and Illinois then followed suit. Since then, many variations have evolved.

Ideally, no-fault insurance eliminates the legal question of wrongdoing and expedites payment while lowering costs for the consumer. Its objective is to change an adversarial three-party system to a mutually supportive two-party system. But the effectiveness, efficiency, and equity of no-fault insurance vary with the many programs now in effect throughout the country.

A good method of judging the efficiency of a state's vehicle insurance laws is to compare their pay-in/pay-out ratios (Table 4-1A,B). To some extent, this equalizes variables such as population density and traffic congestion. The following chart lists those ratios; the higher the ratio, the more cost-efficient the state insurance program. In 1983, the average pay-out ratio of a no-fault state was 50.2 percent; the average pay-out ratio of a traditional state was 43.2 percent.

Table 4-1A

No-Fault Auto Insurance States	Percent
Arkansas	47.4
Colorado	56.7
Connecticut	48.1
Delaware	52.3
Florida	45.7
Georgia	59.2
Hawaii	35.3
Kansas	47.0
Kentucky	56.0
Maryland	53.8
Massachusetts	47.9
Michigan	55.1
Minnesota	50.8
New Jersey	45.0
New York	42.6
North Dakota	50.4
Oregon	54.8
Pennsylvania	54.0
South Carolina	51.5
Texas	47.7
Utah	52.8
Washington	49.2

Table 4-1B

Traditional Auto Insurance States	Percent
Alabama	44.4
Alaska	44.1
Arizona	41.2
California	44.3
District of Columbia	43.3
Idaho	47.2
Illinois	43.1
Indiana	42.7
Iowa	44.0
Louisiana	41.5
Maine	36.9
Mississippi	44.3
Missouri	46.8
Montana	46.2
Nebraska	46.2
Nevada	39.1
New Hampshire	37.2
New Mexico	42.5
North Carolina	45.2
Ohio	42.7
Oklahoma	45.5
Rhode Island	40.5
South Dakota	45.5
Tennessee	42.8
Vermont	39.2
Virginia	40.3
West Virginia	42.9
Wisconsin	45.4
Wyoming	46.6

In a 1984 study by the Office of Economics for the DOT, several conclusions were drawn about no-fault insurance: (1) significantly more motor vehicle accident victims receive auto insurance compensation in no-fault states than in other states; (2) although no-fault states have higher average insurance premiums, the taxpayers in those states save significantly on court costs and on other public legal costs, which no-fault insurance avoids; and (3) compensation payments under no-fault insurance are made far faster than under traditional auto insurance.

There are two types of no-fault vehicle insurance: *no-lawsuit* and *add-on*. The following states and municipalities have no-lawsuit no-fault insurance:

Colorado	Massachusetts
Connecticut	Michigan
Washington, D.C.	Minnesota
Florida	New Jersey
Georgia	New York
Hawaii	North Dakota
Kansas	Puerto Rico
Kentucky	Utah

The following states have add-on no-fault insurance that requires personal injury automobile insurance:

Delaware	Oregon
Maryland	Pennsylvania

The following states have add-on no-fault insurance for which personal injury automobile insurance is optional:

Arkansas	Texas
South Carolina	Washington

In states with no-lawsuit no-fault insurance, a threshold limit is placed on medical expenses before a lawsuit can be filed against the party that caused the accident. This minimum, which varies, is $200 in New Jersey, $400 in Connecticut, $2500 in Colorado, and $4000 in Minnesota. In Michigan, only death, permanent disability, or disfigurement are grounds for a lawsuit. No-lawsuit no-fault also sets maximum medical expenses for personal injury protection (PIP). This is the maximum amount your insurer is liable to you for reimbursement of medical expenses as a result of an accident, regardless of who was at fault. In Michigan, PIP is unlimited; in Colorado, it is $129,925; yet in North Dakota and Hawaii, it is only $15,000. In North Dakota, the threshold limit for instituting a lawsuit is only $1000 in medical expenses, whereas in Michigan, only death, permanent disability, or disfigurement are grounds for a lawsuit. In other words, there is a fine balance achieved between your insurer's legal monetary responsibility to you and the ever-present likelihood of a lawsuit being generated against the insurer of the party at fault. Generally, a high threshold limit lowers both the number of lawsuits and, therefore, the insurance premiums; however, a high threshold limit also makes it difficult for accident victims to receive damages for pain and suffering and related legal actions.

In states with add-on no-fault insurance, there are no restrictions on lawsuits, and these legal actions are easier to come by. However, this is why vehicle-insurance premiums in many of these states are some of the highest in the nation. These states, while adopting the no-fault principle to accident claims, still permit lawsuits as under traditional, or at-fault, insurance laws.

There's no doubt that no-fault vehicle insurance is complex. Remember two points in particular. (1) If you live in a state with a no-fault law, find out how much personal injury protection is available to you under state law. In some cases, you may have to rely on your own personal medical coverage before attaining the threshold amount necessary for the filing of a lawsuit. (2) Check on who is responsible for reimbursement of your collision deductible if you are in an accident that is not your fault. Sometimes, you—not your insurer—will have to go after the other party to collect.

In summary, as the Insurance Information Institute rightfully advises, in states with no-fault insurance, wise insurance buyers should become acquainted with the nuances of their state's law before purchasing vehicle insurance. For specific information on no-fault insurance in your area, contact your state insurance regulatory board. For general expertise on all forms of no-fault insurance, contact:

Office of Economics
Department of Transportation
400 Seventh Street SW, Room 10301
Washington, D.C. 20590
(202) 426-4416

In Case of an Accident . . .

Perhaps the most important item to keep in mind is your legal duty to any and all injured parties. State laws vary, but, for the most part, those involved in a traffic accident have a legal obligation to render reasonable assistance. If you cannot swim, for instance, you cannot rescue a drowning person, but you can notify the proper authorities as quickly as possible.

If your vehicle is involved in an accident, you may not leave the scene until a proper exchange of information has taken place. Should you leave the scene, hit-and-run charges may be filed against you, a serious charge in most states and cities. Laws vary—and ignorance of the law is no excuse—but generally an exchange of names, addresses, phone numbers, license plate numbers, and insurance companies is required. It is also wise to check the driver's auto registration form to see that it matches the information supplied. Also, get the names, addresses, and phone numbers of witnesses.

An Rx for the Road

Ready-made emergency kits are available from drugstores and from hospital and safety-equipment suppliers. But you can pick a few inexpensive items yourself that can handle a wide range of emergencies:

- 4 × 4-inch gauze dressings for cuts, burns, and lacerations
- 2- or 3-inch gauze bandages for holding dressings in place and for wrapping wounds
- Heavy-duty feminine napkins, excellent to help stop heavy bleeding
- 1-inch-wide adhesive tape for securing gauze and splints
- Safety pins for multiple uses
- Scissors for cutting gauze, bandages, and tape
- Double-bed sheet for cutting into slings and bandages
- A blanket for shock victims and for cold weather

Accident Scene Proceedings

All insurance companies require a police accident report, although statutes vary as to whether these must be filed at the accident scene (generally set by the estimated amount of damage). However, if there is any question as to the sequence of events, it is best to have the report filed at the scene, where the attending officer can review the statements in context. If this is the case, it is best to leave the vehicles where they are; otherwise, get them out of the way of traffic. If you leave the vehicles as-is, do not sit in them; in any event, do not stand behind them. The safest place is in front of an accident scene. Even in daylight, place either flares or road reflectors well behind the cars to ward off approaching traffic. And whether day or night, never attempt to divert traffic around an accident scene without illumination.

When speaking with other people at the accident scene, remember that spontaneous and seemingly innocent remarks such as, "I should have been more careful," can jeopardize your case, regardless of whether you were actually at fault. Do not admit guilt, especially when personal injury is involved; speak only with police officers, and do not volunteer incriminating information. Your insurance company will provide for your legal counsel and defense; you can best assist by keeping conversation to a minimum.

Be aware, too, that in states with "per se" drunk-driving laws (laws that define drunken driving on the basis of blood alcohol content rather than driving impairment), if you have been drinking, even though you were not at fault in the accident, you may very likely be arrested for drunk driving. To avoid detection if you have been drinking, know the circumstances under which you can legally leave the accident scene, such as after the completion of the necessary information exchange. *Caution: You risk very serious legal consequences unless you first consult an attorney to determine the validity of these actions under your state laws.*

Report an accident as soon as possible to your insurance company. Weekend accidents should be reported promptly, because most claims are handled on a first-come, first-served basis, and Monday is generally a busy day at claim centers. Nearly all insurance companies have a phone number you can call at anytime of the day or night, any day of the year. If you cannot locate one, your agent should be able to provide you with one or with an alternate procedure.

After all accident scene requirements have been met, do not drive your car until you or someone mechanically competent has determined that the car is safe to drive.

Repair Estimates and Collision Work

A majority of collision claim settlements are straightforward. Four possible scenarios, though, are worth citing.

First, insurance companies have a euphemism for the repair or replacement of depreciated items that, as a result of an accident, are returned to new condition. The term is *betterment,* and in particular, it is applied to items that are not generally replaced or repaired during the course of normal vehicle use, such as interior fabrics, exterior paint, and bumpers. If, for example, your vehicle is 4 years old, and the front end must be repainted because of damage sustained in a collision, an insurance company may figure the average life of the paint job to be 8 years and, therefore, may pay only 50 percent of the repainting costs. This can be a costly surprise *in addition* to the expected collision deductible. You may want to find out how your insurance company handles betterment and take action if necessary.

Second, insurance companies sometimes make deals in negotiating claim settlements. This is termed *allowance.* If a collision leaves your bumper scratched but not seriously dented, the insurance adjuster may offer you an allowance in lieu of a new bumper. The adjuster may, for example, offer $200 towards the deductible if the policyholder forgoes replacement of the bumper. This is possible under any circumstances except those that affect the safety of a vehicle, and in many states, this extends to the replacement of window glass. (Minor window glass damage, though, can now be repaired using an inexpensive, patented process called the *Novus method,* which forces liquid resins into window cracks and is transparent when dry.) Depending on your financial condition, an allowance offer may be tempting, but temper that temptation by considering (1) how it will affect the car's resale value and (2) how the appearance of a damaged car will affect you.

Third, a vehicle may be declared a total loss as a result of an accident. Many erroneously believe this to be when repair costs exceed the market value of the vehicle. A vehicle is totaled, though, when the cost of repairs *plus* its salvage value equals or exceeds the market value of the vehicle. In other words, if a vehicle worth $3500 sustains collision damages of $2500, and that vehicle's salvage worth is $1000 or more, insurance companies declare the vehicle a total loss.

An insurance company would rather pay a policyholder $3500, scrap the vehicle for $1000, and lose $2500 than pay expensive repair bills in an attempt to repair a badly damaged vehicle. Additional legalities could involve both the collision shop and the insurance company if another accident results from faulty repairs. The likelihood of this is greater with a severely damaged vehicle—especially one with unibody construction.

Some body shops specialize in renovating salvaged or totaled vehicles. They buy these vehicles at auctions, repair them, and eventually resell the vehicles. Most states require before-sale inspection of such vehicles and require that the title of ownership reflect that the vehicle has been salvaged. This also gives the owner of a totaled car the option to repair the car. In this case, the owner would have to pay the insurance company the salvage rate and then seek out a shop willing to repair the vehicle.

In most collision work, use of salvage parts is acceptable and will decrease repair costs. On repair estimates, these parts are often referred to as LKQ—like kind and quality, a euphemism for undamaged parts reclaimed from salvage vehicles by junkyards. (In LKQ language, a junkyard is a "recycling facility.")

Check the insurance company's estimate sheet for "economy part" listings, though. These are body panels that are thinner and less corrosion resistant than those of original equipment specifications. Some insurance companies approve of the use of these parts as a cost-saving measure.

Kenneth Myers, product and marketing manager for Ford Motor Company's parts and service division, says 90 percent of these economy parts come from Taiwan. "They use soft metal dies good for stamping out only 15,000 pieces, but they get 25,000 to 30,000 out of one set of dies. They get waviness in the metal and it doesn't fit properly or match with other body parts.

"Ford uses rust protection processes; they don't. Of the body parts we've tested, the *best* have lasted less than 100 hours in our 500-hour salt spray testing designed to simulate five years of weathering under highway conditions."

Myers estimates that 15 percent of all replacement body parts are imitations and that the use of such is on the increase.

The fourth type of collision claim, which involves unibody repair, is without a doubt the most serious of all.

Unibody Repair

Unibody—or "unit body"—repair exemplifies the knowledge lag that can sometimes exist between automotive engineers and garage repair technicians. Many dealership collision shops are well-versed in unibody repair, but 60 percent of all collision repair is completed by independent repair shops. Only an estimated 25 percent of those have the proper unibody-repair equipment. And ever since the late 1970s, nearly all domestic and foreign models have incorporated unibody design.

The entire shell of a unibody car is a stress- and weight-bearing surface. Formerly, car bodies were attached to rigid steel frames that supported the drivetrain and all stresses placed on it under driving conditions. But rigid steel frames often produced net vehicle weights in excess of 4000 pounds; with unibody design, vehicle weight can be kept to well under 3000 pounds. More important, unibody designs are safer in accidents than are rigid-frame vehicles and provide for better economy of maintenance (see Fig. 4-1).

The front and rear sections of a unibody vehicle are designed to collapse on impact, protecting the passenger compartment. The resulting impact, however, travels throughout the unibody, damaging sections that outwardly appear undamaged. Only through use of the proper equipment—generally a laser-beam measuring system—can these damages be detected and corrected precisely. To prevent heat damage to the metal, unibodies require MIG welding, which is cooler than the regular welding or brazing. On the assembly line, robots spot weld parts to very precise specifications; subsequent repairs of damaged parts call for the welds to be made exactly where the factory put them, to maintain the structural integrity of the vehicle.

These measurements cannot be off by more than the thickness of two dimes. Any more than that puts stress on the suspension, the steering, and the metal itself. In an improperly repaired vehicle, a pothole, or even a simple steering maneuver—especially at highway speeds—can cause loss of vehicle control. Poor alignment combined with outdated welding techniques, then, can be deadly.

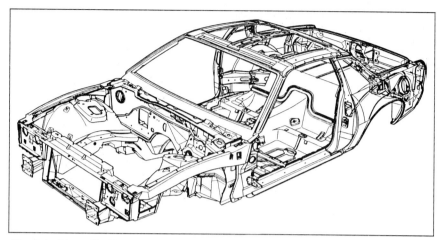

Fig. 4-1 The unibody framework of the General Motors Chevrolet Camaro and Pontiac Firebird models. All unibody designs are integral stress- and weight-bearing structures that require specialized collision repair. Improperly repaired unibodies can be lethal. (*Courtesy Chevrolet-Pontiac-Canada Group.*)

Uninformed repair personnel can destroy the safety built into unibody cars. Some areas of a unibody car are meant to collapse on impact; others are meant to be rigid. Examination of improper unibody repairs has shown that critical parts are sometimes cut into to facilitate hooks that straighten the sheet metal. These parts were then welded back together. Not only does this reduce the metal's ability to withstand stress, but the straightening hooks become so rigid that they could be driven into the passenger compartment like a spear if a subsequent crash were to occur within the same area. Both this and fishplating destroy the integrity of a unibody. *Fishplating,* a "technique" only marginally acceptable with rigid frames, involves welding a piece of metal over a frame separation for the purpose of holding the piece intact.

Initially, automakers were more concerned with the development of unibodies than with their repair. In 1980, the National Association of Independent Insurers reported that unibody cars were being scrapped at a rate 60 percent above the average: although only 34 percent of the cars on the road were of unibody design, they accounted for 54 percent of the cars in salvage yards. Fortunately, both the equipment and the knowledge necessary to repair unibody designs are much more common today than in 1980. A full onslaught of industry-sponsored and vocational school seminars are now being offered on unibody technology and repair (see Fig. 4-2).

In the meantime, it is up to the consumer to find the best repair shop. For legal reasons, insurance companies hesitate to recommend collision-

Fig. 4-2   In addition to providing weight savings, the unibody design is a safety feature. The front and rear structures are designed to absorb impact on collision and collapse like an accordian, protecting the passenger compartment. (*Photo by Mike Spaniola.*)

repair shops; some refuse to altogether. In searching for a shop that is competent in unibody repair, consumers should do the following:

1. Ask about the technicians' training. Look for I-CAR or other training certificates on the wall.
2. Find out what type of welder the shop uses. MIG welders will not damage the molecular makeup of the newer, high-strength, low-alloy steels. Conventional welders will render unibody construction weak and unsafe.
3. Be wary of low estimates. Unibody repair is never inexpensive, but it can be dangerously cheap.
4. If your car cannot be driven, use the police pound for storing it while you check repair facilities. *Don't* let a tow-truck driver decide what shop you choose to do your repair work. Someone may be paying him for sending business their way.

If you are concerned that a past unibody repair may have been done incorrectly, check for the following:

1. Look around the repair area for signs of brass. Although commonly used in collision-shop work, brass should not be used on unibody cars. It has neither the strength nor the durability to hold structural panels together.

2. Check for signs of sudden, uneven tire wear following repair of a unibody. This is an indication that the body was not properly aligned and could result in unexpected loss of control.

3. Check for misalignment, or "dog-tracking." This means that the rear wheels do not follow the front wheels in a straight line. To check alignment, drive slowly through a puddle, then stop the car and examine the tire tracks. They should align, one over the other. If they don't, the body may not have been properly aligned.

If you do have a post-repair problem, notify both the insurance company and the repair facility immediately. Potential liability for negligence provides both with a vested interest in ensuring that the vehicle is repaired properly.

Vehicle Towing

Many new-car owners have found out—the expensive way—that yesterday's chain-and-sling towing methods are not well suited to today's vehicle designs. It behooves new-car owners to familiarize themselves with the manufacturer's recommended towing procedures, because, as vehicles become more complex, simple roadside repair procedures may no longer yield adequate results, and towing will become more common.

Chain-and-sling tow trucks are equipped with a boom that trails the familiar chains and hooks from the back of the truck. Most new cars have plastic molded-fascias that cannot support the weight of a vehicle in tow as well as metal bumpers. Today's cars also have less ground-to-frame clearance and may scrape the ground when towed.

Chain-and-sling hookups can still be used on some newer models if a crossbeam and spacer blocks are used to prevent the chain and sling from making direct contact with the plastic bumper or the fragile underparts. Although automakers do not prohibit use of sling-and-chain towing, most do emphasize that towing instructions in the owner's manual should be followed to the letter. Obviously, it is worthwhile for all car owners to review these directions to better supervise tow-truck operators if the need arises.

Eventually, the chain-and-sling method may be phased out in favor of two alternate methods: wheel-lift and flatbed towing (see Fig. 4-3). Both are now available in most major cities and, again, the prudent driver would do well to know where these operators are located.

The wheel-lift tow truck has a boom that extends horizontally from the back of the truck and supports metal "claws." These slotted arms

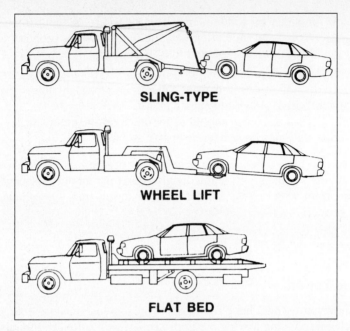

SLING-TYPE

WHEEL LIFT

FLAT BED

Fig. 4-3 In place of steel bumpers, many cars now have fascias made of plastic compounds. Chain-and-sling towing methods can damage these vehicles. Consult your owner's manual; many manufacturers now recommend either wheel-lift towing or flatbed hauling instead. (*Courtesy American Automobile Association.*)

extend under a vehicle and around the front or rear tires. Once the car is in place, the operator raises the vehicle just as a chain-and-sling wrecker would, except that with the wheel lift, only the tires bear the weight of the car. The bumper, suspension, and support rods are left untouched.

In the flatbed method, a vehicle is pulled by means of hydraulics. This is an expensive but superior method of towing; the vehicle is nearly impervious to any towing-related damage. The drawback, though, is that flatbed wreckers require a lot of room in which to maneuver. In side-by-side parking situations, a car may have to be pushed out before it can be towed. Also, as with sling-type wreckers, the height of the towing apparatus prohibits entry into parking garages.

When using either the chain-and-sling or the wheel-lift method, the wrecker operator should secure the front wheels by attaching wheel clamps. A steering-column locking mechanism is not designed for towing.

If a vehicle must be towed either at high speeds or for long distances, be sure to consult the owner's manual instructions. Such towing usually necessitates disconnecting the driveshaft on rear-wheel-drive cars to prevent transmission and axle damage. Front-wheel-drive vehicles should be hoisted from the front, leaving only the rear wheels on the ground. And with either chain-and-sling or wheel-lift towing, check to be sure that there is adequate ground clearance in back; 6 inches is generally recommended.

In all instances, pushing or towing a vehicle yourself is not recommended. In many localities, and especially on freeways, it is illegal, as well. No amount of money saved will ever compensate for an injury or loss of life caused by an amateur attempt at vehicle towing.

On-the-Road Emergencies and Repairs

A lone motorist is stranded on a deserted highway at night, miles from nowhere. . . . After such an experience, an emergency kit would be an automotive forget-me-not.

Nationwide road-service surveys have found that, of all the reasons motorists are usually left stranded, vehicles that won't start (usually because of a dead battery) account for nearly half. Mechanical problems requiring towing waylay about a third; about 10 percent have flat tires; about 3 percent have the keys locked inside; and about 2 percent have run out of gas. (The remainder are classified as miscellaneous.)

At the first sign of car trouble, pull over to the side of the road as soon as it is safe to do so. Leave the car only if you know and trust the neighborhood *and* are relatively sure you can better obtain help by walking than by sitting in the car. Otherwise, put up the hood, turn on the emergency flashers, and tie a white cloth to the roadside door handle. Make extra sure to use your emergency flashers if visibility is limited (by fog or snow); use of either the brake lights or the parking lights may lead drivers right into the back end of your car, because it will appear that your car is still on the road. When someone does stop to help, ask them to call for assistance; you needn't get out of the car.

If you have a flat tire and need to change it yourself, guide the vehicle to the most level area around. Consult the owner's manual as to use of the tire jack and lug wrench. Use of a tire jack is not to be taken lightly; it can be dangerous. As a precaution, it's never a bad idea to familiarize yourself with its use beforehand. As you remove the lug nuts, place them in the wheel cover to avoid losing them. When putting the spare on, do not tighten the lug nuts in a circle, that is, one after another; instead, tighten each lug nut gradually and in a rotation pattern, one across from the other, until all are secure. Never completely tighten lug nuts one at a time.

In your trunk, pack *jumper cables, a flashlight, and two flares or reflectors*. Reflectors have been shown to be more effective than flares, and you can also carry one with you should you have to walk along the roadside for help. It's impractical to carry many different sizes of sockets and wrenches; the simplest tools are the best: regular and Phillips screwdrivers and an *adjustable wrench* are good bets. Also, a length of pipe of the diameter that will fit over your lug-nut wrench will provide extra leverage for "snapping" loose rusted lug nuts.

Carry *a gallon of coolant* (a premixed solution of water and antifreeze will prevent cold-weather freezing) and *window washer solvent.* Do not substitute antifreeze for washer solvent; it will eat away your car's paint job. And a can of *tire sealer,* although it may still leave you with a flat, is better than nothing; hand-operated air pumps can't generate the pressure needed to inflate car tires.

One of the biggest favors you can do for yourself is to stock the correct size of *fan belts* in your trunk. Ask the auto-parts sales assistant to give you the most vital: those that operate the charging system, water pump, and perhaps the power-steering pulleys. Usually one belt operates at least two of these, if not all three. Replacement belts are hard to come by, except in all but the best-stocked service stations, and belts never seem to break near one—or at least near one that's open.

Organize all these items neatly inside a box or other storage container; otherwise, you may never find them again. Two optional items are a fuse replacement kit and a siphon for obtaining gasoline, when all else fails. (This is not advocating the stealing of gas; this assumes you will ask permission first.)

An estimated 3000 people a year accidentally submerge their cars in open water. If this happens to you, remember that the window is your best escape route. The outside water pressure will be too great for most people to open the door until the car is completely submerged. If you have power windows, try to get one open before hitting the water, because the window motor may short out on contact with the water. However, if you cannot exit through the window, pressures will equalize after the vehicle submerges, making the doors easier to open. In any event, you will need to act as quickly as possible; save panic for later.

One for the Road: Alcohol and Driving

As you read the next few pages, someone, somewhere in the United States will die, the victim of another drunk-driving accident. The National Highway Traffic Safety Administration (NHTSA) has estimated that half the population of the United States will become directly involved in an alcohol-related traffic accident at some point. In a groundswell attempt to curb this trend, more than 150 drunk-driving bills were introduced in 37 states in 1982.

Many myths surround drinking and driving. For instance, alcoholics and problem drinkers do not cause the majority of drunk-driving accidents; some may get *arrested* more often for drunk driving, but more than three-quarters of all drunk-driving accidents in the United States involve first, not repeat, offenders—most of whom are under the age of 25.

Alcohol is alcohol, whether you mix it with carbonated beverages, water, or lower-proof liquors. All alcohol, no matter how it is consumed, will get into your bloodstream eventually. Although beer and wine are lower proof (percentage of alcohol multiplied by two) than liquor, ounce for ounce, each is equally intoxicating. Consuming 6 ounces of 24-proof wine, or one 12-ounce can of beer, is not much different from drinking an ounce of 86-proof liquor, either mixed or straight. Cold showers and black coffee will not sober anyone; only time will. Coffee may raise your blood-sugar level, giving you a temporary energy boost, but the alcohol is still in your system, dulling your senses and your reaction time. Likewise, after-the-fact food consumption will not alter your blood alcohol levels, either.

If you are serving alcohol, whether at a private gathering or at a public restaurant, do not automatically refill glasses, and never insist that a person have "just one more." Make nonalcoholic beverages available, so no one need feel embarrassed by having to ask for one. Serve food. Eating leaves less time for drinking, and the longer the period between drinks, the lower the eventual level of intoxication. If you feel that someone has had too much to drink, call a taxi, or take the person home yourself. In addition to the survival of those with whom the driver shares the road, this action is in your best legal interests as well.

Nearly half the states have what are known as "dram shop laws," and in all states, legal consequences exist under alcohol beverage control (ABC) laws, or common-law liability. Not only is the person causing an alcohol-related traffic accident liable for damages, but this can also be extended to public-establishment employees who knowingly serve liquor to intoxicated individuals; in some states, even a private party could be held liable. The latter is more common in states with dram shop laws.

Dram shop laws go back to puritan England. Originally, they were designed to require tavern owners of the day to support the dependents of customers who habitually became intoxicated. (A dram is a unit of measure—0.6 of an ounce—that was commonly applied to alcohol, much the same as the term *shot* is at present.

Under dram shop and similar state liability laws, damages in the millions of dollars have been awarded to victims of drunk-driving accidents. And because many alcohol-related accidents involve those under the age of 25—an age at which one generally has few financial assets—attorneys have shown a marked distinction in suing under dram shop provisions to reach the more lucrative public establishments and private individuals when the legal opportunity presents itself. In other words, aside from the personal or professional empathy you exhibit for drunk-driving victims, your state laws probably provide monetary motivation for curbing excessive alcohol use within your sphere of your responsibility.

Legal Alcohol Intoxication Levels

The legal definition of alcohol intoxication as applied to the use of a motor vehicle is generally determined by a person's blood alcohol concentration (BAC). This can be determined through blood samples or by measuring deep-lung breath. BAC is expressed as the percentage of alcohol in the bloodstream; more precisely, this is the ratio of grams of alcohol per 100 millimeters of blood or per 210 liters of breath. Two-thirds of the states have uniform legal interpretations of BAC levels: .050 or less is not under the influence, .051 to .099 is considered impaired, and 0.10 or more is considered under the influence. Maryland and Idaho set the BAC level at only .080. In states with "per se" drunk-driving laws, a person is driving "under the influence" at specified BAC levels, *regardless* of driving performance.

Alfred J. Farina, a psychologist and researcher with the NHTSA,

KNOW YOUR LIMITS

CHART FOR RESPONSIBLE PEOPLE WHO MAY SOMETIMES DRIVE AFTER DRINKING!

APPROXIMATE BLOOD ALCOHOL PERCENTAGE

Drinks	Body Weight in Pounds								
	100	120	140	160	180	200	220	240	
1	.04	.03	.03	.02	.02	.02	.02	.02	Influenced
2	.08	.06	.05	.05	.04	.04	.03	.03	Rarely
3	.11	.09	.08	.07	.06	.06	.05	.05	
4	.15	.12	.11	.09	.08	.08	.07	.06	
5	.19	.16	.13	.12	.11	.09	.09	.08	Possibly
6	.23	.19	.16	.14	.13	.11	.10	.09	
7	.26	.22	.19	.16	.15	.13	.12	.11	
8	.30	.25	.21	.19	.17	.15	.14	.13	Definitely
9	.34	.28	.24	.21	.19	.17	.15	.14	
10	.38	.31	.27	.23	.21	.19	.17	.16	

Subtract .01% for each 40 minutes of drinking
One Drink is 1 oz. of 100 proof liquor or 12 oz. of beer.

Distributed by the **Office of Substance Abuse Services, State of Michigan** and **Michigan Licensed Beverage Association**

Fig. 4-4   Blood alcohol concentration (BAC) levels are used to define intoxication levels under drunk-driving laws. Know-your-limit cards, generally distributed through state agencies or beverage industry associations, help you to approximate your limit in relation to those used by law enforcement officials. The surest policy, however, is not to drive after drinking. (*Courtesy Michigan Licensed Beverage Association.*)

points out that, on the average, women can consume 15 percent less alcohol than men but still register the same BAC level. "Alcohol is diluted in body water," Farina explains, "and men have more than women, so therefore, the dilution rate is higher in men, which means less BAC impact." A woman's higher percentage of natural body fat is also a factor.

Unfortunately, BAC levels must be generalized for law enforcement purposes, but BAC levels should be defined on an individual basis. A BAC level of 0.10 is generally categorized as about 5 drinks in 2 hours. Although know-your-limit (KYL) cards (see Fig. 4-4) distributed by motor vehicle departments, offices of the secretary of state, or beverage industries serve as good general guidelines, a person also needs to consider weight, height, gender, health, alcohol consumption rate, and meal and modification ingestion.

Two of the most prominent national groups that have increased public awareness of the drunk-driving problem in recent years and that advocate stricter drunk-driving legislation and enforcement are:

Mothers Against Drunk Driving (MADD)
Candy Lightner, Director
669 Airport Freeway, Suite 310
Hurst, TX 76053
(817) 268-6233

Students Against Driving Drunk (SADD)
Robert Anastas, Director
P.O. Box 800
Marlborough, MA 01752
(617) 481-3568

Vehicle Theft

It's no secret that vehicle theft is a major contributor to escalating insurance costs. Most stolen vehicles are stripped for any parts that can be sold—a self-perpetuating situation because insurance companies buy used parts for repairs.

In Detroit, an Oldsmobile Cutlass was stolen and later recovered, with the front clip (the sheet metal from the doors forward) missing. The body shop to which the Cutlass was taken ordered the necessary parts from a local salvage yard. When the front clip arrived, it turned out to be the same one stripped from the car. The parts dealer in Detroit had gotten the clip through a "laundered" source in Toledo, and no complicity could be proven.

This story conveys more than just coincidence. Use of salvage parts once lowered repair costs; today, it is forcing insurance premiums sky-high, and insurance companies are now pushing for laws that prohibit the resale of used body parts for repairs. Don't delude yourself into thinking that your car is "undesirable" for whatever reason. The aforementioned Cutlass was 6 years old and showing it when stolen.

Preventive Measures

These statistics are familiar yet they remain ludicrously stable year after year: 80 percent of all stolen vehicles are left unlocked and unattended; and 40 percent of those had keys left in the ignition. It is more remarkable that insurance companies *honor* claims on such cars. Granted, a professional thief who wants to steal your car will succeed more often than not, but leaving your car unlocked allows amateurs to join in on the booty. A significant number of vehicles are stolen every year as they sit idling at self-service gas stations or in front of convenience stores. So, *take your keys and lock the doors.* Don't leave spare keys "hidden" in magnetic key cases; to a car thief, there's no such thing as an original or a unique spot in which to hide keys. And if you carry a spare set of keys with you, keep them separate from your identification; otherwise, you will lead a thief to both your doorstep and your vehicle.

Because all new cars have interior hood releases, keeping your doors locked prevents ready access to your engine compartment. To a pro, hot wiring is as good as having an ignition key. And a knowledgeable thief can still gain under-hood access unless you literally lock and chain your hood shut, which some owners of high-theft-rate vehicles do; some even remove the ignition-coil wire. You can also park your vehicle with the wheels turned sharply to make a towing theft more difficult. And if you have knobby lock buttons on your car, replace them with the smooth, tapered slip-lock variety to prevent access by coat hanger.

The American Automobile Association (AAA) is a major proponent of etching vehicle identification numbers (VIN) onto auto window glass. Many local AAA offices provide this service free to members. For a nominal fee, some independent repair facilities can also do it. VIN etchings can deter thieves who plan to resell the *complete* vehicle, because doing so would entail replacing all VIN-etched glass, an expensive and incriminating process. VIN etchings are not as effective, though, in deterring the theft of vehicles for salvage parts, in which target items are generally sheet metal and accessories.

Theft-Deterrent Devices

You may rightfully wonder why locking steering wheels do not prevent more thefts. The devices do prevent some amateur thefts, but disabling the mechanism is not difficult and could be described in a paragraph not much longer than this one. So, extra protection, especially in high-risk areas, is often necessary.

A *kill switch* renders a vehicle inoperable, even if the ignition switch is activated. A kill switch is a toggle switch installed somewhere in the ignition wiring harness; its exact location is known only to those who use the car. It is flipped on when the vehicle is in use, and off when it is not. Time is the enemy of a car thief, and if an ignition switch is difficult to jimmy, most thieves will not take the extra time to search for a kill switch.

Another variation of the kill switch is the *fuel-cutoff switch.* A thief may start the car but may get no farther than a block or two before the vehicle stalls.

A *steering-wheel lock* is a metal bar that locks the steering wheel to the brake pedal, making it impossible for the vehicle to be driven. Severing the lock consumes too much time. An *armored collar* is a steel plate that locks around the steering column, protecting the ignition switch. Check with local auto-supply stores about obtaining any of the above items.

Although expensive, *alarm systems* are effective. Alarm systems have been estimated to prevent 60 to 70 percent of all theft attempts. Low-cost units, though, can be a nuisance, going off at the slightest provocation and, usually, at the worst of times (such as in the middle of the night). Better alarm systems incorporate motion sensors and contacts that sense when a hood, trunk, or door is being opened. Motion sensors not only prevent the vehicle from being towed away; they can also thwart thieves attempting to steal hubcaps or wheels or those in the act of breaking and entering. Motion sensors should have adjustable settings to prevent false alarms on windy days. Some alarm systems even have variable volume settings as well. Others incorporate preset alarm delays to give forgetful owners time to shut off the system, before an embarrassing false alarm can sound; some also allow for adjustable exit times as well.

Some alarms operate with keys, others with programmable codes. The more comprehensive alarm systems trigger a kill switch when tampering is detected, and some even flash the vehicle lights on and off for a preset amount of time, making the theft target more apparent to passersby.

Some alarm systems have backup batteries that prevent thieves from disabling the unit by cutting the vehicle's battery cable. Pagers are also available that alert owners when their cars are being tampered with, but their range is unreliable; and unless there's a police officer nearby, the knowledge may be of little practical value to you. Pagers, however, are good backups to alarm systems if you have the money to spend.

In the event that your vehicle *is* stolen, telltale clues help to provide positive identification of the vehicle later. Drop a business card or an old car registration form inside one of the doors, or etch a unique mark in an inconspicuous place—under the carpeting in the trunk, for instance. Such items help to render positive identification if your car resurfaces later with a different paint job or other alterations. And who knows? If you've left behind a form with your name and address on it, a mechanic from 1000 miles away might just give you a call someday.

chapter 5

Dealing with Aftermarket Service and Repair

"After the Warranty Is Gone"

The question "Do you know a good mechanic?" is second only to "What car should I buy?" Typical repair shop selection is haphazard, involving hit-or-miss phone book searches and word-of-mouth referrals. One shop may strike your fancy, but eventually that inevitable something goes wrong, and the search begins again. There's got to be a better way, and there is. But first, check on these potential money-savers.

1. *Check for special policies or recalls on your vehicle.* Either program can save a consumer a lot of money. Both recalls and special policies (warranty extensions) are wide-ranging and may cover *free repair* of anything from trunk hinges to suspension components to complete transmission overhauls. Recall campaigns and, particularly, special policies, are not always well publicized. For example, General Motors still considers *warranty requests* on certain vehicles until 1991, regardless of mileage! (See Chapter 7, "Automotive Special Policies and Recall Campaigns").

2. *Manufacturers are now hearing complaints* through arbitration programs on factory-related repair problems. This could add up to a bottom-line repair bill of *no charge* to the consumer—and most programs go beyond new-car warranty coverage. With the Better Business Bureau's Auto Line arbitration program, for example, most manufacturers agree to hear problems for the lesser of 36,000 miles or 36 months, others for the lesser of 5 years or 50,000 miles. Arbitration programs and tips on how they can save you money are covered in Chapter 2, "Dealing with Manufacturer Warranty and Dealer Service Problems."

3. *Many emissions-control repairs are now warranted for 5 years or 50,000 miles.* This coverage is in effect for most 1981 models and for all models since 1982. These money-saving facts are outlined later in this chapter under the section "EPA Emissions-Control Warranties."

Selecting an Independent Repair Shop: Where Do I Start?

Here is a list of automotive service facilities. A specialized repair source often saves time and money because no one mechanic or repair facility can be all things to all people.

1. *Dealerships* Once a vehicle warranty expires, dealership service departments seldom need to be revisited, unless a problem develops that no one else can solve. Although dealer service is often more expensive than aftermarket alternatives, dealerships generally offer competent, diverse, up-to-date repair service. Routine repairs, such as exhaust system repair, bulb replacement, and general maintenance, etc., warrant neither the added expense nor the expertise of a dealership. All dealers are not created equal, and, as noted in Chapter 1, you need to do your homework in selecting a dealership.

2. *Automotive Electrical Repair Shops* Electrical repair is a highly specialized field of automotive repair in which only the more knowledgeable technicians attempt to make a living. But don't expect these mechanic/technicians to rebuild your transmission although some can and will. These shops may charge more because of their high level of experience and training and the expense of their diagnostic equipment, but, in the long run, it's repair money well spent. Less knowledgeable facilities employ guesswork, trial-and-error methods, and lady luck in solving electrical problems, all of which may leave you stranded with a dead battery, for example, two or three times before the problem is solved.

3. *Axle and Transmission Shops* Drivetrain components are complex and ever-changing: listings of part numbers alone fill dozens of lengthy manuals. Competent drivetrain repair requires exclusive, daily follow-up. This type of repair, when done elsewhere, too often serves as a refresher course or a learning experience for the mechanics—all at your expense.

4. *Muffler, Brake, Tune-up, Exhaust, and Lube Shops* Most of these are national chains operated by local franchisees, and although the home office tries to "clone" each shop, dependability and quality can vary widely with each operator. The main attraction here? Convenient neighborhood locations and relatively prompt service. Don't make the mistake of thinking that these prices are any lower than those at general repair facilities, though.

5. *Tire, Alignment, and Mass Merchandising Repair Shops* The national tire-chain operations (such as General, Goodyear, and Firestone) offer a wide range of services. This is advantageous, because some problems are not readily apparent. The collective corporate girth of these operations may ensure some degree of integrity, but, as with local franchise operations, employee and management quality vary with each location. These shops do have a wealth of home-office support to advise and update mechanical procedures, though.

Mass merchandisers such as K-mart, Sears, and Wards operate auto service centers designed primarily to install the parts their stores sell—batteries, tires, shock absorbers, and the like.

6. *General Repair Shops* This is a catchall category for neighborhood garages and service stations, where everything from tires and batteries to good conversation is available. The latter may be especially handy while waiting for part orders; large inventories are not the norm. Independent repair shops run the gamut from offering a full line of services to handling only your basic lube, oil, and filter jobs. And the mechanic who performs your preventive maintenance so well may not be able to cope with your MacPherson struts, your on-board computer, or your emissions-control system. On the other hand, a competent local mechanic is

worth two elsewhere. Independent repair shops flourish or wither on community reputation; they do not have national ad campaigns to supplement word-of-mouth referrals. Although their knowledge may be less than consummate, the livelihood of an independent is based on doing a good job at a fair price.

7. *Body Shops* In this category, you definitely get what you pay for. If you want a cheap job, some place out there will do it, but don't expect quality.

8. *Vocational or Technical Schools* While getting your car repaired here is a bit unconventional, the engine or body work these schools do often costs less than a quarter of the going market rate. These schools train people in auto repair, and what better way to do that than with cars in need of repair? These schools generally charge for parts only. Not all tech schools, though, are going to jump at the chance to fix your car, and, if they do, it may take a while for them to complete repairs. Going to tech schools is a bit like trusting your hair to a barber college, but give them a thought, nonetheless.

What Do I Look for in Choosing a Repair Facility?

First, impressions are *not* deceiving. Repair shops should be NCO: neat, clean, and organized. A busy multibay garage will never be hospital-clean, but it should be orderly, professional, and businesslike. Spare parts should not be strewn about, the lighting should be bright, and fixtures should not be hung as though an afterthought. Floors and work areas should be unobstructed and free of grease and grime. Diagnostic equipment should look relatively new and well-maintained.

Neatness and organization are not just a matter of appearance. Both indicate concern for detail, ability to manage work projects, and dedication to getting the job done right. Work orders, parts, and tools can be lost in disorganized surroundings, which makes for less efficient and cost-effective repair work.

Do the mechanics use fender aprons (pads to protect the car's finish)? Do they use paper floor mats and plastic steering wheel covers to protect against grease? Does the mechanic offer to road-test the car, or simply take your word on noises, vibrations, and the like? Is the car road-tested after the repair to ensure its effectiveness? Check the odometer to find out. What are the other customers' cars like? Are new and fairly expensive models around, or are most outdated and in poor condition? Cars and mechanics from which people do not expect much are generally found together.

Ask whether the shop uses new or less-expensive rebuilt parts. Many components (such as starters, alternators, brake calipers, and carburetors) can be rebuilt on the premises, and a host of other rebuilt components are available from suppliers. Whether the part is rebuilt or new, all repair work should be warrantied for at least 90 days or 3000 to 4000 miles. Many dealerships do not use rebuilt parts, and this is one reason repair bills are often so costly. Oddly, dealers seldom warranty new-part repairs any longer than repair shops warranty rebuilt parts.

Warranties do not always cover electrical components, the logic being that a faulty electrical component may either mask itself or go bad again because of a not-so-obvious deficiency elsewhere in the electrical system. Again, electrical repairs are best left to automotive electrical repair shops.

Call your local Better Business Bureau (BBB) to check on whether a repair shop has many complaints lodged against it. This will help you to eliminate *really* shoddy outfits from your list: the BBB is not known to withhold recommendation of fair-to-middling businesses. Some automobile clubs maintain listings of repair facilities. The American Automobile Association (AAA), for example, rates repair facilities on staff qualifications, reputation with the BBB and state consumer protection agencies, finances (insurance and bonding), and diversity of repair service. Call a local AAA office or check for their approval sticker in the window of a shop that you may be considering. You may also want to check with your local or state consumer agency. Although they may not be able to recommend shops, they do keep files on problem businesses.

You might also look for service facilities employing repair personnel certified by the National Institute of Automotive Service Excellence (ASE) an independent, nonprofit organization founded in 1972. ASE administers a voluntary program of written tests that measure eight areas of diagnostic and repair skills. The tests are given twice a year at over 270 locations nationwide. To be certified, a mechanic must also have at least 2 years of field experience. Certified mechanics wear a blue and white ASE shoulder patch; repair facilities that employ ASE-certified mechanics usually display the ASE logo (see Fig. 5-1).

ASE tests the following eight repair categories: engine, automatic transmission or transaxle, manual drivetrain and axles, suspension and steering, brakes, electrical systems, heating and air-conditioning, and engine performance. A consumer should not assume, however, that a mechanic with an ASE shoulder patch is certified in all repair categories. A consumer should ask in which area or areas a mechanic is certified. A mechanic who passes all eight tests is certified as a master automobile technician.

All ASE-certified personnel are retested every 5 years. ASE also administers tests to body-repair personnel and to heavy-duty-truck mechanics. It does not, however, attempt to decertify incompetent mechanics; if nothing else, ASE certification indicates that the mechanic has

Fig. 5-1 Look for this logo when looking for service facilities employing mechanics certified by the National Institute for Automotive Service Excellence. Certification involves testing in up to eight areas of vehicle repair and includes periodic retesting. (*Courtesy National Institute for Automotive Service Excellence.*)

some measure of experience. As the complexity of the automobile increases, ASE is working to attract high-caliber individuals to the automotive repair field by sponsoring "career day programs" at high schools. It's a vital step, because some vocational programs at the high school level are little more than detention centers for students who are difficult to place elsewhere.

A push to make October National Car Care Month (actually not a bad time for prewinter maintenance) has gained support from a number of trade publications, the AAA, the National Highway Traffic Safety Administration (NHTSA), and a host of other state and federal agencies. October car care promotions are designed to drum up repair shop business as well as to promote consumer awareness of vehicle safety and maintenance. Perhaps the promotion's greatest value to the consumer is that many repair shops are beginning to pick up on the theme and are offering October price specials. But to avoid being sold a lot of extras, decide ahead of time on your service needs, and the price you're willing to pay— and then stick to it.

When you do find a fair, competent mechanic with whom you've established a comfortable rapport, stick with the individual. Although it may be cheaper to have your muffler replaced elsewhere, send such a repair to that shop. And, while no mechanic can be all things to all cars, if you demonstrate loyalty to the business, you can make a valuable ally—especially in the case of second opinions; often, this can save you more money than any other automotive investment you could make.

Labor Rates and Repair Estimates

Call two or three shops and request a ballpark estimate on the maintenance or repair service you need. Understandably, repair shops may be reluctant to provide price quotes over the phone, but better repair shops know that phone estimates are a part of doing business. And the more competent, efficient, and organized the repair shop, the better able they are to properly estimate repairs—sight unseen. The consumer, on the other hand, should acknowledge that such estimates are not carved in stone but are approximations only. Some of the best repair shops, however, will make only on-premise estimates, and may even charge for them.

Compare the hourly labor rates, too, not just repair estimates. If extra work is required or requested, the difference between a $30-per-hour labor rate and a $40-per-hour rate can make a big difference in your total repair bill.

Repair prices are generally set by flat-rate manuals, which list innumerable repairs on nearly all cars, with the time allotted in tenths of an hour. For example, to replace a muffler on a certain make and model, the time allotment may be 0.8 hour (48 minutes). Many shops split this hourly, or flat, rate with the mechanic. Over the years, flat-rate manuals have been criticized as consumer rip-offs, because repairs that may take only 2 hours, for instance, can be charged out instead at the 3-hour rate specified in the flat-rate manual. Sometimes this promotes hurried repairs to "beat the clock," because a mechanic can work for 8 hours and be paid for 10 or more. Flat-rate pricing, though, helps to weed out incompetent mechanics and encourages productivity—a vital concern to any business. From my dealership experience (and all dealers use manufacturer flat-rate manuals), the mechanics who continually beat the clock were some of the most competent, and, invariably, some jobs require more time than that which is allowed by the flat-rate manual. Often, flat-rate manuals do not compensate for rusted-on bolts, diagnostic work, and ill-constructed engines. In the long run, abolishing the flat rate would only encourage mechanics to stall repairs to pad hours (a tactic not possible with flat rates) and would reward incompetents with larger paychecks, as it would take them longer to complete repairs. The question of whether or not flat-rate manuals rip off the consumer is moot; if consumers sometimes lose money to it, they save as much in the long run as well.

In all instances, it is inadvisable to do business with a mechanic who does not give written estimates. Shop owners and operators who value their reputations find written estimates as much in their best interests as in their customers'. Misunderstandings and "five-o'clock surprises" only harm the image of a reputable garage. Remember to get a copy of the estimate, too; otherwise, having one won't do you much good.

If the estimate does not list complete part and labor costs, there should be a notation stating that your approval is required before the start of any work. Repair approvals can be handled over the phone as long as the mechanic documents the conversation. The customer should get the mechanic's name along with the agreed-upon price quote *and verify that someone in authority at the shop has approved the quote as well.*

Given the complexity of both the modern automobile and today's service legalities, estimates may show only a charge for diagnostic work. Diagnostic fees are based on the shop's hourly flat rate, which could be as high as $50 an hour or as low as $20 an hour, depending on overhead. When the type of repair necessary in unknown, a diagnostic estimate is preferred to a flat-rate manual charge, because it allows a mechanic time to perform tests, and if you've done your homework in selecting a repair facility, you will, in all likelihood, get a good job at a fair price—not cut-rate, but fair.

Cut-rate pricing indicates shortcut repairs, such as brake jobs in which wheel cylinders or caliper pistons are neglected. Some mechanics could lower prices to compete, but they would have to cut corners, and that leads to short-lived repairs and unhappy customers. If you are in doubt about a particular repair price, check your local library for an automotive flat-rate manual. These guides require mechanical aptitude to decipher, but they can still be a good resource.

To prevent repair disputes and to protect yourself in the event of a dispute, save all work orders, including those no-charge second trips back to a repair shop to correct a previous problem. You may need them for backup if the problem lingers. Request the return of old parts, and save them. You may also want to consider paying either by check or by credit card. These methods of payment allow you the option of stopping payment within a few days of the repair job should it prove ineffective. Credit card payments allow more processing time—up to a month in some cases. The Federal Trade Commission allows payment to be withheld in this method for cases of deceptive or negligent repair work only. Also, the repair shop must be within 100 miles of your residence, and the cost must be over $50. You can invoke payment withholding by writing to the respective credit card company. Before doing so, however, contact their customer service number for details.

With body or collision work, determining a fair price is usually straightforward. Many insurance companies have full-time adjusters whose job is to tally up repair estimates. This is also done with flat-rate manuals. When you are pursuing body repairs without the benefit of insurance coverage, nothing beats getting three estimates. Sometimes there will be a wide range in price. If so, ask the repair shop with the higher estimate why another can do it for less, and vice versa. You'll get a bit of an education, a better repair job, and a smaller bill for your efforts. Also, check how long each shop needs to repair your car.

Vehicles of unibody design have caused great consternation among insurers, body-repair personnel, and the consumer—and with good reason. Although unibody design is actually a safety feature, a unibody vehicle can become a coffin on wheels if repaired improperly. Unibody repairs must be carried out with a precision that can be effected only through use of the proper equipment by properly trained personnel.

Most new cars are of unibody design, most foreign makes have been for some time, with domestic makes switching to unibody construction in the mid-1970s. These designs also require towing methods other than the conventional. A great deal more on unibody repair, towing, insurance coverage, claims-handling procedures, and collision shops is contained in Chapter 4.

EPA Emissions-Control Warranties

The U.S. Environmental Protection Agency (EPA) provides consumers with broad protection through two federal emissions-control warranties: the design and defect warranty, and the emissions performance warranty. Both have overlapping provisions, but each has different applications; both, though, are independent of new-car warranty parameters and apply to all subsequent owners of a vehicle, not just to the original owner.

The *design and defect warranty* applies to all motor vehicles manufactured since 1972, including cars, pickups, recreational vehicles, heavy-duty trucks, and motorcycles. The warranty covers repairs to any part in cases in which the defect would cause a vehicle to exceed federal emissions standards. The defect warranty applies for the useful life of the vehicle, which, for cars and light trucks, is defined by the federal government as 5 years or 50,000 miles. For example, a defect warranty can be filed if the catalytic converter on your car rusts out due to defective materials. This warranty applies to all used cars purchased within those time and mileage parameters as well. Proof of scheduled maintenance is not required unless the manufacturer has an objective reason to link the part failure to lack of maintenance.

The *emissions performance warranty* applies to certain vehicles in areas with inspection and maintenance programs (I/M) that meet federal guidelines. The warranty has covered cars and light trucks manufactured since the 1981 model year, and in high-altitude areas (over 4000 feet) since the 1982 model year. The performance warranty is triggered when a vehicle fails the I/M test and the vehicle owner is subject to a penalty (such as being unable to register the vehicle) as a result of that failure.

The performance warranty is also a 5-year, 50,000-mile warranty. For the lesser of 2 years or 24,000 miles, it covers all diagnoses, repairs, and adjustments necessary for the vehicle to pass the I/M test. After this time and mileage parameter, and through the lesser of 5 years or 50,000 miles, the performance warranty covers only those failures traceable to primary emissions-control parts. If related parts must also be repaired or replaced, they are covered as well. For example, if the catalytic converter fails past the 2-year, 24,000-mile point, the performance warranty still covers free replacement of any pipes, clamps, or brackets needed to complete the repair. Parts with scheduled replacement intervals of less than the length of the warranty, such as those in which the manufacturer's instructions say "replace at 15,000 miles or 12 months," are warrantied up to the first

Table 5-1   Primary Emission Control Parts

Exhaust Gas Recirculation (EGR) System
EGR valve
EGR spacer plate
EGR solenoid
Thermal vacuum switch
EGR back-pressure transducer
Sensors and switches used to control EGR flow

Early Fuel Evaporative (EFE) System
EFE valve
Thermal vacuum switch

Air Injection System
Air pump
Antibackfire (diverter) valve or deceleration valve
Diverter, by-pass or gulp valve
Reed valve

Table 5-1   *(Continued)*

Exhaust Gas Conversion Systems

Catalytic converter

Thermal reactor

Oxygen sensor

Dual-walled exhaust pipe

Positive Crankcase Ventilation (PCV) System

PCV valve

PCV solenoid

Evaporative Emission Control System

Purge Valve

Purge solenoid

Fuel-filler cap

Vapor storage canister and filter

Fuel Metering System

Electronic control module or computer command module

Deceleration controls

Fuel injectors, fuel-injection units, and fuel-injection bars developed for feedback EFI and TBI systems

EFI air-flow meter, module, or mixture control unit

Mixture control solenoid, diaphragm, or other fuel metering components that achieve closed-loop operation

Electronic choke

Other feedback control sensors, switches, and valves

Thermostatic air cleaner

Altitude compensator sensor

Ignition Systems

High-energy electronic ignition

Electronic spark advance

Timing advance and retard systems

Miscellaneous Components

Hoses, gaskets, brackets, clamps, and other accessories used in the above systems

Source: Environmental Protection Agency.

replacement point only. This typically includes air and fuel filters, spark plugs, and so on.

In areas with I/M tests, vehicles less than 1 year old are generally exempt from testing and, therefore, no penalty can be imposed upon the owner for failing the test if the vehicle is submitted voluntarily. This, however, would not allow a new-vehicle owner recourse if an emissions-control problem did exist, because the performance warranty applies only if a penalty results from the failure of an I/M test. To allow for these situations, the EPA has a provision that invokes the performance warranty for owners of new vehicles for the lesser of 3 months or 4,000 miles, even though a penalty is not involved. This maneuver may be especially handy for vehicle owners experiencing ongoing performance problems that a dealer cannot readily solve. Submitting the vehicle voluntarily to an I/M test may show a failure, which would then add government pressure on the manufacturer to solve the problem. Often, at the same time, the cause of the drivability problem stands a good chance of being corrected as well.

A vehicle owner seeking emissions-related warranty repair should present the vehicle to a facility that has been authorized by the manufacturer (most often the dealership) to repair the vehicle or its emissions-control system. If the claim is a result of an I/M test, the vehicle owner should provide a copy of the I/M test report to verify the failed status of the vehicle. Test results from official I/M test facilities will always take precedence over those performed by nonsanctioned facilities.

If the manufacturer denies the claim, the denial must be in writing and must explain the basis for rejection. In the case of the performance warranty, federal regulations require either that the vehicle be repaired or that the claim be denied in writing within 30 days; exceptions are made if the I/M program requires a more rapid response or there are conditions beyond the control of the manufacturer. Claims may be denied if the emissions failure was caused by misfueling (use of leaded fuel in a vehicle requiring unleaded), tampering, lack of maintenance, or vehicle abuse.

With either the defect or the performance warranty, consumers who do not agree with the reason for rejection can contact the manufacturer's regional office and ask to discuss it with the customer service manager. If the problem is not resolved, a consumer can seek arbitration (consult Chapter 2) or file against the manufacturer in small-claims court (discussed later in this chapter). The consumer can also write to the EPA:

Warranty Complaint Director
Field Operations and Support Division EN-397F
U.S. Environmental Protection Agency
Washington, D.C. 20460
(202) 382-2633

Consequential and incidental costs (towing, car rentals, lodging) are *not* covered under either emissions warranty. A consumer should nonetheless ask the manufacturer for reimbursement, and can pursue the claim through small-claims court if the request is denied. (Most arbitration programs will not consider a case that involves consequential and incidental costs only.) Exercise common sense, though, and do not rent a car under the assumption that the manufacturer will pay for incidental costs. Inquire first. Remember, the manufacturer has no legal responsibility to reimburse such costs under the emissions warranties but might do so as a courtesy to the consumer.

The emissions warranties also contain provisions for emergency repairs. If a part covered under these warranties causes a vehicle breakdown and it is impractical to go to a repair facility authorized by the manufacturer, reimbursement for temporary repairs is provided if the consumer makes a reasonable effort to get the vehicle to a dealership as soon as possible afterward. For example, should you be stranded miles from a city and an available mechanic informs you that the problem involves an emissions-warrantied part, you are due a refund. However, to prevent giving mechanics carte blanche to make such repairs, only the work required to get the vehicle to a dealership should be performed. To protect your reimbursement rights, nothing of an extensive nature should be undertaken outside of dealership service. The ideal solution is to call a dealership or the manufacturer's regional office for outside repair authorization.

A Primer on Common Repair Needs

Brakes.   You know it's time to have the brakes checked when the brake pedal pulsates or is mushy when pressure is applied, when the tip of your shoe no longer fits between the back side of the brake pedal and the floorboard when the pedal is depressed, when there's the screech of metal against metal on stopping, when the area around the master cylinder is damp, or if you need to add fluid often. Get the brakes serviced! Money is no excuse; a brake job is far cheaper than lawsuits and time lost recovering from an accident. If you don't care, the person you injure probably will.

If the wheel pulls to one side when the brakes are applied, a caliper or wheel cylinder needs checking. Most cars now have disc brakes in front and drum brakes in back. When brake pads (disc) or shoes (drum) are replaced, it is best to have the calipers and wheel cylinders rebuilt to prevent a problem later. These units will leak in time and will ruin the new pads and shoes in the process. Low price estimates on brake jobs usually mean pad and shoe replacements only.

Brake jobs have gotten more expensive because brake pads and shoes are no longer being made from asbestos, but from semimetallics—a combination of steel wool fibers, iron powder, and graphite fused by a plastic resin at high temperatures. The cost is about twice that of asbestos.

Machining drums and discs, while not always necessary, can prevent squealing, pulsating, and pulling. Japanese makes are notorious for front-disc brake rotors that require *major,* expensive surgery to remove. Be aware, though, that on-the-car rotor lathes are available that greatly decrease the cost of these repairs. If your mechanic doesn't know what these are, find one who does.

Conventional brake fluids (DOT 3 or DOT 4) collect water, which often leads to component rust (such as of the calipers and cylinders mentioned above). Have the fluid flushed and replaced when brakes are serviced, or every 2 or 3 years if you're a maintenance freak. Use of silicone brake fluids (DOT 5) is a matter of debate. While DOT 5 prevents water absorption and has a higher boiling point than DOT 3 or 4, silicone fluid may damage brake seals.

Brake lines should be checked with every brake servicing, especially the rubber hoses, which go bad from the *inside* out. Parking brake cables are frequently neglected, and to be kept in working order, the cables should be greased.

The tune-up. In large part, a tune-up today is preventive maintenance. Electronically controlled, high-output ignitions, unleaded gasoline, and copper-cored spark plugs have lengthened the intervals between routine tune-ups, but regular checks of the ignition system are still needed to assure optimal performance and lowest emissions. Emissions-control components, distributor caps, rotors, and spark plug wires need to be maintained, and engine timing and idle speeds (some) need periodic adjustment.

Mechanics who perform tune-ups today should be reading from a manual nearby; otherwise, they are liable to do more harm than good. Not even the engineers who designed today's complex systems can recall all the details. The mechanic should also have some knowledge of electronics. Any number of parts manufacturers and distributors offer clinics to help bring repair personnel up to date. Has the mechanic under your hood attended any *recently*?

The proliferation of automotive electronics has spawned the "replace-the-on-board-computer" syndrome among less knowledgeable repair personnel. Not only is this an expensive proposition, but many times it is unnecessary and solves nothing. The presence of the computer can short-circuit the common sense of even a competent mechanic. Many problems connected with drivability, performance, fuel mileage, or hard starting are caused by internal engine problems or by the computer sensor units. It takes a skilled, knowledgeable mechanic with the proper diagnostic equipment to detect and properly repair these components.

Exhaust systems.   Muffler chains have taken over a large chunk of this segment, not so much because of low price as smart marketing. Many aftermarket suppliers are now offering lifetime guarantees at competitive prices; even factory-issue mufflers are doing likewise.

Have exhaust system components such as clamps, hangers, and connections checked whenever the car is hoisted for routine service. A pair of wide-mouth pliers can be used to judge the thickness of pipes, and this may keep you from having to drag your muffler home between your rear wheels. If *that* happens, an adjacent pipe or hanger usually snaps off, too, increasing the repair bill.

The exhaust system can also be the cause of performance problems, such as those that occur with clogged catalytic converters or petrified heat risers. The exhaust manifold heat riser should be serviced as a part of routine maintenance.

After exhaust system repairs, take the car for a drive and listen for rattles and leaks. Some shops use one-size-fits-all clamps that don't, or they tighten up clamps and hangers one at a time rather than securing all connections gradually, which usually prevents leaks and rattles. So, if you hear either, don't listen to excuses. Have the repair shop readjust the exhaust system.

Lubrication.   At the very minimum, change the oil and oil filter and have the chassis lubed at the factory-suggested intervals. Unfortunately, these intervals are more a marketing pipe dream than anything to which an engineer would admit. Manufacturer recommendations for normal service are fine if you drive over 50 miles a day at freeway speeds and allow your engine a warm-up and cool-down period. The rest of us stop-and-go, short-trip drivers should follow severe-driving service recommendations, which usually require service twice as often.

Given the demands today's engines place on oil, proper maintenance is more important than ever, and this is *not* a marketing scheme. Do yourself a favor and read the section on oil in the next chapter. As to other fluids and gear lubes, consult "Vehicle Maintenance" in this chapter. Taking to heart the advice presented in either section can only save you money.

Starting and charging systems.   Bad grounds are often the cause of mysterious ignition and performance problems, especially on vehicles with computerized ignition systems. The thick, red wire running from the battery is the positive (+) lead, and the black is the negative (−), or ground, wire. Check both and inspect the main ground connection on the engine block. Also check ancillary ground wires attached to the engine compartment and other engine parts; all should be secure and free from corrosion and rust. *Do not pull a battery cable with the ignition switch in the On position.* This can short-circuit the expensive on-board computer—permanently.

Check alternator pulley-belt tension. A loose belt will reduce available battery charge. If the dashboard light or gauge indicates a discharge, the problem most often lies with the charging system, probably with the alternator itself. Too often, battery replacement is the cure-all for starting and charging deficiencies, and, too often, a new battery only cures the symptoms but not the problem. For more information on batteries in particular and on the ignition system in general—*including important battery-related safety precautions*—consult the section on batteries in the next chapter.

Cooling systems.   Today's engines run hotter than their predecessors; there is also less room under the hood for cooling space, and new lightweight materials are less effective than older materials in dispersing heat. Today's cooling systems must be respected for the job they perform—*respected,* not neglected.

The most common cause of overheating is low coolant levels caused by leaks or a broken fan belt. These unexpected problems can be deterred through preventive maintenance. Check the fan belt, hoses, and water pump periodically. If the belt is more than 4 years old, it should be replaced. Cooling system hoses should be checked for cracks, swelling, and loss of suppleness. The water pump will leak when the bearing seals go bad and should be replaced; trying to stop the leaks will not work. And treat your cooling system to new antifreeze every 2 or 3 years. Antifreeze not only inhibits corrosion, but it also lubricates the water pump and raises the boiling point of the coolant.

Some cars now have electric fans to aid with under-hood air circulation after an engine is shut off. Be careful when working around these thermostatically operated fans, so that one does not come to life with your hand nearby.

The cooling system is a very important component, and for this reason, there is a section on cooling systems in the next chapter.

Alignment and chassis work.   This category is no longer fair game for the "$9.95 alignment job." For a front-wheel-drive (FWD) vehicle (which most are, and more will be) expect to pay $20 for two-wheel alignment; for two-wheels referenced to the thrust line, $30; for all four wheels, $40. Anything less, and you may be dealing with incompetents or someone out to fleece you on unnecessary extras once you're lured in by the "unbelievable price."

The most common reason for front-end-alignment comebacks (a second visit for the same service or repair) is that the steering wheel does not center when the car is moving in a straight line. With FWD, a mechanic can no longer adjust the front-end alignment to compensate for the deficiencies of rear-end tracking. Many FWD vehicles do not have the solid rear axle their rear-drive counterparts have; instead, many FWD cars (and some rear-wheel ones as well) have independent rear suspension systems (IRS).

In this situation, all four wheels need to be kept aligned. Should your steering wheel not center *after* a front-end alignment, this fact was ignored, either because the mechanic was unaware of the procedure or did not know how to deal with it.

Properly setting alignment in these situations requires reviewing all suspension components and replacing and realigning the ones that are causing the car to go off-track. This requires specialized equipment and qualified repair personnel. One last point: There is a "tool" on the market called a *strut bender*. Not a single automaker approves of its use. A strut bender utilizes brute force to bring a suspension back into alignment— very handy for mechanics who do not know the proper procedures or who do not care to learn them.

Tires.   This subject is so complex that a whole section has been devoted to it in the next chapter.

A Primer on Common Fraudulent Repairs

Consumer horror stories on this topic abound, and, try as a consumer may, it can be difficult distinguishing the genuine article from the greasy shaft. And, as cars become more complex, opportunities to swindle the unknowledgeable car user will grow.

In a nutshell, avoiding unnecessary repairs is largely a matter of choosing a competent mechanic and a reputable repair shop, which is why this chapter has dwelled on that topic. Service personnel who cheat the customer have generally become accustomed to doing so, not so much out of greed as incompetence. They do not know their profession, or marketing, well enough to earn a living—so they cheat.

There are two sides to every coin, and, in fairness to the automotive repair industry, the typical car is not well maintained, some customers expect 30,000 or more miles of sheer neglect to be altered by a 2-hour repair-shop session—all for under $30 and guaranteed. Also, repairs to certain parts cannot be assured simply by replacing the damaged part itself. For example, if a vehicle has a bad spark plug wire, it is wise to replace all the spark plugs and the distributor cap.

A book that will give you cause never again to trust another repair shop is *Mr. Badwrench,* by Arthur P. Glickman. While *Mr. Badwrench* is thoroughly documented with some very appalling stories, many of Mr.

Glickman's solutions to these problems are to dump them back into the lap of the American public. He suggests that we all need to become automotive activists, that only a public groundswell will finally bring both the automotive repair industry and government to stem the tide of automotive repair abuse.

And he is right. In the meantime, keep a jaundiced eye reserved for the following repairs.

Ball joints. This is the horn of plenty, the veritable cornucopia of automotive repairs. California has even passed laws dealing specifically with ball-joint replacement! This ploy is so old that it is very, very tiring, yet it still works, with little or no variation. This particular ploy is very often accompanied by specials on front-end alignments.

Many a driver has left a car for a front-end alignment only to later hear, "We can't do the work until we replace your ball joints" (uppers, lowers, or both). If you are at the repair facility, this is usually accompanied by a mechanic or two wobbling your front wheels for you to see while displaying well-practiced looks of abject horror.

ADVICE: If you ask what the amount of free play is compared to the factory specifications, the repair personnel will seldom know. Ask, then, how do they know that the ball joints are bad? They will tell you that they know because the front wheels wobble. Again, this is part of the scam, because when a vehicle is on a hoist with the front wheels hanging free, there will always be some free play.

If you have not had any particular problems with the front end—erratic tire wear aside—be very suspicious. A wheel that wobbles on a hoisted car is more likely to have bad wheel bearings than bad ball joints and, in that case, you would have noticed a wheel shimmying or shaking while driving.

When a car is on a hoist, you cannot tell whether a ball joint is good or bad. The loaded ball joint (the one that carries the spring) must be supported in order to determine the amount of slack. This can be done only with the car on the ground and a hydraulic jack (properly placed) supporting the frame or A-arm. In the mid 1970s, a wear indicator was incorporated into some ball joints. Use of this design is sporadic, but if ball joints with wear indicators need replacing, the grease fitting will sink into the ball-joint sockets, making the degree of wear readily visible.

If all of the above checks out in your opinion, you may still be wise to get a second opinion unless you totally trust the garage you are using. This scam is hard to break, and that's why it's been around so long—it's easy and almost always successful. (By the way, at least most shops actually replace the ball joints.)

Idler arms and tie-rod ends. Unless you have been experiencing handling problems or a shimmy, go for a second opinion. If a mechanic warns you that your wheels are about to fall off, stop at the garage, and look for yourself. Even then, a mechanic can loosen things so that your wheels will appear ready to fall off. If your problem is really so urgent that it cannot wait for a second opinion, then rest assured: you would have noticed erratic ride or handling characteristics.

ADVICE: Don't neglect suspension components, but the less you know about cars, the more reluctant you should be to give the OK on these repairs without a second opinion. And *don't* let anyone scare you with "the sky is falling" tactics, either.

With the constant-velocity joints found in front-wheel-drive systems, though, the joint should be replaced if the boot that envelopes it is damaged. In this case, you will not have noticed a problem.

Shock absorbers.   Show me a driver who has ever noticed the difference between worn shocks and new shocks. By the time the original shock absorbers have worn, so will have many other suspension components, such as bushings and grommets, which will nearly negate the effect of new shock absorbers. A vehicle with 20,000 to 30,000 miles that bounces excessively after hitting bumps and on cornering may benefit from new shocks, but probably never again past that point. The bottom line on this is to deal with trustworthy mechanics.

A sagging or leaning car needs more than new shock absorbers (usually springs), and there is *no* sense in installing new shocks until the real problem is fixed. Shock absorbers are hydraulic units that can be compressed by a man of average strength; shocks, then, will obviously not raise up the entire side of a car. Only springs will.

ADVICE: In addition to a bouncy ride, if your tires are wearing in an odd fashion, you may need new shock absorbers to keep proper alignment. And if you need to replace shock absorbers after only 2 years or so of use, then upgrade. If you pull a trailer or other such equipment on a regular basis, try rear air shocks. In any event, try gas-charged shocks for added handling and longevity if your car was not equipped with them originally.

Lifetime guarantees on anything, or low-priced "extended-service programs."   If a front alignment is "guaranteed" (for the life of your car, or whatever), you will eventually be told, "I know we guaranteed your alignment, but we cannot honor the guarantee because you need new [pick one or all of the following] shock absorbers, ball joints, idler arms, stabilizer bars, tie-rod ends . . . (ad nauseam)."

When you go back to have your "lifetime" muffler replaced, you will most likely learn that a rusted pipe is the cause of the noise. (This is not to imply fraud because many times this is simply the way the exhaust system crumbles.) You should be aware of this fact if you are planning to purchase a more expensive muffler solely on the basis of a guarantee. While the muffler may be of superior quality, it won't do a thing for the rest of the exhaust system.

ADVICE: Proceed with caution; better still, proceed to a repair shop that doesn't resort to gimmicks.

Shavings in the transmission pan.   When consumers respond to specials on routine automatic transmission service, the attending mechanic may feign grief while displaying minute metallic particles in the bottom of your transmission pan, and, as though reading tea leaves in the bottom of a cup, predict the untimely demise of the transmission. This line usually begins with, "I don't mean to scare you, but . . ."

ADVICE: Always get a second opinion. Even if you have had a problem with the transmission, it may be something quite minor. Dark, murky (automatic) transmission fluid is more a sign of trouble than the metal shavings normally found on the pan bottom.

Small-change items.   "Shortsticking" is the partial insertion of the oil dipstick to deliberately obtain a low reading in order to sell you a can or two of oil. Another trick is to insert an oil spout into an empty oil can and to go through the motions of pouring it. Modern plastic containers facilitate this nicely.

"Pump-hanging" is practiced by attendants who do not completely hang up the pump handle thereby leaving the pump (and its total price) on standby. For example, if a pump is left running at $5, the next customer will be cheated out of $5 which the attendant will later pocket.

ADVICE: You now have less reason to be angry with the demise of the full-service gasoline station.

Legal Recourse with Service Problems

This section pertains to repair problems with establishments other than dealerships or manufacturers, which are detailed in Chapter 2.

With any repair discrepancy, contact the owner or general manager directly and attempt to mediate a solution; if the facility is associated with a chain or franchise, contact the district or regional office. You may also want to contact the corporate headquarters. When doing so, please consult the Chapter 2 sections "Collecting the Necessary Information" and "Dealing with the Manufacturer's Regional Office." Although both sections apply to automakers, the same letter format, information, and other procedures can be used. Appendix E contains the addresses and phone numbers of the national headquarters for many chain and franchise operations.

You may also want to read the "Government and Consumer Agencies" section in Chapter 2. Federal and state agencies often provide helpful brochures and pamphlets. Privately operated consumer agencies can often suggest attorneys specializing in repair-problem cases or can put you in contact with a consumer who overcame a similar problem.

The similarities between manufacturer and independent repair problems end there, however; there are no arbitration boards or lemon laws. You can do the following, though: (1) take a repair shop to small-claims court, for which you do not need a lawyer; (2) file a civil suit, for which you should have a lawyer; or (3) contact your state consumer protection agency to check for a violation of the law under which the state could prosecute.

Small-Claims Court Procedures

Procedures vary from state to state, but overall, from filing to presenting your case, consumer negotiation of small-claims court is a relatively simple matter. In larger cities (generally those with a population of more than 100,000), local municipal centers administer small-claims court proceedings. In smaller locales, the county may be in charge. Check with your city clerk.

Generally, you must file in the city or county in which the defendant (the person or business you are suing) is located. Filing usually requires completing a one-page form and paying a $10 to $20 filing fee, which should be added to the amount for which you are suing.

The back side of the small-claims court filing form often contains information that tells you what is required. Consumer guides on small-claims court proceedings are generally free for the asking from your local clerk's office. The clerk can advise you on procedures but cannot dispense legal advice. If you cannot afford legal advice, the clerk can direct you to state agencies.

Be sure to inquire about such details as the maximum amount for which you can sue and whether or not case appeals or lawyers are allowed. These items usually vary from state to state and may even vary from locale to locale.

After you file, the clerk's office will issue a copy of the complaint to the defendant, notifying them of the court date. If you have a legitimate complaint, chances are good that the claim will be settled out of court beforehand. In these instances, the very fact that you have filed generally prompts the party to act. Of course, your case must have merit, and you should not expect the mere filing of a claim to prompt recovery.

Under most state laws, you must show a tangible loss before you can file in small-claims court. You cannot, for example, claim the loss of resale value because of a poor collision repair; you can, however, seek reimbursement for the repair *and* the cost of having it redone.

In filing, claim all expenses in addition to the actual loss: rental cars, towing, lodging, phone bills, and the small-claims court filing fee itself. Avoid making frivolous claims, however; they can lessen the impact of a rightful claim, and the defendant may be less likely to settle out of court.

If you have never been to small-claims court and do not know someone who has, you may want to sit in on a session; all cases are open to the public. If that is not possible, arrive early the day of your hearing and listen to the cases that precede yours.

Organize your presentation like a newspaper story; be sure your presentation answers the questions *who, what, when, where, and why* or *how*. Give the dates in order of sequence. If possible, bring the defective part along, and get affidavits or notarized written statements that support your case—this could be the observations of an independent mechanic who has inspected your car. Witnesses are not always necessary; many cases are decided without witnesses. Remember that the court has the power to subpoena reluctant witnesses if necessary; the court clerk can tell you how to go about this.

For the court's use, bring photocopies of all pertinent documents—receipts, correspondence, and any hard copy that speaks for itself, such as the warranty statement on a repair bill.

If there is a deficiency in the small-claims court systems, it is the fact that a lack of court-enforced collection provisions means that not all judgments awarded are actually collected. This should not deter you, though; the benefits of filing in small-claims court far outweigh any disadvantages.

Civil Suits

The following is a general guide to legal recourse in cases of misrepair. The circumstances of each case should be reviewed by an attorney to decide if it is indeed worthwhile to take legal action.

Basically, consumer repair problems fall in one of two categories: *deceptive* repairs or *negligent* repairs. Unauthorized repairs, with or without a written estimate, may be legally construed as deceptive repairs. If the final repair bill is quite a bit more than the estimate, the linkage is obvious, but even if there was no written estimate, courts have ruled this to be an outright attempt to deceive—especially if the old parts were not offered for return to the consumer.

All repair facilities must exercise reasonable care and judgment when repairing a vehicle; failure to do so may be legally construed as negligent repair. The biggest problem for a consumer (and attorney) is to obtain proof, whether of outright negligence or of a mechanic's failure to spot underlying hazards. If, following routine brake service, a vehicle is involved in an accident due to faulty brakes and it is determined that a leaking master cylinder caused the brake failure, the repair facility may be found guilty of negligence for not having diagnosed the underlying defect at the time of the brake job. If a *part* that has been installed is found to be defective, a civil suit can be filed against both the repair establishment and the manufacturer.

With most repairs, expressed and implied contracts and written warranties permit actions under the Magnuson-Moss Warranty Act, which permits recovery of attorney fees. Losses for which a suit may be filed are generally limited to the cost of repairing the vehicle properly plus the cost of the defective repair job. If a vehicle is rendered useless as a result of deceptive or negligent repairs, the fair-market value of the vehicle may be recovered. The cost of using rental cars in the repair interim can also be claimed if the length of repair time warrants such a claim.

Vehicle Maintenance

Phrases such as "well maintained" and "well taken care of" are applied too liberally, especially in selling a vehicle. Regular oil and filter changes, chassis lubrication, and tune-ups do not qualify a vehicle as well maintained. A well-maintained vehicle should have:

- The automatic transmission fluid and its filter changed every 24,000 miles or every 2 years
- The universal joints (if applicable) repacked every 40,000 to 50,000 miles or every 4 years
- The front-wheel bearings repacked every 20,000 to 30,000 miles or every 2 to 3 years (for front-wheel-drive vehicles, both front-wheel and rear-wheel bearings must be repacked)
- The cooling system flushed, cleaned, and refilled with new coolant every 24,000 miles or every 2 years
- A major tune-up, which includes replacing spark-plug wires and overhauling the carburetor and distributor if necessary, at the 50,000-mile mark
- In addition, oil changes; alignments; and belt, filter, hose, and brake servicing must be attended to on schedule

As an extra precaution, the oil in a manual transmission and the oil in the rear-end unit of a rear-wheel-drive car can be changed every 50,000 miles or every 5 years, although this is not as vital as engine or even automatic transmission oil changes because those gear lubes are not exposed to temperature or pollution levels as high as those the engine, and to a lesser degree, the automatic transmission, are exposed to.

Sound fanatical? Sound as though you're the customer in a mechanic's dream? Well, your car will probably survive without the above regimen, but not as long—and certainly nowhere near as trouble-free and dependable—as it will with such maintenance.

The bottom line? If you have a car with which you are happy and you want to maintain that relationship, then maintain the car. If it isn't broken, don't fix it. But don't wait until it breaks, either; maintain it instead.

An excellent book on maintaining your vehicle is *Drive It Forever* by Robert Sikorsky (McGraw-Hill, 1983). The practicality of the suggestions distinguishes this book from others on the same subject. This, combined with an easy-to-read presentation, makes *Drive It Forever* must reading for anyone who is serious about vehicle longevity.

Another good idea is to pick up an occasional copy of, or subscribe to, an automotive magazine. *Popular Science, Popular Mechanics, Home Mechanix, and Family Handyman* update and review practical repairs, typical problems, and conventional maintenance procedures. Publications such as *Road and Track, Car and Driver, Motor Trend,* and *Automotive News* address the business side of the industry and keep the reader abreast of technological advances, recalls, regulations, new models, and prototype development.

Do-It-Yourself (DIY) Tips

The first tip is to locate a manual that deals specifically with your vehicle. Today's automobiles are too sophisticated for generalities; there are more exceptions than there are rules.

Chilton Book Company's automotive guides are very comprehensive. They cover many facets of automotive repair and offer long lists of individual repair guides for both domestic and foreign makes and models. Many bookstores stock or can order these manuals. For a free Chilton catalog call (800) 345-1214.

Your dealer can tell you how to order copies of the factory service manual or check for an order form in your owner's manual. Factory service manuals are more complex than aftermarket equivalents. Factory versions use jargon and procedural explanations that sometimes assume a high level of expertise, and they are often peppered with references to unique factory-issue tools that are beyond both the access and budget of the weekend mechanic. However, if you've gained a familiarity with a certain model over the years, a factory manual can be a real asset.

With either an independent or factory manual, for a modest price—usually $5 to $6—you gain troubleshooting tips that could recoup the cost of the manual many times over. Step-by-step diagnostics found in service manuals can help even the novice, because when a problem occurs, people tend to check the most obvious, rather than the simplest, things first. And "simple" and "obvious" are not synonymous.

If your wiper fluid no longer squirts, it's both obvious and simple enough to check the fluid level. However, if your engine develops a ticking sound, check the oil level first. If your turn signals quit flashing but the bulbs still light, check your fuse box. If your car has fuel injection and the car is hard to start, the problem may simply be the fuel pump relay switch. When this switch fails, an oil pressure sensor switch takes over, but that requires a longer cranking time.

This is not to suggest self-repair, but self-diagnosis can make one more secure when leaving a car for repair. These are but a few of the diagnoses that most anyone can make with the aid of a manual (Fig. 5-2).

Common DIY Items

Armed with the proper manual and a few basic tools, most car owners can accomplish the following. (This list can also double as a prevacation or pretrip checklist.)

- Checking and adding fluids: oil, coolant, battery, brake, transmission, solvent, and power steering.
- Checking, changing, and setting spark plugs, points, condenser, and rotor. Note that changing the distributor cap is not included. Unless you know about firing orders, you can render a vehicle inoperable or do serious engine damage by incorrectly replacing the cap wires.
- Checking and changing filters: air, fuel, and oil.
- Checking and/or changing EGR, PCV valves, and recirculation filters
- Repairing and maintaining the cooling system: flushing, cleaning, refilling, and replacing hoses and thermostat.
- Checking and changing fan belts and windshield wipers.
- Checking and changing light bulbs, turn signals, headlights, and fuses.
- Adjusting tire pressure (including spare if applicable).
- Washing and waxing. Frequent washings prevent rust better than do frequent waxings. In other words, don't put off washing your car until you can also wax it. A neat trick in staving off rust is to use a clear silicone caulk to seal around chrome strips and mirror-to-body-type attachments. This is where most surface rust is likely to start. Just apply a bead along those surfaces as you would caulk to a window frame and let dry. It won't harm paint surfaces. For more tips on interior and exterior care, consult Chapter 3, the section "Selling a Used Car."

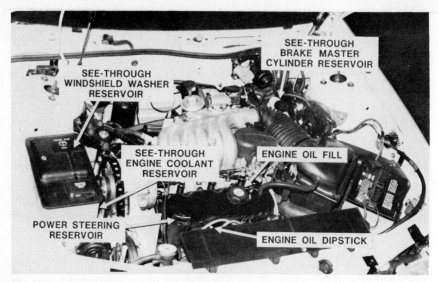

Fig. 5-2 Don't let under-hood prospects frighten you from attempting simple maintenance. Some cars, like this Ford Taurus and the Mercury Sable, are designed for easy consumer access; use of transparent materials allows for visual checks of some fluid levels, too. (*Courtesy Ford Motor Co.*)

Here is a bare-minimum list of tools to have on hand. If you do not already have these on hand, then spend for these tools as they will be used: sparingly.

- Two long and two short screwdrivers, one each of flat- and Phillips-head design
- A pair of adjustable pliers
- An oil-filter and a spark-plug wrench
- A starter set of ratchet, box-end, and open-end wrenches and extensions (metric dimensions or U.S. customary depending on vehicle year)
- A tire pressure gauge and a set of thickness (feeler) gauges
- A small set of hex (allen) wrenches
- A long-necked funnel

A helpful tip for rookies: Clockwise rotation is the direction in which a clock runs, that is, left to right. Clockwise movement of a threaded object tightens it. Therefore, clockwise motion is *going on* (as time is an ongoing process). Counter clockwise motion is the opposite (coming off). Another way to remember this principle: Right is tight; left is loose.

(There are very few exceptions; one, however, is the left-handed lug nuts found on Chrysler products some years ago.)

Another good DIY idea is to take instant photos of an item before it is disassembled and during critical repair steps. This provides a reference point when the inevitable happens and you can't remember what went where.

Before rendering your vehicle inoperable, be as certain as possible that the replacement part(s) fit. Also, because it's difficult to anticipate all parts needs, make sure that someone is available to make a parts run for you if necessary. In locating difficult-to-find parts, especially those for older and low-production vehicles, the monthly publication *Hemmings Motor News* (Box 100, Bennington, Vermont 05201) is a good reference.

Cautions

Never use a bumper jack to raise a vehicle for the purpose of working underneath. Don't risk maiming yourself for the sake of an oil change. Invest in an appropriately weight-rated scissor jack or a hydraulic jack. And to prevent the car from rolling, be sure the transmission is in gear with a manual or in park with an automatic. Always block the wheels.

If you use the parking brake on a regular basis, set it as well. If you normally do not use the parking brake, it may seize up when applied and not disengage when you release it.

Scissors jacks are especially useful, because you can keep one in your trunk and throw away the tire jack. No matter what automakers will tell you, tire jacks are *not* very safe for changing tires. Ask anyone who has had to buy a new brake drum or rotor to replace the one that broke when the car fell off the jack.

Don't wear loose-fitting clothes; they can become entangled in the fan belts, possibly dragging you into the engine compartment. Don't wear jewelry or watches; they can catch on protruding bolts and wires (usually when a person is jerking an arm away as a reaction to an electrical jolt or the touch of a hot part). You can severely sprain a finger or wrist, not to mention damage the jewelry.

Read and follow all product label directions. Some products may eat away the finish of your car should they come in contact with it; others give off hazardous fumes. Be sure you know the do's and don'ts beforehand. Keep a dry chemical fire extinguisher in the work area, either one that is rated type B or an all-purpose type ABC. (Class A fires involve such materials as wood and paper; class B fires involve petroleum-based products; and class C fires are electrical.)

Store gasoline in safety-rated containers only. These should have spring-loaded caps that prevent all spillage, but still allow fumes to vent.

The filler neck should have a flame arrester; the tank itself should be short and stout, so that it will not overturn easily; and the container should be clearly labeled. While researching an article on child-poisoning prevention, I spoke with a man whose son had drunk from a soft-drink bottle in which gasoline had temporarily been stored. The child was spared serious injury because the father (1) saw his son drinking from the bottle, and (2) had the number of the local poison control center handy. For a listing of U.S. Poison Control Centers, contact the Division of Poison Control, 5600 Fishers Lane, Room 1345/HDF 240, Rockville, Maryland 20857, (301) 443-6260.

This is by no means a complete list of cautions. I do not know of any such list in existence. But if there is a complete list somewhere, I am sure it begins with the simple directive to *use common sense!* And if the attainment of that commodity has always been a struggle for you, stay away from vehicle repair.

Nifty Car Products

Listen to This Idea

For those who want more than a warning light and gauges, there is the Auto Alert Voice Warning System, which uses voice-synthesis electronics to tell you "Parking brake is set," "Check engine temperature," "Check your engine oil," and twelve other items involving component checks.

The system is reputed to be easily self-installed and is warrantied for 1 year. The cost is $180 from the Sun Electric Company, 1560 Trimble Road, San Jose, California 95131.

Now Hear This!!!

Blaupunkt car stereos have an ARI circuit that ensures you'll never miss important announcements. ARI stands for Autofahrer Rundfunk Information, which is German for "motorist radio information." In wide use throughout Europe, ARI circuits detect a special subcarrier signal that certain stations add to their broadcasts when they're announcing traffic information or bulletins.

You can't hear the ARI signal, but it will put a cassette tape into the pause mode just long enough for a listener to hear the data; then it bounces the stereo back to the tape. The radio must be left on, but the volume can be turned completely down. The ARI will boost the volume as announcements are made and then return the radio to silence.

Blaupunkt sells these units for about $200; they hope to license the design to automakers so that standard car radios will contain ARI. Surprisingly, many major cities have at least one radio station that is ARI-activated. Your town may be one. Check with the closest office of the Federal Communications Commission.

This Idea Will Make You a Fan

A broken fan belt can be bad, bad news because replacement availability is so erratic. The Bull Ring from England will get you several hundred miles in a pinch. This cut-to-size emergency replacement belt does not require any tools to install. The only thing you need is the heavy-duty razor blade that's included. The Bull Ring is available from Fleet Resources, Inc., 414 County Street, New Bedford, Massachusetts 02740 (enclose $4.95).

Running on Empty

Goodyear and Pirelli have developed a rim that substantially resists tire roll-off in case of deflation. This type of rim has asymmetric ridges, or humps, at opposite points on the wheel near the rim flange that keep the bead on the rim should the tire deflate. It does not, however, provide long-term run-flat capability. Such wheels are now standard on some high-performance European models, and the patented concept is being made available for use by the industry worldwide.

An En-Deering Device

The Austrian-made Sav-A-Life deer alert is actually two whistles, each about the size of your thumb, which can be attached to your car's front bumper. The whistles emit frequencies which people can't hear but which deer and dogs, up to a quarter-mile away, can. Some corporations use them on their service vehicles. Your local hardware store may carry them. Or write Sav-A-Life, Inc., Box 1226, New York, New York 10025 (enclose $26.95).

Give This Gadget a Hand

Beep 'n' Keep resembles a miniature cigarette lighter that attaches to your key chain. The device calls to you if you misplace your keys, leading you to them. Four evenly spaced hand claps within a 20- to 30-foot radius activate the device. Les Kacev, a partner in the design and development of the product, said he used whistle activation "until I realized that not everyone could whistle."

The unit is self-contained and operates on two 1.5-volt camera batteries that are user-replaceable. It weighs less than 1 ounce and even has a LED which flashes to the proper hand-clapping beat if you haven't got a good sense of rhythm. Many luggage and department stores stock Beep 'n' Keep. For the nearest location, call (415) 331-5338.

Now, Why Didn't I Think of This One?

Worried that thieves will find your new state-of-the-art car stereo as impressive-looking as you do? For $2.49 you can get the Decoy. It's a molded plastic insert that transforms the dial-cassette door of your valuable stereo into a very ordinary-looking and undesirable AM car radio. Write to Kustom Kreations, 19316 Londelius, Northridge, California 91324.

Oh, My Aching Back!

The Backsaver II lumbar and kidney support cushion provides support with an inflatable inner bladder and foam pads. A hand pump inflates the cushion to the desired firmness. Backsaver II costs $39.95 and is available from Foremost Designs, 522 Broadway, Lorain, Ohio 44052.

chapter 6

Ⓐ Primer on Selected Vehicle Systems and Components

"The Very Heart of the Matter"

Your car is a companion of sorts, and the better you understand a companion, the better you get along. Pets are companions, and when people first take one home, they read books on the subject and talk at length with breeders. But a car? As long as it starts. . . . Well, you *might* wash it next week. We know pets depend on us, but we view ourselves as depending on cars. And that, perhaps, is why we neglect to learn more about them. We fail to see that our cars really do depend on us, and that when one breaks down, it's often not the car that's undependable, but the owner.

Tires

Only four spots of a vehicle touch the ground, and the condition of each reflects the overall performance, economy, and handling of the vehicle. You can help to maximize tire life by simply checking the air pressure once a month. Next to oil and antifreeze levels, drivers most often neglect the air pressure in their tires. In fact, unless a tire is low, it probably never gets checked at all. Tire industry and auto club surveys have shown that 50 to 80 percent of us drive around on underinflated tires. "Underinflated tires waste one gallon in 20 because your rolling resistance is increased," the Detroit-based Automotive Information Council reports. And those of us who have attempted to push a car with a flat tire, or to ride a bicycle with an underinflated tire, can attest to that fact. Underinflated tires also lead to premature wear from overflexing and overheating. There are safety aspects, too: underinflated tires can cause handling and braking problems, especially at freeway speeds.

In short, tire condition and inflation pressures affect the way in which your car rides, handles, and performs. And that's a big chunk of the pie to neglect!

Tire pressure is measured in pounds per square inch (psi). The manufacturer's recommended psi for your tires is listed in the owner's manual and on a sticker either on the driver-side doorjamb or on the back of the glove compartment door. Tire pressure should be checked cold, generally after no more than 3 miles of driving. Tires heat up from tread-to-road friction, and heat inflates readings. Tire pressure is also altered by outdoor temperature (about 1 psi for every 10° Fahrenheit), and about 1 psi a month is lost through normal driving use. Tire pressure can also be lost if valve stems are not capped. These small screw-on caps are often viewed only as a nuisance and are discarded, but they protect the valve-stem cores from dirt, salt, and water corrosion.

Don't judge the inflation pressure visually, either; overinflation causes as many problems as underinflation. Use of a tire gauge is important, because (1) radial tires can deceive the eyes with their "flat" profiles and (2) wear and tear may render service station air meters inaccurate. Also, if tire pressures are checked monthly, tire wear can be better monitored: Are the tires wearing unevenly? Are there sidewall defects (cracks, bubbles)? Tread-wear indicators are incorporated into tires. They appear as horizontal "bald spots" running across the tread. Early detection not only increases vehicle safety but can save on mechanical repairs and tire wear. Tread-wear indicators, or "wear bars," begin to appear when a tire has $\frac{1}{16}$ inch of tread left (Fig. 6-1). For more precise readings, service personnel use tread-depth gauges.

The Tire Industry Safety Council, which represents over a dozen major tire manufacturers, has a $2.75 glove compartment tire safety and mileage kit that includes an air-pressure gauge, a tread-depth gauge, four tire valve caps, and a 12-page "Consumer Tire Guide." It's a very handy kit at a very reasonable price. Write to the Tire Industry Safety Council, Box 1801, Washington, DC 20013.

Tire Rotation

The reasoning behind tire rotation is to ensure that all four tires wear evenly (Fig. 6-1). Mass production methods cannot produce tailor-made suspension systems; the mass production of vehicles is instead guided by acceptable component tolerances. What this means is that unless a vehicle's suspension components are periodically tuned (front-end alignment is but one of these adjustments), the laws of physics cause each wheel to wear its own tire differently.

Tire rotation compensates for each wheel's unique tread print. With proper rotation, tires may go thousands of miles farther than they would otherwise. For the consumer, tire rotation has become a confusing issue. Some mechanics are no longer sure of what is right or wrong, and rather than deal with the nuances, they do not provide tire rotation service as part of routine maintenance.

The confusion over tire rotation stems from the widespread use of radial tires (now standard on most vehicles) and the increasing use of front-wheel-drive (FWD) power trains. Prior to FWD, front tires steered and back tires provided traction—this allowed a rather even distribution of the work load. However, braking has always been harder on front tires, and now FWD requires double duty of front tires: they provide both traction and steering also. Some manufacturers put longer-wear tires up front to compensate for the extra demands of FWD; these need not be rotated, so check to see if your tires are of this type.

The preferred rotation pattern for FWD vehicles is simply to put the rear tires on the front and vice versa without switching sides. This is known as *straight-line,* or *parallel,* rotation. The spare is not used. Rear-

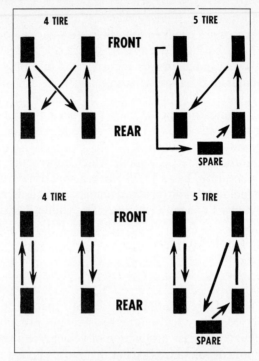

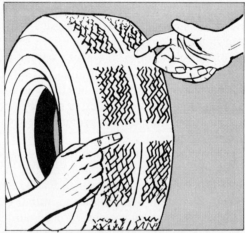

Fig. 6-1 (*Top*) Here are the patterns of vehicle tire rotation recommended by the Tire Industry Safety Council. Tire rotation provides for safe, even wear and longer tread life. Tires should be rotated every 6000 to 8000 miles, or sooner if irregular wear develops. (*Bottom*) All new passenger car tires are required by Federal law to contain "wear bars" as illustrated. The bars appear as smooth bands when the tire has worn to the danger level, $\frac{1}{16}$th of an inch or less. When these wear bars appear, it's time to replace the tires. (*Courtesy Tire Industry Safety Council.*)

wheel-drive vehicles should use the standard "X" pattern for tire rotation, using the spare to replace the most worn of the four (if, of course, the spare is not the inflatable space-saver variety).

In any event, the *tire* manufacturer's recommendation on both tire rotation and tire pressure is the final word. If either you or your mechanic have any doubts, contact the local manufacturer's office for advice. These offices are usually listed in the phone book, or a local distributor can give the number to you. Addresses and phone numbers of the national headquarters of major tire manufacturers are listed in Appendix E.

Wheel Balancing

Improperly balanced tires, front or back, cause irregular tread wear that lessens the overall life of tires and suspension components and make for a rough, vibrating ride at higher speeds. (Out-of-round tires and those with tread separation will cause similar vibration and should be replaced. These defects often produce rippled or bulging sidewalls.)

Tires and wheels (rims) must be balanced as one unit; there are three methods for doing so: bubble balancing, dynamic balancing, and computer-assisted balancing.

With bubble balancing, a tire is mounted on the wheel and then placed horizontally on a stand which has a central pivot point. A tire is balanced when a bubble in a small cross-hair indicator on the stand comes to rest in the dead center. This is accomplished by placing lead weights around the tire rim until the bubble centers on the cross-hair indicator.

Dynamic balancing is done by rotating the tire assembly on the vehicle with a machine at about 40 to 50 miles per hour. This improves wheel-balancing results, because all tire assembly components are balanced as a unit—brake drums, rotors, lug nuts, bearings, etc. These parts are balanced at the factory, but it's beneficial to rebalance the entire unit when new tires are added.

Computer-assisted balancing is done at driving speeds, but with the wheel off the car. As the tire spins, a computer program analyzes the required balance points and weights. It is the only wheel-balancing method that actually determines whether the weight(s) should go on the outside or *inside* of a wheel. With bubble and dynamic balancing, weights are placed on the outside of the rim.

Tire Buying: Classifications and Ratings

Over half of all new tires are purchased through independent tire dealers. Independents generally have the widest range of prices and tires because they stock a variety of brands. Manufacturer retail outlets (General, Goorich, Goodyear, Firestone, et al.) sell only their respective brand names. Tire manufacturers sometimes offer direct factory discounts to their namesake distributors, which lowers prices considerably. In short, it definitely pays to shop around for the best price when buying tires. And always get the *complete* price—installation, balancing, and mounting.

Tire jargon can numb a normally healthy sense of curiosity; it confounds most consumers. However, keep in mind the following: most tires are made in three layers and are constructed according to one of three basic designs.

Of the three layers, the outermost layer, the tread, is the most familiar. Underlying the tread is a layer of belt plies, and underlying the belt plies is the third layer—the body plies. The tread layer provides traction, the belt plies reduce road surface "squirm," and the body plies give a tire its shape and support. (Road surface squirm is similar to the motions involved in making a pencil erasure, and just as the eraser wears down, so will tire treads.)

The three basic construction designs are radial, belted bias, and bias (Fig. 6-2).

Radials are constructed so that the body plies run perpendicular to the tire tread (horizontally); the belt plies run in the same direction as the tire tread (vertically). This construction gives rigidity to the tread area and maximum flexibility to the sidewall. The belt plies restrict road surface squirm, which maximizes tread life. (Radial tires with fiberglass belt plies are known as glass-belted radials; those with rayon plies as rayon-belted radials.)

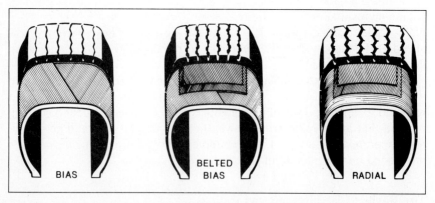

Fig. 6-2 These cutaway views show the ply and belt construction patterns commonly used in the manufacture of bias, belted bias and radial tires. Bias tires have two overlapping diagonal plies, but lack the overlapping belts of a belted bias tire; the belts limit road squirm and increase tire life. The inner ply of a radial tire is circular, which along with use of belts, provides for maximum tread wear. (*Courtesy Tire Industry Safety Council.*)

Belted bias tires have body plies that run at about a 35-degree angle to the tire treads; two or more belt plies run diagonally to one another under the tread. This construction adds stability, and the belt plies reduce road surface squirm, which improves tread life.

Bias tires may have two, four, or more body plies that run diagonally to one another. Bias tires lack the belt construction found in radials and belted bias tires, which is one reason the tread wears sooner.

Over 60 percent of all tires sold today are radials, about 25 percent are of simple bias design, and nearly 15 percent are belted bias. Generally speaking, radial and belted bias tires last two to three times as long as bias tires, with radials delivering better highway gas mileage and overall tread life.

If you need tires for a car used primarily for short distances around town, a two- or four-ply bias tire should do; for more extensive use and a "soft" ride a belted bias tire with polyester reinforcement is best; for an even more durable, though somewhat stiffer-riding tire, buy nylon-belted bias tires; and for maximum longevity for all driving applications, buy radials.

The Department of Transportation (DOT) Uniform Tire Quality Grading System gives tires three test ratings: (1) a numeric tread-wear grade; (2) an A, B, or C rating on traction; and (3) an A, B, or C rating on heat resistance. (A is highest and C is lowest.) These ratings are found on the information sticker glued to the treads of new tires and/or are molded into the tire sidewall. Note that these standards do not apply to deep-tread, snow, or space-saver tires or to those for use on rims of a diameter of 12 inches or less.

Traction ratings are based on how quickly a tire can stop on wet surfaces. Heat resistance is based on how well a tire dissipates road-friction heat. Average tread life is assigned an arbitrary value of 100 for purposes of comparison; thus a DOT quality grade of 200 means the tire has tested to last twice the average.

DOT tread-wear grades compare tires tested under like conditions. But because these tests cannot possibly compensate for such variables as under- or overinflation, alignment, driving habits and locale, suspension maintenance, and so on, attempts to convert tread-wear grades to figures indicating the approximate number of miles a tire will last are not recommended.

A better way in which to use tread-wear grades is to divide the grade number by purchase price. For example, if tire A costs $50 and is rated at 150, and tire B costs $65 and is rated at 200, the tread-wear values are nearly equal. Tire A costs 33.3 cents a point, and tire B costs 32.5 cents a point. Temperature and traction ratings should then be taken in account. Highway driving would call for a more heat-resistant tire; inclement weather would call for a tire with better traction; in many cases, you may need both. To meet both your budget and driving needs, it may be better to buy a tire with good temperature and traction ratings rather than heavily weighting your purchase decision on tread life, especially in the case of older cars which may be sold within a year or two.

Also check a tire's maximum load rate, which is molded onto the sidewall of every tire. Take the weight of your car, add to it the average weight of both occupants and cargo, and divide the total by 4: the result should not exceed the maximum load rating of an individual tire.

On General Motors vehicles, factory-issue tires, built to General Motors specifications, have a tire performance criteria (TPC) number molded into the sidewall. The initials TPC are followed by a four-digit number. When purchasing another set of tires, a distributor can use the TPC number to provide tires that will meet original equipment specifications. (As a side note, GM also designates these radials as snow tires, but in states requiring snow tires for winter driving, check to make sure the tires comply with local government standards.)

On FWD and 4WD vehicles, all-weather, all-terrain tires, usually designated as M/S, M&S, mud & snow, etc., should suffice. All-weather tires, especially on FWD vehicles, are preferred over snow tires; snow tires wear quickly on dry roads and do not aid in traction on ice. If used, a pair of snow tires go up front on FWD vehicles, but studded snow tires and tire chains are what really make the difference in traction under extreme winter conditions.

Once you have decided on which type of tire best suits your need, you have tire size to contend with. Tire size is molded onto the outer sidewall. Tires on the same axle must be of the same size, and radials should not be mixed with bias or belted bias tires. When replacing all four tires, it is usually best to stay with the same size tire that originally came with the car. Those who prefer the appearance of larger or wider tires need to scrutinize wheel-well, or "tub," clearance before committing their money to a venture that may literally bottom out or cause excessive wear of suspension components.

Tire manufacturers refer to the *aspect ratio* of a tire. The more nearly round the tire, the more nearly equal the rim-to-tread height of the sidewall is to the width of the tread and the closer the aspect ratio is to 100. A tire with a wide tread pattern and low rim-to-tread height has a low aspect ratio (Fig. 6-3). Tires with an aspect ratio approaching, say, 50 appear "squat," with very little sidewall but very wide treads. Low-aspect-ratio tires improve traction at the expense of riding comfort; high-aspect tires ride more smoothly but they do not corner or grip the road as well.

A few tire sizes are still classified alphanumerically. An example of an alphanumeric rating is FR78-14. The first letter (F) indicates the load

Fig. 6-3 The Camaro (*top*) sports some very good examples of low-aspect-ratio tires. Note how narrow the sidewalls are compared to the tread width. The VW van (*bottom*) has high-aspect-ratio tires; the sidewall height is nearly equal to the width of the tread. (*Courtesy Chevrolet Motor Division/Volkswagen of America.*)

rating (the farther down in the alphabet, the higher the load rating); the second letter indicates construction type (R = radial, B = belted bias, D = diagonal bias). The first number (78) is the aspect ratio, and the last number (14) is the rim diameter in inches.

Most tire sizes today are classified in ISO-metric, and more will be as the International Standards Organization (ISO) consolidates U.S., European, and Japanese tire ratings. In the United States the prefix P indicates a passenger-car tire, and T indicates a temporary or space-saver spare tire. The prefix LT usually indicates a light-truck tire, although, load rating permitting, many light trucks in noncommercial use are equipped with P-metric tires.

The domestic ISO-metric designation P185/80R13 indicates a tire 185 millimeters in width with an 80 percent aspect ratio of radial (R) construction for use on a 13-inch-diameter rim. European size classifications (Euro-metrics) for the same tire may omit the P, the 80, or both. Some European tires also carry speed ratings: H for high speed and V for very high speed. The omission of either letter, or an S rating, indicates normal speed. A normal-speed radial, for example, a 155SR12, is for use up to 113 mph (180 km/h); a high-speed radial is safe for speeds up to 130 mph (210 km/h); and a very-high-speed radial, an ER/70VR14, for example, is safe for speeds above 130 mph. Between the high and very-high speed ratings are T and U, but these ratings are not widely available in the U.S.

Keep in mind that OEM (original equipment manufacturer) tires are not always capable of the same top-end speeds as that of the vehicle on which they are placed. In 1978, both a U.S. automaker and a tire manufacturer were held liable for the death of a Louisiana driver who—even though drunk and speeding—was killed when a tire blew out after the car reached a speed over 100 mph. The court ruled that the tire manufacturer knew that the standard tires on the car were only good for speeds less than 85 mph and that the vehicle manufacturer knew the car was capable of 140 mph.

Finally, independent tire dealers are no longer required to register tires for buyers, as was once the case. If you request such registration, however, some dealers will do it for you. In event of a recall, registration helps the manufacturer to ensure direct and timely contact with consumers. Registration cards are kept on file for a federally mandated 3 years.

A tire registration code is a group of letters and numbers molded onto the sidewall. For example, DOT WOKAABCD 325 is translated as follows: DOT = Department of Transportation, WO = a DOT manufacturing code, KA = tire size, ABCD = various manufacturer codes, and 126 = the date the tire was made, the twelfth week of 1986. Because tire ID numbers are usually found on the inner sidewall of the tire, get the numbers before the tires are placed on the vehicle.

Retreads

Today's retreads can represent a good value for the money. The key is finding a good dealer, and the Tire Retreaders Industry Bureau (TRIB) has a toll-free number (800-368-5757) to help you locate one. TRIB recommends buying only retreads offered with a written warranty.

Batteries

There are two kinds of automotive, or storage, batteries: conventional and maintenance-free. Conventional batteries require the periodic addition of water; maintenance-free batteries are sealed and do not. Conventional batteries use lead-antimony grids. Antimony depletes water from the electrolyte, which is sulfuric acid diluted in water. The development of lead-calcium grids enabled production of maintenance-free batteries by eliminating antimony use.

Battery grids, whether lead-antimony or lead-calcium, are pasted with active materials (Fig. 6-4). The grid is then classified as a plate. The addition of sponge lead creates a negative plate; lead dioxide, a positive plate. Negative and positive plates are stacked together along with separators to form an element; each element produces 2 volts. Combine six elements and you have today's 12-volt battery.

In the presence of the electrolyte, the plates produce a chemical reaction that results in the flow of electric current (voltage). As this reaction continues, the acid in the electrolyte combines with the active material on the plates to form lead sulfate; water is produced as a by-product. If the reaction continues to the point at which only lead sulfate and water

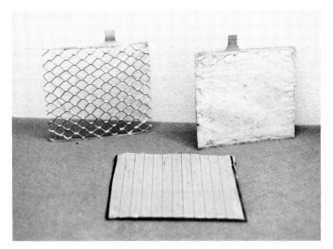

Fig. 6-4 A lead-calcium battery grid (*left*), a battery plate (*right*), which is a grid with the active material applied, and a separator sleeve (*foreground*) used to separate the negative from the positive battery plates. (*Photo by Mike Spaniola.*)

remain, the result is a dead battery. Recharging stimulates production of sulphuric acid from the lead sulfate, which (1) restores the electrolyte solution and (2) converts the plate materials back to their original sponge lead and lead dioxide compositions. This permits the chemical reaction needed to produce voltage to recur.

Battery Safety Precautions

Storage batteries should always be kept clear of possible ignition sources, such as sparks and flames, especially during recharging. A battery that is recharging is not "storing" electricity; instead, a chemical reaction that produces highly volatile fumes is taking place.

The positive (+) and negative (−) electric terminals in a car battery— similar to ends, or poles, of a magnet—repel one another when put in mutual contact and may cause a violent explosion. *Never cross the negative and positive terminals with metal objects or the positive terminal with the sheet metal of the car,* which is a negative ground. The danger of an explosion is never more prevalent than when "jumping" a battery (Fig. 6-5).

Seeing is believing, and the National Society to Prevent Blindness reports that an average of 20,000 people are injured in car battery accidents each year; two-thirds sustain eye damage. The excruciating pain of trying to keep healing eyelids from adhering onto one's eyeballs need not be personally experienced to encourage safety when working around a storage battery.

The society recommends *using safety goggles and gloves* when working around automotive, or storage, batteries. Safety goggles protect the eyes from stray particles and battery acid, and rubber gloves prevent the absent-minded transfer of corrosive particles from hand to eye.

Never attempt to jump-start a battery if the fluid is frozen. In all cases, observe correct jump-starting procedures. Before attaching the battery cables, be sure both batteries are of the same voltage (most vehicles use 12-volt ones). Always begin by connecting the positive terminal of the booster battery to the positive terminal of the discharged battery. Next, standing on a side away from the battery and keeping the cables away from the carburetor, fuel line, or any moving part, connect the negative terminal of the booster battery to the engine block of the stalled car. Start the donor car, then the stalled car. Disconnect the cables by first removing the negative end on the engine block, the negative on the booster battery, and, finally, the positive cable. For 25 cents, the National Society to Prevent Blindness (79 Madison Avenue, New York, NY 10016) has an under-hood sticker which details battery safety. It's worth looking into.

WARNING
BATTERIES PRODUCE EXPLOSIVE GASES

NO SMOKING

WEAR EYE PROTECTION

Keep sparks, flames and cigarettes away from batteries at all times. Wear eye protection. Don't lean over batteries during jump-starting. See owner's manual for instructions.

JUMP-START INSTRUCTIONS

Be sure: vent caps are tight and level...damp cloth, if available, is placed over vent caps...vehicles are not touching...both electrical systems are the same voltage. **Don't Jump-Start If Fluid Is Frozen!**

ATTACHING THE CABLES
(Do in order listed):

1 Clamp one jumper cable to positive (+) terminal of discharged battery wired to starter or solenoid. Do not allow positive cable clamps to touch any metal other than battery terminals.

2 Connect other end of positive (+) cable to positive (+) terminal of booster battery.

3 Connect one end of the second cable [negative (−)] to other terminal [negative (−)] of booster battery.

4 Make final connection on engine block of stalled engine (not to negative post) away from battery, carburetor, fuel line, any tubing or moving parts.

Connect Cables as Shown

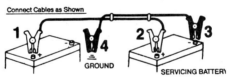

GROUND

SERVICING BATTERY

5 Stand back from both vehicles. Start car with good battery—then start the disabled car.

6 Remove cables in reverse order of connections beginning by first removing cable from engine block or metallic ground.

PREVENT BLINDNESS®

NATIONAL SOCIETY TO PREVENT BLINDNESS
79 MADISON AVENUE, NEW YORK, NY 10016

Copyright 1984 by National Society to Prevent Blindness

Use CAUTION and SAFETY EYEWEAR
when jump-starting vehicle.

Place in glove compartment or
other clean, dry location.

Fig. 6-5 This is an example of the under-hood battery warning sticker available from the National Society to Prevent Blindness. Heed its cautions. (*Courtesy National Society to Prevent Blindness.*)

Battery Maintenance

Tap water is acceptable for use in conventional batteries, provided that it is not "hard water," which has a high mineral content (iron content, especially, will ruin a battery). If your tap water is hard, use distilled water. The most accurate, practical, and safest way to add water to a battery is to use a bulb syringe.

Do not add water when the outside temperature is below freezing unless you drive the car immediately following. Otherwise, the water will freeze before becoming part of the electrolyte solution, seriously impairing your battery. A fully charged battery will freeze at $-83°$ Fahrenheit; a weak battery, at $0°$ Fahrenheit. (A hydrometer is used to measure the specific gravity of the electrolyte to determine the charge of the battery. A fully charged battery will read 1.265 at $80°$ Fahrenheit. Some maintenance-free designs incorporate a color "eye" which informs you of the battery's current charge.)

If your battery is more than 3 years old, it's a good idea to have it checked for cranking power, especially prior to winter. At the same time, the alternator circuit can be checked to ensure that the battery is being properly recharged. Remember, even if a battery *appears* to be sealed, it may not be "maintenance-free." True maintenance-free batteries are constructed of lead-calcium grids. If you're unsure which type you have, check with the manufacturer or distributor.

Terminals of conventional batteries have to be cleaned periodically, due to acid vapors which vent from the filler caps and from the electrolyte of an occasionally overfilled cell. Before proceeding with cleaning, though, plug any battery cap vents (the hole in the center of each cap) with round toothpicks to prevent the neutralizing solution from entering the battery. Then, wearing a pair of rubber gloves and safety goggles, remove the white powdery acid buildup from the terminals, hold-down clamps, and battery cables by applying a 50:50 solution of baking soda and water. This neutralizes the caked-on acid deposits. (An old trick of repair shops was to drop Alka-Seltzer into a battery: the consequent foaming would rival that of a rabid dog and the mechanic would have another battery sale.) After cleaning, use petroleum jelly on battery terminals and cables to slow the recurrence of acid deposits.

Road vibrations can loosen and cause premature shedding of the active plate materials found on the grids. To help eliminate the impact of vibration, check that the battery is tightly secured by the hold-down straps or brackets provided; otherwise, overall battery life may be severely reduced.

Maintenance-free batteries are just that: there are no access caps to spew forth noxious fumes that eat away hold-down bars and terminal connections. However, some maintenance-free batteries are vented, so a periodic check of these connections is advisable. Overall, though, the use of lead-calcium grids in maintenance-free batteries has greatly reduced battery care without compromising quality and longevity.

Some vehicles have a warning light for the charging system. Putting the key in the Start position will turn on the warning light (generally labeled or depicted as "battery," "volt," or "−/+"), which should turn off as the engine starts. Be certain that the warning light appears during engine starting; otherwise, have it checked. It could spare your being stranded due to a dead battery.

Battery Purchasing

The typical car battery is not designed to withstand extremes of discharging and recharging (known as *cycling*). "High-cycling," or "deep-cycling," batteries are manufactured for use without a charging system because they can bounce back from an extreme discharge without damage. These batteries are generally found in emergency and delivery vehicles, to name two types, and are a necessity in most marine applications. They are also more expensive. But unless vehicle operation causes abnormal battery discharge—extensive idling or accessory use with the engine off—a general-purpose automotive battery will suit the majority of drivers.

When shopping for a new battery, there are two factors to compare in relation to the price: (1) cold-cranking amps performance and (2) warranty. Battery warranties are expressed in months, such as a 36- or 48-month battery, but *in all applications, battery warranty is a secondary purchase consideration.* Compare cold-cranking amps (CCA) first. CCA ratings measure a battery's capacity to operate in cold-weather, and cranking over a cold engine is the hardest task a battery must perform. CCA ratings are expressed numerically, generally ranging from 275 to 650 for general-purpose 12-volt automotive batteries. The rating of the new battery should not be lower than that of your present one.

All chemical reactions are greatly influenced by ambient temperatures, and those that occur in car batteries are no exception. At low temperatures, the reaction is slow and less power is produced. For example, at 0° Fahrenheit a fully charged battery provides only 40 percent of the energy it would provide at 80° Fahrenheit. A half-charged battery can provide only one-fifth its rated power at 0° Fahrenheit. And in addition to the loss of available power in cold weather, battery recharge is undercut during winter months by extensive use of headlights, heater blower fan, and rear-window defrosters, especially at idle.

Another battery rating is that of reserve capacity, which is measured in minutes. Reserve capacity ratings are relative to CCA ratings, so that one comparison should suffice. If your trade-in battery is not the original one that came with your vehicle—and particularly if you have been experiencing ongoing battery problems—consult the owner's manual, check a part listing, or call your dealer to obtain the correct CCA rating.

Gasoline

Gasoline can be refined and blended in numerous ways, and the resulting octane rating, volatility, alcohol, and lead content affect both engine performance and longevity.

Better gasoline is highly refined and contains beneficial additives; these qualities are lacking in bargain brands. You get what you pay for, and gasoline is no exception.

Octane Ratings

Octane prevents spark, or engine, knock. Prior to the use of unleaded gasoline, the general public was unfamiliar with the sound of spark knock; today, it's all too familiar. Spark knock is produced by a random combustion chamber explosion ignited by high internal engine temperatures.

High-octane gasoline (a 90-plus octane number) can prevent spark knock, because the temperature at which it detonates is higher. This is why spark knock was rare when engines ran on leaded gasoline—the octane number was higher.

High-octane gasoline will not increase horsepower or improve fuel economy, though, and in the majority of cases, it is best to stick with the octane rating recommended by the manufacturer. Even in cases of spark knock, the real problem is usually with engine tuning; although frustrated mechanics may tell you otherwise.

The octane number found on gas station pumps is an average of the two ways in which octane is rated. One rating method provides the *motor* octane number; the second, the *research* octane number. The motor octane number (M) is derived under a heavier engine load than the more clinically derived research octane number (R). The gas pump octane number, which generally ranges from 87 to 95, is produced by using the (R + M)/2 average.

Because gasolines are blended, even those of the same octane rating can vary your car's performance (Fig. 6-6). If, for example, the most volatile portion of the blend has a low-octane number, spark knock can result; if the most volatile portion of the blend has a high-octane number, spark knock will cease. A consumer can determine this only by trying different brands of gasoline.

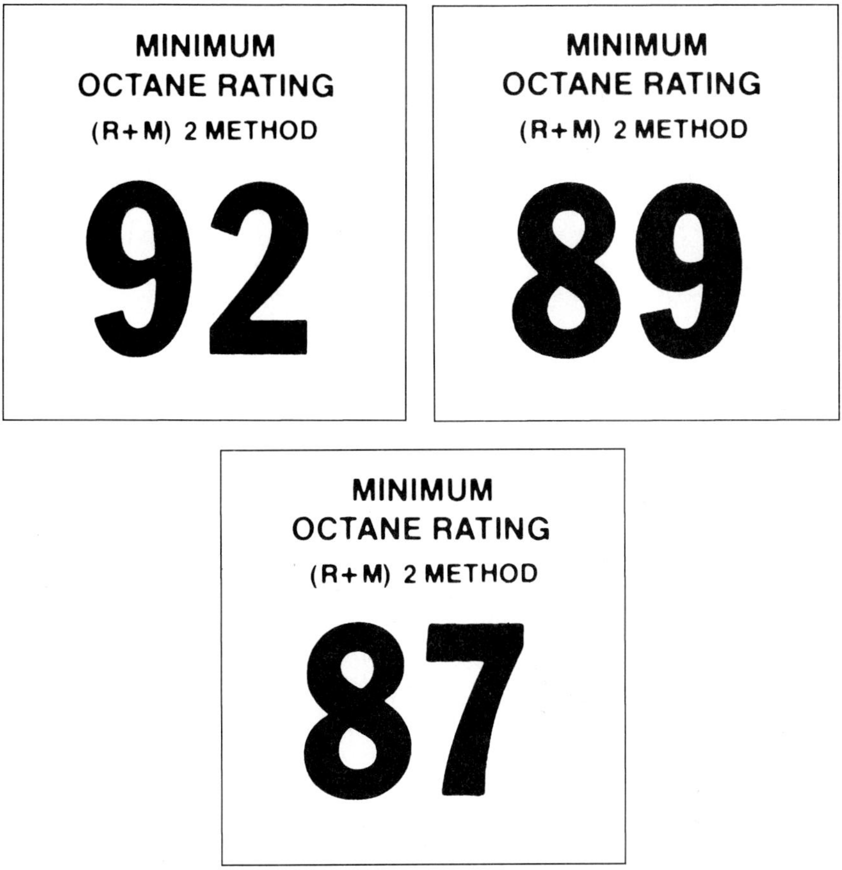

MINIMUM OCTANE RATING (R+M) 2 METHOD **92**	MINIMUM OCTANE RATING (R+M) 2 METHOD **89**

MINIMUM
OCTANE RATING
(R+M) 2 METHOD

87

Fig. 6-6 What you see is not always what you get. These gasoline pump stickers were bought for $1 each from a supplier who said, "Some unscrupulous station owners slap a 92-octane sticker on pumps [dispensing] gas mixed with kerosene and alcohol. That's how some stations price gas so low."

Excepting diesel engines, vehicles beginning with the 1975 model year use unleaded regular gasoline with an octane rating of 87. Vehicles made in the early 1970s usually make do with either leaded, low-lead, or unleaded regular; drivers of these vehicles should experiment with each fuel for best results. Vehicles that once used leaded premium should be fueled with a mix of half regular and half unleaded premium of a 92-plus octane rating.

Cans labeled octane booster, available at many auto supply stores, do not boost octane per se. Instead, most of these liquid solvents help eliminate combustion chamber deposits which are the primary cause of spark knock and autoignition. Use of these solvents more often than every 6000 miles or so can melt plastic fuel system parts and cause fuel pump diaphragms to wear prematurely. Instead, use detergent gasoline to prevent combustion chamber deposits.

For vehicles requiring high-octane fuels, the only real octane-boosting additive is tetraethyl lead, but it is highly toxic and assuming you could buy it, which you cannot, it would take a death wish to get near it— let alone mix it with your gas. Major refineries are developing additives that duplicate the lubricating properties of tetraethyl lead. Other alternatives are liquid petroleum gas (propane or butane) or aviation fuel. For street use, however, a more rational (and legal) approach would be to reduce engine octane requirements by retarding the timing, redoing the distributor curve, or rejetting the carburetor.

Leaded and Unleaded Gasolines

The retail sale of leaded gasoline to the general public is being phased out by the U.S. Environmental Protection Agency (EPA). Leaded fuel will still be available for off-road applications such as racing.

Leaded gasoline, when added to a vehicle that should use unleaded only, poisons the catalytic converter and renders a majority of smog-control equipment ineffective. Leaded gasoline is a major source of airborne lead poisonings, and high levels of lead in the bloodstream also cause high blood pressure.

According to the EPA, adding leaded fuel to unleaded-only vehicles increases exhaust emissions by up to 400 percent. The EPA estimates that approximately 16 percent of drivers resort to this practice, usually to save a few pennies a gallon on the price difference between unleaded and leaded gasoline. To do so, though, is penny wise and gallon foolish, considering that the replacement of a "lead-poisoned" catalytic converter is a $200-plus job. In addition, carburetor and valve damage can also result. Leaded fuel in an unleaded system will also plug exhaust gas recirculation valves, fuel-control system components, and foul spark plugs, all of which increases fuel consumption and lays the foundation for expensive repairs. And in areas requiring idle short tests, you will void your 5-year/50,000-mile warranty on emissions-control parts and will have to pay for the repairs out of pocket.

Unfortunately for the law-abiding and environment-conscious consumer, unleaded gasoline is sometimes deliberately mixed with the leaded variety to increase wholesale profit margins. For the same purpose, gasoline may also be cut with methanol, an alcohol not favored for use in automotive fuel. Spot tests of gas samples by the EPA in many areas throughout the United States found that over 25 percent of service stations were selling something other than what the pump was labeled. The practice proliferates because such tactics are difficult for the consumer to detect, and even if vehicle damage results from the use of tainted fuel, repair reimbursements often require a "Philadelphia" lawyer.

"Proving a certain station was *the* one is extremely tough," states Frank O'Connor of Detroit's Wayne county EPA branch. He adds that although station owners are responsible for what they pump, doubts arise as to whether it's the station owner, the local oil company, or even the delivery-tank truck operator who caused the problem. "In the case of unleaded being mixed with leaded, the problem sometimes occurs when one station tank is full, so a driver might mix leaded with unleaded just to complete the delivery."

Although the EPA will send out inspectors in answer to an individual's complaint, the EPA will not test gasoline for an individual, and therefore, the agency is of little help in proving gas-station liability. Private testing firms will perform lab work on gas samples from individuals, but their prices range from $75 to $250, with the more expensive being the court-admissible test. You may also want to contact a local college or university; sometimes these institutions will analyze at a fraction of the cost.

Realistically, though, for the consumer, an ounce of prevention is worth a gallon of cure. Plumbtesmo paper, distributed by Gallard-Schlesinger Chemical Manufacturing Company of Carle Place, New York, can detect the presence of lead in gasoline. Plumbtesmo paper is similar in ways to litmus paper. A strip of Plumbtesmo paper is moistened and held inside your tailpipe, usually with a clothespin or a small clamp. If lead is detected, the paper will turn pink to a near red, depending on the amount of lead detected. The American Lung Association provides Plumbtesmo paper at no charge to those who write to either a local branch or to the American Lung Association headquarters at P.O. Box 596-CB, New York, New York 10001.

Alcohol-Blended Gasoline

Gasoline is also mixed with alcohol, generally either ethanol or methanol, but there are legal limits as to the percentage. The EPA states that gasoline can be blended with up to 10 percent ethanol and with up to 12 percent methanol—although three percent methanol is the limit most often cited by automakers in new-car warranty terms.

Gasoline legally mixed with ethanol can be sold as *gasohol*. *Ethanol*, or ethyl alcohol, is extracted from grain, mostly corn, and blends better with gasoline than other types of alcohol. *Methanol*, or methyl alcohol, is extracted from wood, coal, and natural gas, but does not blend well with gasoline. Its main attraction is that it is cheap to produce.

Why should you be concerned whether your gasoline is being diluted with either ethanol or methanol? Methanol, for one thing, can melt plastic carburetor parts and may damage other critical parts as well. All major automakers, both foreign and domestic, very much discourage the use of methanol; some, such as Chrysler, Mazda, and Mercedes, will not warranty damage caused by use of methanol-diluted fuels. And *all* automakers only scantily approve of the use of ethanol-blended gasolines; AMC, for example, warns of fuel system corrosion. Automakers point out that use of ethanol blends can degrade starting, driveability, and fuel-efficiency. Unfortunately, only two states—Michigan and California—require pump notices of alcohol blending.

According to a listing by Mort Schultz in the October 1985 issue of *Popular Mechanics,* seven major refiners do not add alcohol to their fuel: Exxon, Gulf, Marathon, Mobil, Shell, Sohio, and Union. He rightfully adds, though, that fuel tampering can occur "after it has left the province of the fuel company."

There are inexpensive kits available that enable consumers to determine the percent of alcohol in fuel. Although the kits cannot distinguish between the various types of alcohols, it can give a consumer the *percentage* contained. One such fuel tester, the "Alcohol Detection Kit" by Kent-Moore (part no. J 34353), for example, will separate the alcohol mixture from the gasoline by dissolving it in water. The volume of the water-alcohol solution corresponds to percentages provided with the kit. The procedure is simple and takes only a few minutes. Write Kent-Moore at 29784 Little Mack, Roseville, MI 48066 or phone (313) 774-9500.

You can also detect alcohol in gasoline through use of a "martini tester," a product sporadically available through liquor stores, government agencies for liquor control, or supply wholesalers of restaurants or bars. These eyedropper styled testers contain small plastic balls that float if alcohol is present in gasoline (due to differences in specific gravity).

None of these inexpensive tests is intended to be scientifically accurate, and once again, besides obtaining a receipt whenever you buy gas, there is little else you can do to prove station liability for damages incurred due to improper pump blends. But these tests can alert consumers to curtail use of tainted gasoline before any serious damage results.

Sometimes, too, water will be found in a gas tank. Many car insurance policies will cover the claim minus your comprehensive deductible; check with your agent.

Fuel Filters

Changing fuel filters has always been a part of routine maintenance, but it has never been as important as it is with today's fuel-injected and diesel engines. The precise tolerances of today's fuel systems require very fine filtering action, and consequently, fuel filters are more susceptible to clogging. When this occurs, fuel flow to the engine is severely restricted and overall engine performance is affected, especially in the form of engine hesitation when traveling at high speeds.

Oddly enough, one fact about changing fuel filters that is seldom mentioned, even in service manuals, is that fuel systems are pressurized; consequently, before changing the fuel filter, you should loosen the gas-filler cap. This prevents fuel from spurting all over you and the engine, making filter changing safer and easier; that is, if you can find the filter.

With some late-model fuel-injected and diesel engines, a service manual is a near necessity just to locate the fuel filter before you can even hope to change it. The fuel filter could be underneath the car near the gas tank; in the trunk behind a panel; in the passenger compartment; or—believe it or not—under the hood (but usually well disguised). On engines with carburetors, the fuel filter is generally attached to the carburetor at the point where the fuel line connects, and by using two wrenches to "crack" the fuel-line nut loose from the carburetor body, you can get to the fuel filter.

And to help prevent fuel system contamination, avoid buying gas when the delivery-tank truck is filling a station's underground reservoirs. During delivery, sediments and water, which are normally deposited safely at the bottom of these reservoirs, may swirl to the top and into the pumps from where it can then pass into your tank. Similarly, sediment and water can also be at the bottom of your fuel tank, which is why you should avoid frequent driving at near-empty fuel levels.

Spark Plugs

The explosions that power a vehicle occur in alternating patterns within the combustion chamber of the engine cylinders. This sets the pistons in each cylinder into motion. In a four-cylinder engine, two combustion chamber explosions equal one revolution (Fig. 6-7); in a six-cylinder engine, three combustion chamber explosions equal one revolution, and so on. These alternating charges produce an effect similar to that of peddling a bicycle, forcing the pistons through sequential up-down motions that rotate a crankshaft connected to the transmission and on out to the drive wheels. This entire system is known as the drive- or power-train assembly.

Spark plugs are the final link in the voltage discharge system that powers these cylinder combustions. If your car has a tachometer, you know that your engine typically ranges from about 500 to 5000 revolutions per minute. Given that one revolution requires two, three, or four sparks, depending on the number of engine cylinders, the life of a spark plug is not an easy one. (Diesel engines use "glow," and not spark, plugs.)

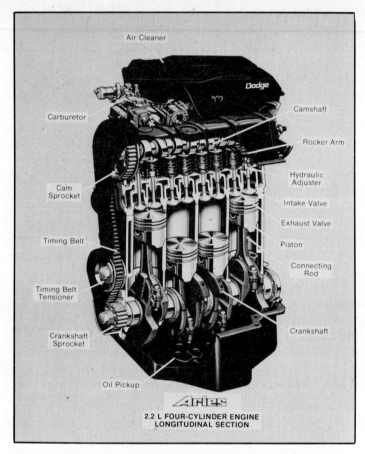

Air Cleaner

Dodge

Carburetor

Camshaft

Rocker Arm

Cam Sprocket

Hydraulic Adjuster

Intake Valve

Exhaust Valve

Timing Belt

Piston

Connecting Rod

Timing Belt Tensioner

Crankshaft

Crankshaft Sprocket

Oil Pickup

2.2 L FOUR-CYLINDER ENGINE
LONGITUDINAL SECTION

Fig. 6-7 This cutaway diagram of a 4-cylinder engine depicts the major parts and components discussed in this chapter. The exact location and presence of certain items will vary from engine to engine, depending on design, displacement, and manufacturer. (*Courtesy Chrysler Corp.*)

The threaded end of the spark plug resides in the interior of the combustion chamber; it is threaded in from outside the engine. The internal tip of the spark plug is gapped at a preset specification expressed in hundredths of an inch. The voltage that surges through the plug jumps across this gap, igniting the fuel-air mixture in the cylinder chamber.

Spark plugs themselves generally don't cause, but merely reflect, problems. If the ignition system is defective or fails to provide enough voltage, if the fuel system is too rich, or if an engine burns oil, a spark plug will foul. Furthermore, the rate at which a spark plug dissipates heat plays an important role in this process.

Spark Plug Characteristics

The primary function of a spark plug is to ignite the combustion chamber gases, but it must do so within a heat range that is neither too hot nor too cold. The ideal spark plug has a heat range that prevents both autoignition and carbon fouling.

If the spark plug's heat range is too hot, the spark plug tips will reach autoignition or preignition temperatures, causing premature wear or damage to engine components. (Preignition is spark knock, the metallic pinging or rattling noise heard on acceleration. Autoignition is engine run-on after the key is turned off.) If the spark plug heat range is too cold, the spark plug tips will become covered with fuel, or carbon, deposits, which increases emissions and decreases fuel-economy.

Heat range is determined by the rate at which heat is dispersed from the center electrode, a metal rod located in the center of the spark plug. From this center electrode, voltage is passed over a gap to the side electrode, the process by which the fuel mixture is ignited, producing an immense amount of heat. Shielding a part of the exposed lower portion of the center electrode is a ceramic coating referred to as the insulator tip. A long, thicker insulator tip retains heat much the same way that added insulation does for a home, resulting in a hotter plug; a short, thinner insulator tip produces a cooler plug (Fig. 6-8).

Power-train engineers, who design and test engines, must choose a spark plug with a heat range that provides good all-around performance: city and highway, in hot and cold weather. If your driving is less random, a hotter or colder plug may be better suited for your application. Generally, cooler plugs are better for high speeds and hot climates; hotter plugs, for stop-and-go city driving, colder climates, and preventing carbon- and oil-fouling in older engines.

If you have a problem with autoignition while the engine is tuned and other variables such as gasoline have not solved the problem, you may want to try a spark plug one or two ranges colder. Should the plug prove to be too cold, engine performance will become erratic when the plugs begin fouling—you will then need to experiment with a plug somewhere in midrange.

With older engines, gas-burning efficiency is lost through wear on components, and oil will probably begin seeping its way into the combustion chambers. In this application, you may want to go up a couple of heat ranges from the original plug recommendation. If autoignition occurs, back off one heat range.

Bear in mind as well that the ignition coil plays a large role in getting the correct voltage to the spark plugs, and that with vehicles more than 5 years old, a weak ignition coil can cause excess plug fouling. The coil

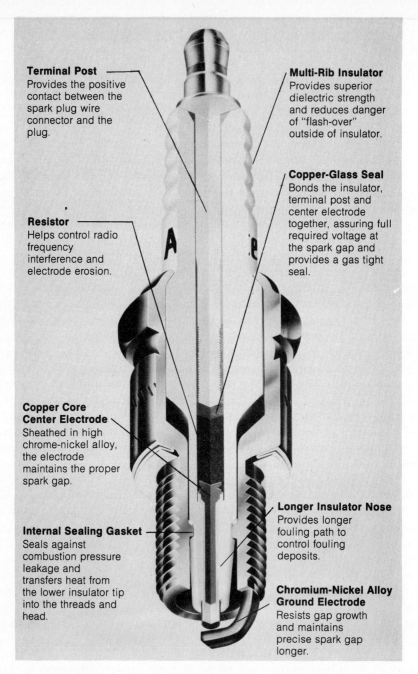

Terminal Post
Provides the positive contact between the spark plug wire connector and the plug.

Multi-Rib Insulator
Provides superior dielectric strength and reduces danger of "flash-over" outside of insulator.

Copper-Glass Seal
Bonds the insulator, terminal post and center electrode together, assuring full required voltage at the spark gap and provides a gas tight seal.

Resistor
Helps control radio frequency interference and electrode erosion.

Copper Core Center Electrode
Sheathed in high chrome-nickel alloy, the electrode maintains the proper spark gap.

Longer Insulator Nose
Provides longer fouling path to control fouling deposits.

Internal Sealing Gasket
Seals against combustion pressure leakage and transfers heat from the lower insulator tip into the threads and head.

Chromium-Nickel Alloy Ground Electrode
Resists gap growth and maintains precise spark gap longer.

Fig. 6-8   Cross-section of a spark plug. (*Courtesy Fram/Autolite.*)

boosts the 12-volt battery system to as high as 30,000 volts. At 30 mph, this is done about 100 times a second. Coils are relatively inexpensive and with a modicum of common sense are self-serviceable.

As to heat-range selection, auto-parts personnel or your mechanic should be able to guide you. In general, the higher the spark plug number, the higher the heat range. For example, with AC Spark Plugs, an R45TS is three ranges hotter than an R42TS; the same comparison with Champion, RBL15Y to RBL9Y; with Motorcraft, ARF52 to ARF22; and Autolite, 26 to 23. Do not experiment with heat ranges on a whim. Stick with the manufacturer's recommendation unless you have a specific problem that you are trying to solve, and keep in mind that you may violate new-car warranty terms. Do not mix spark plugs of various heat ranges, either.

The R in many spark plug numbers indicates resistor plugs, which prevent voltage discharges from interfering with radio reception and, more recently, with the electronic feedback of the engine itself. Using resistor plugs is nearly mandatory today for that reason, and even with older engines, using resistor plugs does not affect performance in any way.

Until recently, most spark plugs had center electrodes made of a nickel alloy. Today, spark plugs with copper-cored center electrodes are becoming commonplace.

Copper-cored plugs date back to 1942, the year AC Spark Plugs first patented the design for wartime aviation use. Copper-cored plugs took to the wing because of their superior sparking and antifouling properties. Although the cars of that day did not require this special ability, today's smaller engines do. They run cooler at low speeds and hotter at high speeds, situations that predicate spark plug fouling and preignition. And lead-free gasoline requires spark plug temperatures 150° to 200° Fahrenheit hotter in order to burn carbon formation from spark plugs. Because copper-cored plugs provide a wider heat range than nickel-alloy plugs, they resist fouling better.

A platinum electrode spark plug, which further resists fouling, is also available. Bosch, the West German manufacturer, uses a unique design for its platinum-coated electrode plug. The plug uses a single, small-diameter pin (0.3 mm) on the plug's ceramic nose. The platinum plug has not only wider heat ranges than copper but better wear characteristics as well. Further development of the platinum plug may produce a lifetime spark plug.

Both copper-cored and platinum-coated plugs are available for most engines, and can be substituted for nickel-alloy plugs. Just be careful in matching heat ranges; auto-parts personnel, your mechanic, or dealer can assist you. Platinum plugs cost about twice as much as copper plugs, and copper plugs cost about twice as much as the conventional nickel-alloy plugs. The platinum and copper plugs are bound to come down in price as their use becomes more widespread. (Bosch, in fact, no longer makes chromium-nickel electrode plugs.)

Changing Spark Plugs

The modern spark plug is not designed for perpetual life—not yet, anyway. While today's electronic ignition systems add longer life, the engine temperatures subtract from that. Spark plugs are battered by high-combustion temperatures that can reach 4000° Fahrenheit. Combustion deposits accumulate on internal surfaces, and plugs become worn.

Spark plugs should be checked at least every 10,000 to 15,000 miles in cars with electronic ignition systems, and they should be replaced at these intervals in cars with conventional point-condenser distributors. If you want better engine performance, a fresh set of spark plugs is the best of bets. Although some engines require a contortionist to get at certain spark plugs, changing spark plugs is usually easy enough. Moreover, for today's breakerless ignition systems, a change of plugs can often put new life and pep back into your vehicle.

If you change your own plugs, remember that a spark plug is basically a hollow shell and does not need tightening much past the point of initial resistance. To avoid misthreading spark plugs located in difficult-to-reach spots, use a length of small-diameter rubber hose. Place it over the ceramic on the wire end of the plug, and use it to guide the plug into place. Some spark plugs have a small, circular metal O-ring gasket at the base of the threaded tips; this allows the plug to seat properly and prevents the side electrode from intruding too far into the combustion chamber, a condition which could damage both plug and engine. Before installing the new plug, check if this gasket is in place; if it is missing on a new plug, use one from an old plug.

You should also check the gap size between the center and side electrodes before installing the plugs. This is done with a flat, or feeler, gauge. In the mid-1970s wide-gap plugs were introduced, designed to be compatible with electronic ignition systems and to ignite the leaner combustion gas mixtures required to meet emission controls. Spark plugs of pre-1970s vintage generally required gaps of 0.035 inch; today, the gap varies from 0.060 to 0.080. Your owner's manual and service and parts manuals all list the exact gap required per engine.

Every used spark plug tells a story, and the following pictures paint a thousand words. These photographs can help in determining optimum plug type and heat range by providing clues as to the mechanical condition of the engine(Fig. 6-9).

Engine Oil

If there were an award for the most neglected but most vital automotive component, engine oil would be the undisputed grand-prize winner. In fact, with fewer full-service gas stations around, some manufacturers are considering increasing the engine oil crankcase capacity just to compensate for driver neglect of engine oil levels.

The average driver has an even worse attitude when it comes to changing engine oil. Haven't got the funds to spare? Consider that frequent oil and oil filter changes help ensure the longevity of your vehicle with an efficiency few other maintenance procedures can duplicate. A $15 oil and filter change can keep that $10,000-plus car around tens of thousands of miles longer.

In early 1984, *Consumer Reports* surveyed 3300 owners of cars having more than 100,000 odometer miles. More than half had oil and filter changes every 3500 miles or less; few of them waited more than 5000 miles to climb on the odometer before the change. And, yes, automakers recommend change intervals for oil and oil filters of 7500 miles for many late-model cars, but this is more a marketing enhancement than anything of an engineering nature. Under severe driving conditions, automotive warranties mandate oil and oil filter changes twice as often.

Severe driving conditions are, for all practical purposes, "normal" driving conditions: frequent starts and stops; short engine warmup; and shutting off and restarting the engine after less than 10 miles of driving. Under these conditions, automakers generally recommend changing your oil and oil filter at intervals of no more than 3500 miles or every 3 to 4 months. Engine oil does not "wear out"; its additives break down over a period of time and use.

The internal combustion process that powers your car produces water, acids, hydrocarbons, and resins. By-products not eliminated through the tailpipe travel into the crankcase and, if not neutralized, will pit and collect on engine parts, eventually and inevitably reducing engine longevity, performance, reliability, and fuel economy. This process occurs regardless of the age of an engine. However, deposits are neutralized and suspended by additives in engine oil, so that the by-products flow throughout the system without damaging the engine. When oil is left in too long, this function is lost. The oil will continue to suspend harmful engine contaminants but only until its saturation point is reached, at which point pitting and collecting will begin. Keeping the engine oil level full (as indicated by the dipstick measurement) helps avoid contamination, because the addition of even one quart of new oil adds fresh additives and increases suspension properties of the entire system.

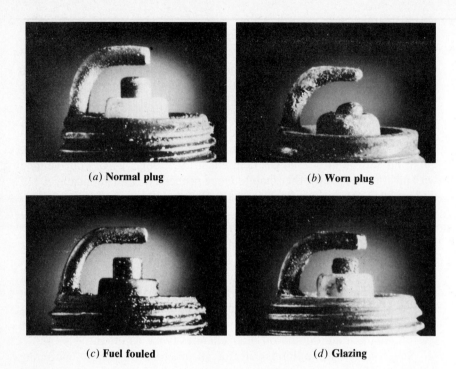

(*a*) **Normal plug**   (*b*) **Worn plug**

(*c*) **Fuel fouled**   (*d*) **Glazing**

Fig. 6-9   Spark Plugs: (*a*) A slight tan color and some electrode and insulator erosion are normal. (*b*) This plug needs replacing because the side and center electrodes have worn. The wear has increased gap size, which will cause fouling because the wider gap demands extra voltage. (*c*) Unignited fuel has coated the entire plug tip and insulator nose. A fuel-fouled plug should not be dried out and reused because the plug has been shorted out. Common causes of fuel fouling include carburetion (fuel mixture) or ignition system problems (such as with the plug wires, distributor cap, sensor units, or ignition coil). (*d*) A common cause of engine misfire, glazing results from fuel deposits that have literally melted and shorted out the spark plug. This occurs on hard acceleration of a vehicle typically used in stop-and-go traffic, without first allowing deposits to burn away through gradual acceleration. (*e*) Carbon-fouled plugs are caused by low-speed driving or extended idling. These plugs can be cleaned, regapped, and reused if insulator and electrode wear are minimal. However, carbon fouling can also occur because of worn plugs. (*f*) Preignition results in spark knock, which

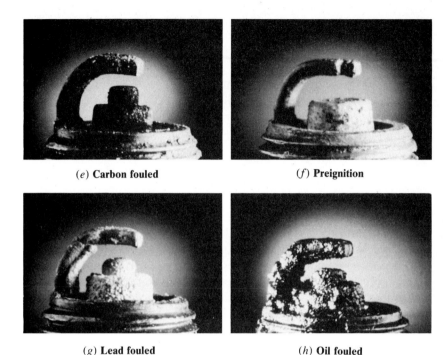

(*e*) **Carbon fouled**   (*f*) **Preignition**

(*g*) **Lead fouled**   (*h*) **Oil fouled**

occurs when high combustion-chamber temperatures cause random ignition of the air and fuel mixture in the combustion chamber. Advanced ignition timing, engine overheating, ignition system problems, and use of low-octane fuel all cause preignition. (*g*) This occurs when leaded fuel is substituted for unleaded fuel in modern engines. In older engines still requiring the use of leaded fuel, this is caused by loss of cylinder compression and valve train wear. An engine overhaul is generally required to correct this problem. (*h*) Wear on piston rings, valve seals, and guides causes excessive amounts of crankcase oil to enter the combustion chamber. Of the oil that does burn off, a heavy deposit is left behind on the plug, shorting it out. Eventually, raw oil soaks these caked-on deposits. An engine overhaul is required to correct the problem. (*Photographs courtesy of Fram/Autolite, Fram Division.*)

The oil filter should also be changed every time the oil is. With today's full-flow oil filters, all engine oil must first pass through the filter before it is returned to the engine. If the filter clogs, a small bypass valve returns dirty oil directly. Therefore, it is false economy not to change both oil and oil filter at least every 3500 miles or 3 to 4 months. Enough said. To the heart of the matter: the oil itself.

Motor Oil Terminology

Selection of the proper service classification oil is important in maintaining new-car warranties. Look for the phrase "meets or exceeds all car manufacturers' warranty requirements." Fortunately, for the layperson, this is written on the oil container in plain English.

Beyond that point, oil is rated in two ways: American Petroleum Institute (API) and the Society of Automotive Engineers (SAE). API ratings consist of two letters that denote oil quality, whereas SAE ratings are numerical and denote oil viscosity relative to ambient, or outdoor, temperatures.

An example of an API oil rating would be SF or CD. The letter pair beginning with the *S* indicates oil for use in spark-ignition engines; the pair that begins with the letter *C* indicates oil for use in diesel, or compression-ignition, engines. The second letter indicates the number of oil additives. The farther along in the alphabet the second letter, the higher the oil quality. Unlike food additives, oil additives are highly desirable.

SA and SB oils are not applicable to today's cars.
SC is considered the first modern oil, formulated for high-performance V-8s. Today, though, it is meant for use only in engines built before 1967.
SD has more engine-protecting additives than SC and can be used in engines built before 1970.
SE oil was formulated for emissions-control engine designs of the mid- to late-1970s.
SF is an improved version of SE and is of special importance if your car has a turbocharger.
CC and—more often—CD are acceptable ratings for diesel engines.

The proper API-rated oil for an engine is usually stamped on the dipstick. Note that the additional additives of SF allow longer intervals between oil changes and higher engine temperatures; SF also includes an antiburning additive to prevent by-product buildup on turbocharger bearings. No matter the year of your car, you can always use SF-rated oil to preserve its mechanical integrity the best.

SAE numbers indicate motor oil viscosity, a measure of an oil's thickness relative to atmospheric (that is, outdoor, or ambient) temperatures.

The higher the viscosity number—30, 40, or 50—the better the oil for use in hot weather; a lower viscosity number coupled with a *W*—20W, 10W, or 5W—indicates an oil suitable for cold-weather use. Driving circumstances and conditions determine exactly which SAE(s) are the most appropriate.

Multiviscosity oils often enable a driver to use one oil the year round. The viscosity rating 10W-40 indicates an oil suitable for use in both hot and cold weather. (To be exact, 10W indicates outdoor temperatures as low as 0° Fahrenheit, and the 40, ambient temperatures up to 100° Fahrenheit.) Not all oils have detergent additives, so in addition, check for the letters HD, which indicate "high-detergent" properties.

In selecting oil, *follow owner's manual recommendations.* For example, General Motors began telling its customers to use no more than a 10W-30 oil in many of its cars beginning from the model year 1984. Chrysler, starting with its 1986 models, began recommending use of 5W-30 motor oil in many of its engines. To demonstrate the effect of oil viscosity, Chrysler found in cold room tests that 5W-30 oil improved starting time 39 percent and improved cranking rpms by 14 percent, as compared to 10W-30 oil. In all cases, though, abide by owner's manual recommendations, and if in doubt, check with the dealer. But after the warranty expires and as the car continues to age, you may want to go up one step in viscosity during the summer (20W-40) for better lubricating properties and one lower in the winter (5W-30) to facilitate cold-weather starting. This assumes, of course, that you change your oil frequently enough to facilitate this. (And you know you should!)

"New Wave" Oil

For decades, the service classification and viscosity numbers of oil were confusing enough. Now, we have the more expensive friction-modified (graphite) and synthetic oils with which to contend as well.

Friction-modified oils contain minute specks of graphite (nearly 80 of them side by side would be barely visible) or molybdenum disulfide (moly, or $MoS2$). These minuscule particles pass through the oil filter easily, but in the closer tolerances of the engine, they slide apart sideways (much as a spreading deck of cards) and thereby reduce engine friction, or, in engineering parlance, "the coefficient of friction number."

Due to the "slipperiness" of these oils, they can also improve fuel economy. ARCO graphite oil, for example, has been shown to increase fuel mileage between 4 and 8 percent in various tests. Belying the superior lubricating properties of these friction-modified oils is the black color of these oils; it's normal, however. These oils also offer all the same additives and multiviscosity ratings found in conventional oils.

Synthetic oils are considerably more expensive than either conventional or friction-modified oils. Synthetic oils, however, outperform all other engine oils at high engine temperatures. When overheated, conventional oils leave a gummy residue that is detrimental to engine longevity; synthetic oils do not. These synthetic oils are thinner and are *not* recommended for new-engine break-in periods or for engines with high mileage, nor should they be mixed with oils containing either graphite or MoS2. And although synthetic oil manufacturers claim intervals of oil change in excess of automaker recommendations, you risk voiding your new-car warranty by extending the intervals.

Oil and Oil Filter Changing

Change oil hot. Hot oil suspends contaminants better and drains more thoroughly. Do not tighten either the oil-pan bolt or oil filter beyond a firm initial resistance. Even though you are dealing with a liquid, massive torque is not required to prevent leaks; you can damage the oil-pan bolt, oil pan, and/or oil filter by overtightening.

On the engine side of the oil filter is a round, rubber gasket that is vital to proper sealing. Take a bit of clean oil, and rub it along this gasket surface before installing the filter. Check that the gasket from the old filter came off and is not stuck to the engine block. If the old gasket is stuck to the engine block, be sure to remove it before installing the new filter.

Check that you have replaced the oil-pan drain bolt before refilling the engine with oil. The oil-pressure indicator, light or gauge, should respond within seconds; if not, do not gun the engine. Instead, turn the engine off and check the oil level and look for leaks. (In rare cases, you may have to remove the oil filter and prime the oil pump: using a squeeze pump, squirt 5 to 10 drops of oil into the oil filter housing base, and replace the filter.) After the engine has warmed up, check the oil level and look for leaks once again. Finally, be sure to dispose of the used oil properly, either at a recycling center or gas station, but never down a storm drain, please.

If your vehicle is equipped with an oil-pressure warning light (this light is usually labeled *OIL* or emblazoned with a graphic that vaguely resembles a dripping genie's lamp), it should light with the ignition key in the Start position. This is done so that you can check whether the bulb has burned out. If the light does not come on, have it replaced as soon as possible. Both warning lights and gauges are triggered by an engine oil-pressure sending unit. If the unit fails, a gauge will quit working, but warning lights will not provide a clue, because the bulb itself will still light on starting. Have a mechanic check the sending unit every so often if your vehicle is equipped with a warning light.

*If the oil-pressure light activates while driving, or should the gauge reading drop, and there is an accompanying engine knock, turn the engine off **immediately**!* If the light flickers or the gauge drops when accelerating or stopping, you're low on oil. The real urgency begins when the engine starts knocking, a situation in which you are playing for all the marbles.

The Cooling System

The main function of the engine cooling system is to remove excess heat and maintain proper engine operating temperatures. If an engine runs too hot, oil viscosity is altered, detergent action is inhibited, and varnishlike internal engine deposits form; at worst, burned valves, scored pistons, and damaged bearings could result. If an engine runs too cold, wear on the cylinder walls can increase up to eight times the norm. Fuel will also vaporize, decreasing gas mileage and increasing engine oil pollution, which decreases the lubricating properties of an oil.

The normal operating temperature of most late-model engines is approximately 200° to 230° Fahrenheit. A small saucer-shaped unit called a thermostat is responsible for bringing the starting temperature of an engine up to normal as quickly as possible, but from that point, many other elements make it possible for an engine to function at temperatures well above the boiling point.

Checking Coolant Level

Fortunately, you no longer have to remove the radiator cap to check the coolant level on most late-model vehicles. Many now have coolant overflow reservoirs made of plastic, which is sufficiently transparent to allow a visual check by comparing the fluid level with the "hot" and "cold" lines molded on the sides of these containers.

The entire cooling system is pressurized. Opening a radiator cap when an engine is hot causes a rapid pressure drop, which, in turn, causes the coolant to boil violently. Depending on ambient temperatures, an engine may remain well above 200° Fahrenheit for a half-hour or more after being shut off, so judge internal temperature by radiating heat, not by time. Better yet, never remove a radiator cap when the engine is hot. Besides, you should never add coolant to a hot engine (to include normal operating temperature), because cold water in a hot engine can crack the engine block and/or components. If you must add water when an engine is hot, add the water slowly while the engine runs at a fast idle. (WARNING:

When doing so with a 1970 to 1979 Ford car or light truck or van with an automatic transmission, always set the parking brake firmly. These transmissions can shift into reverse accidentally, which has resulted in hundreds of injuries and over a hundred deaths; please use extreme caution.)

How Important Is Antifreeze?

Plenty important. Not only does it protect against cold-weather freezing, but it also lubricates the water pump, provides anticorrosive, antirust properties, and helps keep the cooling system cooler in summer. Of course, all good things must end, and similar to oil, these properties wear thin and need replacing approximately every 24,000 to 36,000 miles or every 2 to 3 years.

The preferred dilution rate is half ethylene glycol, half water, which lowers the freezing point to about −34° Fahrenheit and raises the boiling point to 226° Fahrenheit. Should boiling ever occur, the water will boil off first, increasing the ethylene glycol concentration. (Oddly enough, pure ethylene glycol will turn into a gel at only −8° Fahrenheit, so a mixture of water is essential for maximum cold-weather protection. If an engine block freezes, the expansion of the ice will crack it.)

By the 4-year or 45,000-mile mark, it becomes more than a matter of simple maintenance to have the cooling system flushed and refilled. Many antifreeze additives will have been depleted by that time, and this often leads to water pump, radiator, heater core, thermostat, and other problems for the cooling system that are often attributed to normal wear and tear. This needn't be if you renew the coolant.

If tap water in your locale is hard, that is, high in mineral content, it's best to use demineralized (softened) water. The minerals in hard water can leave deposits throughout the cooling system and may even react with other chemicals to form corrosives. Automotive water filters (truck dealers usually stock them) are available for situations in which hard water must be used.

Many new cars now have some type of aluminum component in the cooling systems. When purchasing an antifreeze, check that it contains aluminum corrosion inhibitors.

If you flush the system yourself, *dispose of the expelled coolant properly* via a toxic dumpsite or through the facilities of a service garage; *do not leave it to sit out uncovered.* Ethylene glycol is highly toxic, but it has a sweet taste. It may tempt animals and children, and 1 ounce can kill a 15-pound dog. Also, if the coolant drains near foliage or onto the lawn, it will kill either.

Along with the coolant mix, the radiator cap plays an important role in controlling engine temperatures. The purpose of the cap is to pressurize and, thereby, raise the boiling temperature of the coolant. Each point of pressure that the cap produces will raise the coolant boiling temperature about 3° Fahrenheit. A cap that places the coolant at 12 pounds of pressure will raise the boiling point of the coolant from 226° to approximately 260° Fahrenheit.

A radiator cap has two valves. The pressure valve seats against the radiator filler neck under spring tension until it reaches its pressure rating (12 pounds was used in the above example). It will then open and allow the coolant to enter the overflow reservoir to prevent excess pressure from damaging engine components. The other valve is vacuum-operated. The pressure drop that is created when an engine is shut off forms a vacuum (a suction) that would collapse hose lines if air were not allowed to enter the system via this vacuum valve. Therefore, should you ever need to replace a radiator cap, be sure it is of the correct specified relief pressure. Also, check the rubber base of your present cap; if chipped or cracked, it should be replaced.

Underheating and Overheating

If your car's heater isn't hot during cold weather, it's very possible that the engine thermostat needs to be replaced. A relatively inexpensive operation, you may want to try replacing it yourself if you have a service manual. Most modern engines use a 195° Fahrenheit thermostat, while older models use a 180° or 160° Fahrenheit thermostat. This rating is stamped on the thermostat itself.

Instead of replacing the thermostat, some people in cold weather will place cardboard over the radiator to increase heat production. This is not wise because automatic transmission cooling lines also run through the radiator in separate passageways. The ventilation thus blocked by the cardboard can cause the transmission to overheat. The consequence of spending $300 to repair a transmission to avoid replacing a $5 thermostat is ridiculous, to say the least. (You may see trucks and buses using cardboard, but other variables are involved here, one of them being that most of these vehicles have manual, and not automatic transmissions.)

Overheating is a more common and complex problem to dissect. However, there is one certainty: If your car overheats while in operation, shut off the engine as soon as possible. You run the risk of severe damage, otherwise. Until you can pull over, set the dashboard temperature controls in the full-heat position and set the blower fan on high speed. If the car has a belt-driven fan, put the transmission in neutral as often as possible, and rev the engine. This increases coolant circulation (if a broken fan belt is not the cause of the overheating, that is) and heat dispersion and reduces the engine load. Bear in mind that this is only a *tempo-*

rary cure to relieve the *symptoms* of an overheating problem. By no stretch of the imagination is it to be viewed as "solving" the problem.

If your vehicle is equipped with a cooling system warning light—typical forms of the light include the words TEMP or HOT or a rendering of a thermometer—check that the light comes on when the key is in the Start position. If not, have it checked. Unfortunately, this test will not disclose whether the engine sending unit, which controls the bulb in all other modes, is operable. To be on the safe side, it's a good idea to have a mechanic check it periodically—coolant change intervals would be an easy way to remember this. If your vehicle has a gauge, you needn't worry; a gauge either works or it doesn't.

Overheating is usually caused by low coolant levels due to a leak in the system, a broken fan belt, or dirty cooling system components. Cooling systems which are not flushed and refilled with new coolant at manufacturer-recommended intervals, or sooner, can develop clogged passages that restrict coolant flow and overall cooling efficiency. The end result of such neglect is having to recore the radiator and backflush the system to restore normal operating temperatures. This is, of course, preventable through regular maintenance.

Also, keep the radiator core clean of bugs and other road debris. To depict how clogged a radiator core can become, imagine the number of squashed bugs that have been removed from the windshield over the years. This same number become impaled upon the radiator core as well and, unless removed, will increasingly hamper air flow. Taking a garden hose or a spray wash "wand" and spraying through the radiator from the engine compartment will remove a majority of the core debris. Avoid hitting the core itself when spraying. A radiator may appear rugged, but it's a fragile series of thin hollow tubing that winds through the radiator frame. It ruptures easily.

If the cooling system leaks, locate the exact spot before randomly using stop-leak additives. Stop-leak products not only will do nothing for a leaking hose but may also clog passages. Hose leaks are not always obvious, and some require flexing before a crack or split shows itself. Be careful not to let a leak catch you off guard and squirt up at you. Should the leak occur near the end of a hose, a *temporary* measure is to slice off the leaking portion with a knife and refasten the remaining length of hose. But, as common sense would dictate, it is better to replace the hose as soon as possible—if it started to leak once, it will probably do so soon again elsewhere.

If the leak is coming from the water pump area, replace the pump. All water pumps leak as internal seals and/or bearings wear out, and if the fan wobbles, you have a water pump that is really on its last leg, leak or no leak.

If there is water coming from the back of the engine block at the point where it attaches to the transmission or from down one of the sides of the engine block, you probably have a leaking freeze plug. If there is no sign of an under-the-hood leak, check underneath the carpeting on the passenger side of the car. If it is wet with a very filmy feel accompanied by an unpleasant odor, you have a leaking heater core. If the tailpipe exhaust is white or if your oil is the consistency and color of mayonnaise, sorry, but you have a crack in the block and/or a blown head gasket.

These latter conditions, as well as a leaking radiator, warrant the use of stop-leak additives, because at that point, you have nothing left to lose—at least temporarily—but follow label directions. Too much can clog vital engine passages.

Automotive Additives

P. T. Barnum was either in the wrong business or just slightly ahead of his time. For nearly as long as there have been automobiles, there have been quick-fix cures. Like patent medicine shows of the old west, some automotive concoctions offer little more than false hope.

And hope springs inexpensive when your car isn't running right. What's a few bucks when you're faced with a potential $100-plus repair? Could this be the time-honored marketing philosophy behind many "cure in a can" products?

There are legitimate additives, but be careful. Beyond being worthless, some may cause greater problems than the ones they pretend to solve. Especially when human nature dictates "if a little doesn't work, a lot will." Not quite. In trying to stop a radiator leak, if one can of stop-leak doesn't work, two or more cans may well seal part of your cooling system shut and still leave you with the leak. With additives, more is never better, and never may be better yet.

Gasoline Additives

Certain additives can be beneficial. Composed mainly of solvents and alcohol, fuel additives can remove deposits and ensure against water buildup and winter gas-line freeze. Fuel-injected engines, which are more susceptible to dirt and buildup than engines with carburetors, may especially benefit. In any case, use these additives infrequently—once, maybe twice a year. Using them more frequently than that can dissolve plastic fuel-system parts and fuel-pump diaphragms. And when applicable, check that the additive is compatible with catalytic converters too.

If you use a detergent gasoline or a detergent oil and keep your car in relatively good tune, gasoline additives will not be necessary. At any rate, gasoline additives are no substitute for proper maintenance. This includes the periodic replacement of the fuel filter, especially on fuel-injected engines. And if you keep your gas tank at least half-full during cold weather to avoid gas tank condensation, you'll probably never need gas-line antifreeze, which contains methanol.

Diesel Fuel Additives

There are plenty of frustrated diesel owners willing to try anything short of converting to gasoline engines. So, plenty of snake oils have popped up on the aftermarket.

Cold-weather starts are better aided by battery and fuel filter heaters than anything in a can. Unless you and your diesel are caught in a cold snap with nonwinterized diesel fuel, forget additives. The antigels found in them can cause combustion-chamber pitting.

On the other hand, you may want to try a can of diesel fuel biocide to stave off the fungus growth that flourishes on diesel fuel in the presence of water. This slime can plug your fuel system, and once it is detected, your fuel system must be professionally cleaned. Biocides are for use as preventatives, not cures.

Last, always use a high-grade diesel fuel. It is lowest in abrasive- and corrosive-sulphur content and contains more passenger-car types of additives.

Oil Additives

These products can increase the amount of residue left behind by oil itself and can cause premature clogging of hydraulic lifters and other engine parts. During colder weather, engine-oil thickeners can inhibit starter cranking to the extent that your vehicle may not start. If you have an oil burner, you may want to try a can, but the above cautions still apply.

There are other oil supplements that claim sludge-removing abilities, extra additive strengths, and gas-mileage improving properties. Some sludge removers may work (plain kerosene is just as effective), but some of this sludge is usually holding deteriorating gaskets together in older engines and plugging potential oil leaks elsewhere too. You may be pulling a finger out of the dike, so to speak. Instead of adding extrastrength oil supplements, save your money, apply it toward more frequent oil changes (every 3 months or 3000 miles), and use an API-rated SF oil.

Stop-Leak Additives

Stop-leaks are available for engines, transmissions, power steering units, cooling systems, and everything else that is user-serviceable. Try a can if you like, but repeated use (which is actually a misuse of the product if you read the directions carefully) can inadvertently clog passages and ports without sealing the leak.

Real folly is the use of a stop-leak product before the source of a leak is located, especially in the case of the cooling system. If a leaky water pump, hose, or connection is the cause, you could very well be left stranded when one of those problems finally lets loose, because stop-leak won't solve them. And water-pump lubricants and rust inhibitors are found in antifreeze; buy a can of that instead. Better still, flush and then refill your entire cooling system.

chapter 7

Automotive Special Policies and Recall Campaigns

"If at First You Don't Succeed, Try, Try Again"

Try as we may, getting it right the first time is a more noble goal than it is a practical one. But the ways in which automotive manufacturers go about correcting or improving past production and manufacturing deficiencies is sometimes more pragmatic than noble. Automotive special policies and recall campaigns certainly have one common denominator: both issues stir up controversy unrivaled by anything else within the automotive industry.

In a general sense, special policies and recalls are similar; both usually provide the vehicle owner with repairs or replacements at the manufacturer's expense, and both are usually initiated because of a high failure rate of a component or the potential for such failure. But the two programs are administrated differently, and when comparing one special policy to another, or one recall to another, more exceptions are gathered than rules. Special policies and recalls both require consumer participation, though. And for your efforts, you can save not only money but, sometimes, lives as well.

Special Policies: Warranties You "Auto" Know About

From time to time, most domestic and foreign manufacturers issue special policies, usually in the form of a service bulletin to its dealerships. Judging from the past three things seem to be true of special policies: (1) anything in or on a vehicle may be covered—from power-train components to body finish to window regulators and even trunk lid hinges; (2) vehicles up to 5 years old (in some cases, even older) may still have some sort of warranty coverage under the terms of a special policy; and (3) you may never know of special policy coverage unless you ask.

Exactly What Are Special Policies?

Although there are similarities, *special policies are not recalls.* Keep that point in mind. Special policies are issued on parts or components that malfunction either because of a manufacturing or a production problem. A manufacturer may then extend the warranty on that particular part or component only, authorizing its repair or replacement without charge to the customer, *but only when and if the defect occurs.* This fact distinguishes a special policy from a recall. *With recalls, the part or component in question will be repaired or replaced regardless of its present condition or time and mileage parameters.* With special policies, the warranty coverage applies only within the time and mileage parameters allotted by the manufacturer.

The issuance, redemption, and substance of special policies vary with the manufacturer and the components involved. Terms of the warranty are at the discretion of the manufacturer. For example, a manufacturer notes a high failure rate of power-window motors. Examination reveals poorly manufactured armature brushes that tend to fail at about the 30,000-mile mark; however, the new-car warranty extends to only 24,000 miles. As a show of good faith, this particular manufacturer acknowledges that the failure is caused by a manufacturing deficiency and extends warranty coverage on that particular component *only* for up to 36,000 miles. (If such a part or component is still being used in assembly, its use is discontinued. This is referred to as a "running model change.")

The exceptions are defects that involve safety or emissions controls. In these cases, a recall campaign would either be ordered by the federal government or undertaken voluntarily by the manufacturer.

Special policy notifications are distributed through the manufacturer's regional offices. In turn, these offices alert the dealership service departments within their region. (A zone, or regional, office is a local branch of a manufacturer's national headquarters that assists with customer relations and provides dealer network support.) Dealerships may be the only public source of special policy information and, consequently, consumers may unwittingly pay for repairs elsewhere that are covered by special policies. This is especially true in the case of older vehicles, which are seldom taken in for dealer repair. These deficiencies have earned special policies the label of "hidden warranties."

Consumer Problems with Special Policies

The primary consternation for consumers is the lengths to which manufacturers sometimes go in *not* publicizing special policies. Many consumers learn of these policies only through a visit to the dealership or from an employee of the manufacturer. Manufacturers are concerned that if word spreads of a special policy, eligible owners might demand that dealers repair the part or component whether or not the defect had yet occurred. It could be argued that if manufacturers had felt such action was necessary, they would have issued a voluntary recall.

In some instances, manufacturers do mail special policy notices to owners, but a large consumer problem here is that special policies affect second and third owners, too, who are not on manufacturer mailing lists. Compounding these oversights, few second and third owners of vehicles ever see the light of dealership service departments and, therefore, unaware of a special policy, often chalk up a defect to wear and tear and pay for the repair out-of-pocket.

There is another problem here, too. Sometimes, aftermarket repair shops tell a consumer that a part is warrantied, but ask for permission to proceed with the repair work, saying that the manufacturer will reimburse the consumer later. This is a very risky proposition. To avoid getting stuck with the repair bill, the consumer should first contact the dealership or the manufacturer's regional office (consult Appendixes A and B).

Clarence Ditlow, director of the Center for Auto Safety in Washington, D.C., states that the center receives many complaints from consumers who are unaware of special policies—including first owners who should be on the manufacturer's mailing list.

"Anytime you have a 'secret' policy out there that affects your car, and you don't take advantage of it, you're just throwing money away. The further down the ladder you go," Ditlow says in reference to second and third owners, "the greater the problem of getting information. A manufacturer is probably a little more willing to tell a first owner about a special policy than a second owner, simply because they think, 'This first owner bought a car from us, and maybe he or she will buy another from us if we're nice to them.' "

Special policies can easily be kept in the dark as well. Ditlow cites the example of a 1978 Ford special policy that warrantied rust repairs on Fords that year beyond the new-car warranty parameters. Ditlow claims that Ford was so concerned about the expense of honoring the warranty, that not only did they fail to notify owners, they told only their district offices about the policy. Ford dealers were not even informed of the policy.

Other policies may acknowledge a problem but limit responsibility. Take the case of 1984 to 1985 Cadillacs with 4.1-L engines. General Motors acknowledged that these engines might leak coolant into the crankcase, which would impair engine oil lubrication and could result in severe engine damage. Cadillac's special policy allowed for a change of oil and filter, installation of an engine-oil supplement, and a change of the ethylene-glycol engine coolant to include a cooling-system sealant free of charge to owners with the 4.1-L engine. GM supplied literature including service schedule labels and extended the warranty on the 4.1-L engine to 4 years or 50,000 miles. One owner rightfully lamented, "That isn't much consolation to people like me, who spent more than $20,000 with the idea of keeping the car 7 or 8 years."

Although the Federal Trade Commission and the National Highway Traffic Safety Administration (NHTSA) frown on the current handling of special policies, neither organization has yet gone beyond basic federal surveillance.

The General Motors–Federal Trade Commission Agreement

General Motors, through a compromise agreement with the Federal Trade Commission (FTC), maintains an expanded arbitration program that is in effect through the year 1991 for vehicles manufactured from 1974 through

April 26, 1983. This agreement applies to some 21 million General Motors vehicles regardless of age or mileage. The program involves submitting a claim through GM's arbitration process, which is operated by the Better Business Bureau, as described in Chapter 2. An arbitrator renders a decision based on the documentation and presentation of the claim by the consumer and the defense presented by a GM representative. The proceedings are informal, and attorney involvement is not necessary.

Present owners may arbitrate for either reimbursement or repair of any of the following components. Past owners may arbitrate for *reimbursement* of the repair of any of the following components. You will need a repair receipt, but *you need not still own the vehicle.* Once again, this expanded arbitration program applies to General Motors vehicles manufactured from 1974 through April 26, 1983.

1. Turbo Hydra-matic 200 automatic transmissions used in a number of rear-wheel-drive vehicles beginning with the 1976 models. These transmissions allegedly have several defects that cause them to wear out prematurely. Repairs here can run as high as $600.

2. Camshafts and lifters in 305- and 350-CID V-8 gasoline engines produced in plants operated by Chevrolet since 1974. The FTC blames the premature failure of these components on the fact that some motor oils did not protect against excess wear and that GM did not disclose in owners' manuals which types of oils were required. Repairs average $400 to $800.

3. Fuel-injection pumps or fuel injectors in the 350-CID V-8 diesel engines produced in plants operated by Oldsmobile since 1978. The FTC said that GM did warn buyers of the danger of water contamination and that, in some cases, a water filter is needed to prevent corrosion that could cause the fuel-injection pump to fail, necessitating repairs of $300 to $500.

GM also consented that *any owner of a GM vehicle with a power-train problem can seek warrantied repair* through GM's arbitration program, *regardless of mileage,* provided the vehicle is still owned by the person filing, through November 21, 1991.* These power-train+ components are defined as follows:

> Cylinder blocks and heads and all internal parts, including camshafts and lifters, manifolds, timing gears, timing-gear chains, or belts and covers, gaskets, water pumps, fuel pumps, and diesel-injection pumps, turbocharger housings and internal parts, turbocharger valves, seals, and gaskets

---

* Neither agreement requires that the vehicle be maintained by a GM dealer or mechanic, but commercial use of a vehicle excludes it from the agreement.

+ The power-train definition in the consent order is more limited than the warranty; that is, no drive shaft or differential coverage is included.

Transmission cases and all internal parts, torque converters, vacuum modulators, seals and gaskets, transmission mounts, transfer cases, and all internal parts, seals, and gaskets

J. David Hudgens, General Motors customer relations and service spokesman in Detroit, said that owners who encountered component problems in vehicles covered under this agreement can first visit their dealer and do not necessarily need to seek arbitration. Of course, if the dealer or zone office representative denies warranty coverage or does not, in your opinion, present a legitimate offer, you will then need to pursue arbitration. For more on the GM-FTC agreement and the corresponding Better Business Bureau arbitration program, Auto Line, see Chapter 2.

The Lowdown on Tracking Down Special Policies

Both General Motors and the Ford Motor Company, through agreement with the FTC, now make many of their policy adjustments available to the owners of the vehicles affected. This applies to any vehicle manufactured either by the Ford Motor Company (Lincoln, Mercury, etc.) or by General Motors (Buick, Chevrolet, etc.).

General Motors agreed to make special policies affecting vehicles from the 1982 through the 1991 model years available for public inspection at dealerships. GM also publishes indexes and quarterly updates of special policies. Both are available from your GM dealer or by calling (800) 551-4123.

Ford owners should call (800) 241-FORD and request bulletins for their particular year, make, and model. Any applicable special policies will be forwarded to you. To keep customers updated, Ford keeps all names on their mailing list for 1 year.

Beyond these two manufacturers, locating special policies becomes an ill-defined and nebulous procedure. For example, I wrote an article on special policies for a national magazine a few years back; however, when the editors and I tried to contact the various manufacturers—as a consumer would—the process became so involved and uncertain that it literally defied description, and the article was never published. Score "1" for the manufacturers, a big fat goose egg for the consumer.

Perhaps the best way to check for special policies is by starting with your dealership, the manufacturer's regional office, or both. If people with whom you speak do not seem to understand the term "special policy" (a term known to cause temporary amnesia), try "policy adjustments," "warranty extensions," "service bulletins," "extended coverage," or any combination of these words (see Figs. 7-1 and 7-2). Even though you may finally be on the same wavelength, do not expect much;

CHEVROLET
PRODUCT SERVICE PUBLICATIONS
ORDER FORM

CATEGORY	DESCRIPTION	QUANTITY	PRICE EACH	TOTAL $
MISCELLANEOUS PUBLICATIONS	1983 Index and Summaries		FREE	
	1984 Index and Summaries		FREE	
	1985 Index and Summaries		FREE	
	1986 Index and Summaries (Available 1/2/86)		FREE	
	Service Manual and Owner Publications Order Form		FREE	
INDIVIDUAL PRODUCT SERVICE PUBLICATIONS Note: Please List Only One Bulletin Number per Line. Your First Product Service Publication Costs $3.00; Each Additional PSP Costs $1.00.	Bulletin Number - *	1	$ 3.00	$
	Bulletin Number - *	1	$ 1.00	$
	Bulletin Number - *	1	$ 1.00	$
	Bulletin Number - *	1	$ 1.00	$
	Bulletin Number - *	1	$ 1.00	$
	Bulletin Number - *	1	$ 1.00	$
	Bulletin Number - *	1	$ 1.00	$
	Bulletin Number - *	1	$ 1.00	$
	Bulletin Number - *	1	$ 1.00	$
	Bulletin Number - *	1	$ 1.00	$
PAST PRODUCT SERVICE PUBLICATIONS	All 1983 Publications		$ 40.00	$
	All 1984 Publications		$ 45.00	$
	All 1985 Publications		$ 50.00	$
	Special 3" Binder (Holds One Year)		$ 10.00	$
SUBSCRIPTION SERVICE	1986 Model Year (First Shipment – December 1985)		$ 90.00	$

	Total Order	$
Michigan Purchasers — Add 4% Sales Tax	**Michigan Sales Tax**	$
	Grand Total	$

*Orders cannot be filled without the appropriate bulletin numbers. These numbers may be found in the PSP Index.

Orders will be mailed within 10 days of receipt. Please allow adequate time for postal service.

Make check or money order (NO STAMPS) for this amount payable to Helm, Incorporated.

NOTE: Please fill in order form and MAIL TO:

HELM
Post Office Box 07130
Detroit, Michigan 48207

Name of Purchaser [Please print clearly]

Street Address   Apt. No.

City, State and Zip Code

This is your shipping label   Please print clearly

FROM . . .
HELM
Post Office Box 07130   Return Requested

CHEVROLET MANUAL
DISTRIBUTION DEPARTMENT
DETROIT, MICHIGAN 48207

FOR
          Name

          Street Address   Apt. No.

          City, State and Zip Code

PLEASE COMPLETE SHIPPING LABEL   ORD-86 (7 85)

Fig. 7-1 All General Motors Divisions make service bulletins available to consumers who request them. Bulletin indexes and summaries are free, but there is a charge for some individual service bulletins. (*Courtesy Chevrolet Motor Division.*)

C-15

CUSTOMER INFORMATION SYSTEM

CUSTOMER TECHNICAL SERVICE BULLETIN

 Automatic Transaxle

All vehicles need repairs during their lifetime. Sometimes Ford issues Technical Service Bulletins (TSBs) and easy-to-read explanations describing unusual engine or transmission conditions which may lead to costly repairs. Often a repair now can prevent a more serious repair later. Information provided in TSBs is designed to assist you and your dealer in the correction of unusual conditions. Ford Motor Company and its dealers are pleased to provide you this TSB because . . . it could save you money.

FLYWHEEL FLEXPLATE FRACTURES

Car Indentification

This TSB could apply to the following car lines: 1983-84 Escort/Lynx/EXP/LN7, and 1984 Tempo/Topaz equipped with the automatic transaxle transmission.

Description

The condition of flexplate fractures may be caused by excessive stress being induced by a tolerance stack-up of the automatic transaxle case and rear of engine block face.

Symptoms

The condition outlined above will cause a knocking sound at the rear (left side) of the engine when starting the engine, and at all speeds. This sound will usually become louder as the flexplate fracture spreads.

Consequences

This condition could ultimately result in the complete separation of the outer portion of the flywheel flexplate which would prevent starting of the vehicle.

Repair Procedures

Removal and replacement with the revised flexplate may be performed by following the procedure outlined in the 1983-84 Escort/Lynx/EXP/LN7/Tempo/Topaz Car Shop Manual, Powertrain, Volume E, Section 21-08.

Estimated Costs

Part No.	Description	***Class	**Price
E43Z-6375-A	Flywheel (1983 vehicles equipped with converter drain plug)	C	$ 68.29
E53Z-6375-A	Flywheel (1983-84 vehicles not equipped with drain plug)	B	$ 68.28

Estimated Cost of Repair

Model	Labor (Hrs)	*Labor	**Parts	Total
1983-84 Escort/Lynx/ EXP/LN7	3.4	$105.40	$68.29	$172.69
1984 Tempo/Topaz	5.8	$179.80	$68.28	$248.08

**Parts prices are the current suggested list prices (September, 1984) and do not include local Sales Tax.
***Parts Classification is for dealer reference.

Adjustable Terms

Reimbursable during period of warranty coverage.

NOVEMBER, '84 021/100184/6/R

Ford

Fig. 7-2 A Ford Motor Company customer service bulletin outlines a special policy on an automatic transaxle for the 1983 to 1984 Escort, Lynx, EXP, and LN7 and the 1984 Tempo and Topaz. Ford provides these bulletins free of charge and will mail updates as well. (*Courtesy Ford Motor Co.*)

instead, you will probably be asked whether you have a problem with your vehicle. If you reply that you simply would like some information, chances are that you'll then be told to be more specific. In other words, the runaround is on! I sincerely hope that you fare better.

You can also write to the NHTSA and request copies of any special policies that apply to your vehicle:

The National Highway Traffic Safety Administration
Technical Reference Division/NAD-52
400 7th Street
Washington, D.C. 20590

Include in your request the year, make, model, and vehicle identification number (VIN). The VIN can be located on your registration, on your title, or on the metal inlaid tag at the corner of the driver's side of the dashboard.

Now let me turn the podium over to the manufacturers themselves, and let *them* try to explain it!

Manufacturer Views and Applications of Special Policies

Gerard N. Murphy, president of the Automotive Consumer Action Program (AUTOCAP), which is operated through the National Automobile Dealers Association (NADA), states that special policy coverage is for "inordinate problems" that occur very soon after the purchase of a new car or are too unusual or severe to be considered "par-for-the-course repairs." Murphy adds, "If your air conditioning malfunctions at 25,000 miles, inquire as to why it went out so soon. Don't just drop off the car and say, 'Fix it'; ask if there is a policy adjustment in effect."

J. David Hudgens said that a special policy generally means "that we will repair the designated component if it proves defective within the specified time and mileage constraints. A policy may be issued for situations in which a failure is traced to a manufacturing or production process. Corporate policy is to send out letters to owners and service bulletins to alert our dealer network." What should consumers do if they have unwittingly paid for a repair covered by one of these policies? "A consumer should then take his receipt and contact their local zone office," says Hudgens. (GM zone offices are listed by division: Buick, Cadillac, Chevrolet, Pontiac, and Oldsmobile.)

Ford Motor Company parts and service public affairs manager Thomas Rhoades said that notification letters are sent to owners "just like a recall, and we also release it to the news media to reach as many people as we possibly can.'' Rhoades believes that Ford keeps a well-updated list of owners and that it is highly unlikely that very many owners are unaware of special policies. He suggested that consumers get in touch with their local district office to check for special policies if they suspect that one exists and says that (Ford) ''will figure out what district they're in, and the person responsible for that area will handle it.'' Ford has about 30 district offices throughout the country, and Rhoades stated: ''If a consumer has a problem, a district office representative will visit the customer's dealership to try and resolve it. This factory representative has the power to decide whether something will be warrantied or not. We advise [consumers] to start with the dealership, as it is in the dealer's best interest to make sure a customer is satisfied.''

Thomas O'Neill, manager of Chrysler's warranty administration, also said that the dealer or zone office is a good place for Chrysler customers to check for special policies. ''We provide within the owner's manual . . . a listing of zone offices across the country, and [other] customer relations information. Of course, any customer who has what he might deem an extraordinary failure would be prudent to . . . contact any manufacturer. The best way for a customer to get satisfaction is to start at the local level. Go to a dealer and ask for assistance, and if the dealer doesn't seem to be able to help him, then he's got the zone office to . . . help him. The customer relations number in Detroit is considered a last resort for problems that cannot be handled by the zone office at the local level.''

A spokesperson at the American Motors Corporation (AMC) corporate headquarters in Southfield, Michigan, said that AMC does not issue policy extensions but that customer complaints are considered on their individual merit. If an inordinate problem develops, AMC suggests first contacting the dealer and then, if necessary, the AMC regional office listed in the owner's manual. He also added that customers can make an appointment to discuss their problem with a regional AMC customer service manager, if they so desire.

Kurt Antonius, assistant manager of corporate public relations for American Honda, defined a special policy as a ''warranty extension for a specific component'' that has caused ''problems in the field. For reasons of customer satisfaction and confidence, we extend the warranty on that specific component.'' Honda has a ''free fender program'' for owners of 1979 Accords, under which Honda will, at the company's discretion, replace fenders that have rusted prematurely because of corrosives such as road salt. ''We don't ask everyone to bring their car in, because that's not necessary. But if people have had a failure, they will still be covered under an extended warranty for that component.''

Antonius said that product updates are also issued ''if a newer, better part is available to replace one in the field. We had a new vacuum hose for '83 Preludes, and we sent out a product update for people to bring . . . in their cars and get a new vacuum hose and the car would run smoother at idle." Antonius explained that this was accomplished by mailing letters to "Honda owners of record," which the company gets from state registration departments. He advises that for *any* service problem, the customer should see the dealer first. If the dealer does not resolve the problem, the customer should then contact the zone office. Antonius added that zone offices have the power to make warranty decisions for American Honda.

Toyota uses the term "good will" to describe its interpretation of a special policy. Matthew Morales, national customer relations analyst for Toyota, described this as a "grass-roots philosophy" that has proven to be a bona fide policy for the corporation. He also said the Toyota policy is a "trendsetter" among automakers. "We don't have any special policies. Each of our 12 regional offices across the U.S. has a budget—which we call good will—and if they see a particular problem, they can reimburse the customer as they see fit. And that is strictly up to each region; there is no specific policy outlining that from national headquarters. The district service manager," Morales said, "is in charge of each region, and he decides if a problem is covered by warranty, or maybe they'll provide a partial reimbursement, or they may reimburse them totally out of good will."

A spokesperson for Volkswagen of America at its headquarters in Troy, Michigan, reported that the company does not issue special policies. "We don't extend warranties on certain parts. Should a VW owner, though, experience an inordinate problem after the new-car warranty period, that owner is advised to contact customer assistance. "There may be certain circumstances where we may feel what we should pay, because it's a manufacturing or production problem, but that would be handled on an individual basis."

The national warranty manager for Nissan said, "We have issued special warranty extensions from time to time—maybe 4 to 6 in the last 5 years—and when we do, we mail notices to owners of vehicles affected by the policy." As to how a Nissan owner might check on special policies, he replied, "There are two ways. First we recommend they see their local dealer, and if there is any problem, we have customer relations managers in each of our regional offices as well as at our national headquarters."

When contacting a manufacturer's regional office, have on hand the year, make, model, and VIN. The addresses and phone numbers for domestic manufacturer national and regional offices are listed in Appendix A; for foreign manufacturers, they are listed in Appendix B.

Automotive Recall: More Than a Trip Down Memory Lane

Recall campaigns are either initiated voluntarily by the manufacturer or ordered by the federal government. Mandatory recall campaigns are associated with either emissions or safety defects. The NHTSA oversees vehicle safety standards, and the U.S. Environmental Protection Agency (EPA) monitors emissions-control compliance.

The Department of Transportation (DOT) established the NHTSA in 1966. Since its inception, the NHTSA and automotive recalls have been a political hotbed. From time to time, a manufacturer belittles the importance of a suggested recall; the federal government, in turn, sometimes complains of manufacturer obstruction; and consumers deride recalls that take years before finally being enforced.

Recalls are costly. In the wakes of the infamous X-car and passenger diesel engines, Roger B. Smith, chairman of General Motors, said that in 1982 the company spent $33 million on recalls. Recalls also spawn numerous automotive liability suits. In 1983, the Ford Motor Company estimated product lawsuit claims totaling more than $7.9 billion. Automotive liability has become a lucrative practice. In 1978, there were 8 jury verdicts of more than $1 million; by 1981, the number had soared to 30.

Recalls also tarnish the corporate image. They can shake a consumer's confidence in a manufacturer for years to come and can cause declines in both sales and investor funds. For both profit and prestige, recall can be a four-letter word.

Safety Recalls

If a safety defect is discovered, the manufacturer must notify the vehicle owners, dealerships, distributors, and the NHTSA; the NHTSA is responsible for monitoring corrective action. Compliance must be within the guidelines of Federal Motor Vehicle Standards, which sets minimum performance levels for vehicle safety components—brakes, tires, and lighting, for example. It also regulates items such as safety belts, child restraints, energy-absorbing steering columns, and motorcycle helmets.

Generally, a safety-related defect is a problem that exists in a vehicle or item of vehicle equipment, is common to a group of vehicles of the same design or manufacture, and poses an unreasonable risk to safety.

Once a recall campaign begins, owners are notified by first-class mail that they can get their vehicles fixed free of charge at the dealership. (The law gives the manufacturer three options for correcting the defect: repair, replacement, or refund. Obviously, vehicle manufacturers choose the repair option.) In the recall notice, the manufacturer must explain the potential hazards a defect may pose to consumer safety. Names of vehicle owners are obtained from state motor vehicle offices.

The statute of limitations for *initiating* the recall of a vehicle is 8 years. Beyond that point, if the government or manufacturer discovers a safety defect, the manufacturer must make that fact public, but the manufacturer does not have any legal responsibility to warranty the repair of the defective part or component. If you buy a used car, however, and discover that a recall notice was never answered by a previous owner, the vehicle is still eligible for the repair even if it is more than 8 years old. In other words, recall provisions initiated before the 8-year statute of limitations remain in effect indefinitely.

If you want to find out whether or not a recall is still in effect on a vehicle you currently own, start with an affiliated dealership; many have computerized referral files linked to a national data base. (For example, the Ford Motor Company has OASIS, the on-line automotive service information system.) You will need to supply the make, model, and year of the vehicle along with the VIN. If the dealership cannot help you, contact the manufacturer's regional office nearest you (Appendixes A and B), or you can contact the NHTSA directly:

Office of Defects Investigation (NEF-10)
National Highway Traffic Safety Administration
Department of Transportation
400 Seventh Street SW/Room 5326
Washington, D.C. 20590
(800) 424-9393; within the 202 area code, call 426-0123
Hearing-impaired, call (800) 424-9153; within the 202 area code, call 755-8919
(Spanish-speaking operators are also on duty.)

If you believe that you have an automotive safety problem, contact the NHTSA at the above address. When you report a safety-related problem, you will be asked your name and address and will be mailed a preaddressed postage-paid questionnaire that asks for information needed by the technical staff of the NHTSA (see Fig. 7-3). Upon receipt of the questionnaire, the agency will evaluate the information and will check your description of the defect. If the problem you report is already under investigation, your complaint will be added to the case file. When the agency receives similar reports from a number of people, an engineer begins an investigation. If you describe a problem that is unique to your vehicle or a problem for which no failure trend is yet apparent, your report is placed in a computerized complaint-retrieval file. These cases are reviewed periodically, and if several reports are received describing

Form Approved: O.M.B. No. 2127-0008

US Department of Transportation **National Highway Traffic Safety Administration**	VEHICLE OWNER'S QUESTIONNAIRE	The Privacy Act of 1974 Public Law 93-579 This information is requested pursuant to authority vested in the National Highway Traffic Safety Act and subsequent amendments. You are under no obligation to respond to this questionnaire. Your response may be used to assist the NHTSA in determining whether a manufacturer should take appropriate action to correct a defect. If the NHTSA proceeds with administrative enforcement or litigation against a manufacturer, your response, or a statistical summary thereof, may be used in support of the agency's action.

FOR HQ USE ONLY

ODI NO.	HL NO.

OWNER

LAST NAME	FIRST NAME & MIDDLE INITIAL	TELEPHONE NO. *(Area Code)* Work – Home –

STREET ADDRESS	CITY	STATE	ZIP CODE

VEHICLE INFORMATION

VEHICLE MAKE & MODEL	MODEL YEAR	BODY STYLE	VEHICLE IDENTIFICATION NO.

ENGINE SIZE (CID/CC/L) _____ ☐ FUEL INJECTION ☐ GAS ☐ DIESEL	MILEAGE	DATE PURCHASED _____ ☐ NEW ☐ USED	DEALER'S NAME AND ADDRESS	AIR CONDITIONED ☐ Yes ☐ No

VEHICLE SPEED AT FAILURE _____ ☐ Parked	NO. CYLINDERS _____	POWER STEERING ☐ Yes ☐ No	POWER BRAKES ☐ Yes ☐ No	TRANSMISSION ☐ MANUAL *(Speed)* ☐ 3 ☐ 4 ☐ 5 ☐ AUTOMATIC TYPE _____

FAILED COMPONENT(S)/PART(S) INFORMATION

COMPONENT/PART NAME(S)	LOCATION ☐ Left ☐ Right ☐ Front ☐ Rear	FAILED PART(S) ☐ ORIGINAL ☐ REPLACEMENT	MILEAGE(S) AT FAILURE(S)	NO. OF FAILURES

DATE(S) OF FAILURE(S)	DESCRIPTION OF FAILURE(S)

FAILED TIRE INFORMATION

MANUFACTURER	TIRE NAME	SIZE	TYPE FAILURE

CONSTRUCTION ☐ Belted ☐ Bias ☐ Radial	FAILED TIRE ☐ Original ☐ Replacement	BELT MATERIAL ☐ Steel ☐ Fiberglass ☐ Aramid ☐ Rayon	LOCATION ☐ Right Front ☐ Right Rear ☐ Left Front ☐ Left Rear ☐ Spare	DOT IDENTIFICATION NO. *

*The identification number consists of about ten letters and numerals following the letters DOT usually located near the rim flange on the side opposite the whitewall or on either side of a blackwall tire.

APPLICABLE ACCIDENT INFORMATION

ACCIDENT ☐ Yes ☐ No	NO. INJURIES	NO. FATALITIES	

DESCRIPTION OF ACCIDENT

SIGNATURE OF OWNER	DATE

HS Form **350** (Rev. 3/84)

Fig. 7-3 If you believe that your vehicle has a safety defect, you should report it to the National Highway Traffic Safety Administration (NHTSA). The NHTSA will then send you the above form from which it will further investigate your complaint. (*Source: NHTSA.*)

the same problem, the agency begins an investigation to see if there is a potential safety defect.

A copy of your questionnaire is forwarded to the manufacturer of the vehicle, together with a request for the manufacturer to investigate the problem. After an investigation by the NHTSA, if the problem is judged to have widespread potential as a safety defect, a formal investigation is begun. The manufacturer is notified, and the public is generally alerted via press releases. If the formal investigation bears out a potential safety defect, the manufacturer and any other interested parties meet publicly to present additional data and views. If the conclusion still indicates that a problem exists, and if the manufacturer refuses to recall affected vehicles, the NHTSA can order the recall. The manufacturer is given the opportunity to appeal the decision, though, before enforcement proceeds.

Emissions-Control Recalls

The EPA began surveillance of vehicle emissions-control standards in 1971. The agency issues recalls when necessary to ensure compliance with exhaust and evaporative emissions standards. As with safety recalls, repairs are to be completed at the manufacturer's expense.

Surveillance programs include tests of in-use vehicles. These are randomly selected vehicles that have similar engine operating characteristics and emissions-control systems and are of like make and model year. Testing is generally done with vehicles 2 to 3 years old. The EPA selects a target group of vehicles and then randomly solicits an in-use sample from private citizens. Letters are mailed explaining the program, and all participation is voluntary. If an individual chooses to participate, that person is usually provided with a loaner vehicle in addition to the free maintenance work that will be performed on the vehicle. The sample vehicles are then set to manufacturer specifications and tested for emissions levels. The results of such testing determine whether or not the EPA will recommend a recall. Usually a manufacturer representative also takes part in these tests.

Emissions standards become more stringent each year. Late-model vehicles are expected to meet more strict emissions standards than those in earlier years, thus improving air quality with each passing year. In addition, manufacturers are also required to meet corporate average fleet economy (CAFE) standards. CAFE standards determine vehicle gas mileage for vehicles under 6000 pounds. These standards are set to improve fuel economy year by year on an across-the-board basis for all vehicles manufactured by a given company. Recalls are never imposed, however, to enforce CAFE standards; instead, fines adding up to millions of dollars can be imposed. In 1985, when all major domestic automakers except Chrysler failed the CAFE standards, the determining formula was refigured, lowering the 1985 requirement by about 1½ gallon per mile.

Answering a Recall Notice

Federal authorities estimate that half of all recall notices go unanswered. Some blame the ambiguous and deliberately confusing language sometimes found in the letters manufacturers issue to announce a recall campaign. One such notice read "Loss of front braking at a time when minimum stopping distance is required could result in vehicle crash without prior warning." Or, translated, your front brakes might give out during sudden stops. The translated version imparts a sense of urgency, which the original copy downplays.

A survey conducted in 1980 for the NHTSA showed that the most common explanations consumers give for not responding to recall notices were (1) they didn't have time, (2) they found it to be inconvenient, (3) they were too lazy, (4) they didn't think there was anything wrong with the vehicle, and (5) they didn't believe the recall was important.

The granddaddy of all recalls was the 1978 government-mandated recall of Firestone steel-belted radial 500 tires for a tread-separation problem. Only about 40 percent of the 14.5 million units affected were returned in answer to the campaign. Figures like these are difficult to interpret. I owned a car with a set of those tires, but because I was not the original purchaser of the tires, I never knew about the recall. That is until the tires, true to form, started to blow apart one by one. This was indeed a dangerous situation, and it was not until I went to a Firestone outlet to question the problem that I learned of the recall. *In short, it's not a bad idea to call the NHTSA or the EPA just to find out if there is a recall that affects your vehicle* (and the safety of those who use the car).

In general, recall announcements can be confusing for several reasons. Some owners first learn of a recall through media announcements, but it may be up to a month or so before the actual recall notice arrives in the mail. Also, parts need to be distributed to the dealerships, and mailing lists need to be compiled. Then again, not all vehicles of the same make and model year are always involved in the same recall. Sometimes only vehicles manufactured at certain plants or those assembled with components from a certain manufacturer are affected by a recall. In these cases, if you do not receive a notice and are concerned, you can check with an affiliated dealership. This is especially advisable in cases of second or later vehicle owners. Although manufacturers use Department of Motor Vehicle records for the mailings, these lists are not always up to date. And in the event of a voluntary recall, the manufacturer may use owner mailing lists only.

If your vehicle is involved in a recall, to limit inconvenience, call the dealership ahead of time to check on their work load. Not only do the recall repairs themselves add to the daily work schedule, but many recall respondents decide to catch up on maintenance and other repair needs as well. Consequently, not all dealers consider recalls an inconvenience. Said one, "Sure, we feel bad if a customer has problems with a car we sold them, but we find the recalls can mean extra business for us." Added another, "Some people don't even change their oil. So when there's a recall, suddenly there's a tremendous generation of service traffic because people who wouldn't normally get their cars checked bring them in. It's a great opportunity for our service department to do some extra work." Some dealers even end up selling cars to recall respondents, all of which adds another dimension to being on the safe side: answer recall notices promptly, but when doing so, don't wander into any new-car showrooms.

Appendixes

Appendix A Domestic Automotive Manufacturers

Appendix B Foreign Automotive Manufacturers: U.S. Locations

Appendix C Better Business Bureau Locations

Appendix D AUTOCAP Locations

Appendix E Consumer Automotive Manufacturers and Suppliers, Agencies, and Organizations

Appendix F Federal Government Automotive Agencies

The information in the following appendixes may be out of date by publication date and should be checked against local telephone directories.

appendix A

Domestic Automotive Manufacturers

American Motors Corporation

National Office

Manager, Owner Services
American Motors Sales Corporation
14250 Plymouth Rd.
Detroit, MI 48232
(313) 493-2341

Zone Offices

Atlanta Zone Office
1640 Stone Ridge Dr.
P.O. Box 718
Stone Mountain, GA 30086
(404) 491-3233, 3265

Boston Zone Office
420 Providence Hwy.
Westwood, MA 02090
(617) 392-5633

Chicago Zone Office
1600 Busse Rd.
Elk Grove Village, IL 60007
(312) 364-8601, 8605

Dallas Zone Office
7900 Embassador Row
P.O. Box 47326
Dallas, TX 75247
(214) 689-9734

Denver Zone Office
5005 Lima St.
Denver, CO 80239
(303) 373-5800

Detroit Zone Office
24100 Southfield Rd.
Suite 100
Southfield, MI 48075
(313) 827-7870

Kansas City Zone Office
8915 Quivira Rd.
Overland Park, KS 66215
Mail: P.O. Box 283
Shawnee Mission, KS 66201
(913) 677-7850

Los Angeles Zone Office
23046 Avenida De la Carlotta
P.O. Box 30710
Laguna Hills, CA 92654
(714) 855-3533, 3534

New York Zone Office
444 Saw Mill River Rd.
P.O. Box 500
Elmsford, NY 10523
(914) 997-2823, 2824

Philadelphia Zone Office
1450 Grandview Ave.
West Deptford, NJ 08096
Mail: Mid-Atlantic Industrial Park
P.O. Box 1000
Woodbury, NJ 08096
(609) 853-4457, 4458

Pittsburgh Zone Office
750 Commonwealth Dr.
Warrendale, PA 15086
(412) 776-7254

Washington Zone Office
1751 Old Meadow Rd.
P.O. Box Drawer AA
Westgate Research Park
McLean, VA 22102
(703) 790-3031, 3032

Chrysler Corporation

National Zone Office

National Owner Relations Manager
Chrysler Corp.
P.O. Box 1718
Detroit, MI 48288-1718
(313) 956-5970

Zone Offices

Los Angeles Zone Office
P.O. Box 3019-C
Anaheim, CA 92803-3019-C
(714) 870-4000

Pleasanton Zone Office
P.O. Box 5009
Pleasanton, CA 94566-0509
(415) 484-0646

Florida Zone Office
P.O. Box 13428
Orlando, FL 32809
(305) 352-7402

Georgia Zone Office
1100 Circle 75 Pkwy.
Suite 850
Atlanta, GA 30339
(404) 953-8880

Illinois Zone Office
P.O. Box 1102
Itasca, IL 60143-1102
(312) 773-7780

Kansas Zone Office
6901 W. 63rd St.
Suite 205
Overland Park, KS 66202
(913) 831-6670

Louisiana Zone Office
P.O. Box 73168
Metairie, LA 70033
(504) 455-1433

Maryland Zone Office
P.O. Box 3130
Landover Hills, MD 20784
(301) 464-4040

Massachusetts Zone Office
P.O. Box 50
Natick, MA 01760
(617) 655-2810

Denver Zone Office
P.O. Box 39006
Denver, CO 80239
(303) 371-1330

Michigan Zone Office
P.O. Box 3000
Troy, MI 48007-3000
(313) 879-3600

Minnesota Zone Office
P.O. Box 1231
Minneapolis, MN 55440
(612) 553-2546

Missouri Zone Office
P.O. Box 278
Hazelwood, MO 63042
(314) 895-0731

Phoenix Zone Office
P.O. Box 35666
Phoenix, AZ 85069
(602) 866-6090

Syracuse Zone Office
P.O. Box 1207
Syracuse, NY 13201-1207
(315) 432-4041

Tappan Zone Office
P.O. Box 500
Tappan, NY 10983
(914) 359-0110

Ohio Zone Office
P.O. Box 41902
Beaverton, OR 97075
(503) 641-4170

Pittsburgh Zone Office
Box 4599
Pittsburgh, PA 15205
(412) 777-3600

Wayne Zone Office
3 Great Valley Pkwy., E.
Suite 201
Malvern, PA 19355
(215) 251-2990

Tennessee Zone Office
P.O. Box 18008
Memphis, TN 38118-0008
(901) 365-4701

Dallas Zone Office
P.O. Box 110162
Carrollton, TX 75011
(214) 242-8462

Houston Zone Office
363 North Belt
Suite 590
Houston, TX 77060
(713) 820-7062

Ford Motor Company

National toll-free number for customer assistance: (800) 241-8450

National Office

Manager, Owner Relations Operations
Ford Motor Company
P.O. Box 1805
Dearborn, MI 48121
(313) 337-6950

District Offices

Atlanta District Office
P.O. Box 105003
Atlanta, GA 30348-5003
(404) 763-6440

Boston District Office
Maine, New Hampshire, Vermont,
 Massachusetts, Rhode Island,
 Connecticut
P.O. Box 587
Waltham, MA 02254-0244
(617) 895-1000

Buffalo District Office
Upper and Western New York,
 Northern Pennsylvania
P.O. Box 220307
Charlotte, NC 28222-0307
(704) 554-4501

Charlotte District Office
North Carolina, South Carolina
P.O. Box 220307
Charlotte, NC 28222-0307
(704) 554-4501

Chicago District Office
Northeastern Illinois,
 Northwestern Indiana
2225 W. North Ave.
Melrose Park, IL 60160-1191
(312) 681-6500

Cincinnati District Office
Southern Ohio, Southern West
 Virginia, Eastern Kentucky,
 Southern Indiana
P.O. Box 6308
Cincinnati, OH 45215-6308
(513) 563-3120

Cleveland District Office
Eastern and Northwestern Ohio,
 Northwestern Pennsylvania
P.O. Box 41035
Brecksville, OH 44141-0035
(216) 526-6900

Dallas District Office
Northern Texas, Oklahoma
P.O. Box 110037
Carrollton, TX 75001-0037
(214) 323-9900

Denver District Office
Colorado, Wyoming, Western
 Nebraska, Southwestern South
 Dakota, Utah, Southern Idaho,
 Northeastern Nevada,
 Southeastern Oregon, Montana
P.O. Box 5588
Terminal Annex
Denver, CO 80217-5588
(303) 291-4610

Detroit District Office
Michigan (except Upper Peninsula)
P.O. Box 775
Wixom, MI 48096-0775
(313) 337-9900

Houston District Office
South Texas
P.O. Box 827
Houston, TX 77001-0827
(713) 680-4260

Indianapolis District Office
Central and Western Indiana
Southeastern Illinois
P.O. Box 19448
Indianapolis, IN 46219-0448
(317) 353-8251

Jacksonville District Office
Florida, South Georgia
P.O. Box Y
Jacksonville, FL 32203-0576
(904) 783-7777

Kansas City District Office
Western Missouri, Kansas
P.O. Box 501
Shawnee Mission, KS 66201
(913) 888-0141

Los Angeles District Office
Southern California, SE Nevada
P.O. Box 4680-P
Anaheim, CA 92803-4680
(714) 520-8300

Louisville District Office
Western Kentucky, Central
Tennessee, South Central Indiana
P.O. Box 32080
Louisville, KY 40232-2080
(502) 456-3700

Memphis District Office
Arkansas, Western Tennessee,
Northern Mississippi,
Northwestern Alabama
P.O. Box 8347, Hollywood Station
Memphis, TN 38108-0347
(901) 454-7270

Milwaukee District Office
Wisconsin (except Northwestern
corner), Michigan (Upper
Peninsula)
16535 Bluemound Rd.
Suite 350
P.O. Box 267
Brookfield, WI 53005-0985
(414) 785-3100

New York District Office
Northern New Jersey, Eastern
New York, Southeastern New
York, Long Island
U.S. Highway 46
Teterboro, NJ 07608-1177
(201) 288-9421

New Orleans District Office
Southern Mississippi, Louisiana,
Southwestern Alabama
P.O. Box 8630
Metairie, LA 70011-8630
(504) 454-6764

Omaha District Office
Western Iowa, Central Eastern
Nebraska, Southeastern South
Dakota
P.O. Box 37433
Millard Station
Omaha, NE 68137-7433
(402) 334-4750

Philadelphia District Office
Northeastern Pennsylvania,
Southeastern Pennsylvania,
Southern New Jersey, Delaware
P.O. Box 816
Pennsauken, NJ 08110-0816
(609) 662-8021

Phoenix District Office
Arizona, New Mexico, Western
Texas
P.O. Box 844
Phoenix, AZ 85001-0844
(602) 266-8500

Pittsburgh District Office
Southwestern Pennsylvania,
   Northern West Virginia,
   Southeastern Ohio
Manor Oak Two
Suite 910
1910 Cochran Rd.
Pittsburgh, PA 15243-1254
(412) 928-2939

St. Louis District Office
Southern Illinois, Eastern Missouri
P.O. Box 24575
St. Louis, MO 63141-0575
(314) 569-4455

San Jose District Office
Northern California, Southern
   Oregon, Western Nevada,
   Hawaii
P.O. Box 4002
Milpitas, CA 95035-2002
(408) 262-9110

Seattle District Office
Alaska, Washington, Northern
   Idaho, Northern Oregon
10604 N.E. 38th Pl.
Suite 215
Kirkland, WA 98033-7995
(206) 244-5800

Twin Cities District Office
Northwestern Wisconsin,
   Minnesota, North Dakota,
   Northern South Dakota
P.O. Box 9303
Minneapolis, MN 55440-9303
(612) 887-4290

Washington District Office
Maryland, Northern Virginia,
   Southern Virginia, Eastern West
   Virginia
P.O. Box 703A
8051 Gatehouse Rd.
Falls Church, VA 22046-1503
(703) 698-1900

General Motors Corporation

Buick—Cadillac—Chevrolet—Pontiac—Oldsmobile—GMC Truck & Coach

Buick Division

Central Office

Buick Motor Division
Customer Assistance Center
902 East Hamilton Ave.
Flint, MI 48550
(800) 521-7300

Buick Division Zone Offices

Atlanta Zone Office
5730 Glenridge Dr.
Atlanta, GA 30328
Mail: P.O. Box 50309
Atlanta, GA 30302
(800) 521-7300

Boston Zone Office
1776 Heritage Dr.
North Quincy, MA 02171
(800) 521-7300

Buffalo Zone Office
445 Evans St.
Williamsville, NY 14221
(716) 633-1200

Charlotte Zone Office
2100 Rexford Rd., Suite 100
Charlotte, NC 28211
Mail: P.O. Box 11937
Charlotte, NC 28209
(800) 521-7300

Chicago Zone Office
475 Alexis R. Shuman Blvd.
Mail: P.O. Box 3001
Naperville, IL 60566
(800) 521-7300

Cincinnati Zone Office
155 Tri-County Pkwy.
Mail: P.O. Box 465611
Cincinnati, OH 45256
(800) 521-7300

Cleveland Zone Office
Westgate Plaza Bldg., Suite 405
20325 Center Ridge Rd.
Rocky River, OH 44116
(800) 521-7300

Dallas Zone Office
130 E. Carpenter Freeway
General Motors Bldg., Suite 175
Irving, TX 75062
Mail: P.O. Box 660116
Dallas, TX 75266
(800) 521-7300

Denver Zone Office
Writers' Three
Suite 600
1780 S. Bellaire St.
Denver, CO 80222
(800) 521-7300

Detroit Zone Office
3031 W. Grand Blvd.
Suite 505 New Center Ave.
Detroit, MI 48232
Mail: P.O. Box 33120
Detroit, MI 48232
(800) 521-7300

Houston Zone Office
6535 S.W. Freeway
Houston, TX 77074
Mail: P.O. Box 183
Houston, TX 77001
(800) 521-7300

Jacksonville Zone Office
Center Bldg., Suite 115A
7825 Baymeadows Way
Jacksonville, FL 32216
(800) 521-7300

Kansas City Zone Office
10800 Farley
Suite 270, GM Bldg.
Overland Park, KS 66210
Mail: P.O. Box 23342
Kansas City, MO 64141
(800) 521-7300

Los Angeles Zone Office
2625 Towngate Rd., Suite 300
Westlake Village, CA 91361
Mail: P.O. Box 5003
Westlake Village, CA 91359
(800) 521-7300

Memphis Zone Office
5865 Ridgeway Pkwy.
Suite 103
Memphis, TN 38119
(800) 521-7300

Milwaukee Zone Office
250 N. Sunny Slope Rd.
Suite 210
P.O. Box 950
Brookfield, WI 53005
(800) 521-7300

Minneapolis Zone Office
7600 Parklawn Ave.
Suite 408
Edina, MN 55435
(612) 830-4121

Newark Zone Office
9 Sylvan Way
P.O. Box 3002
Parsippany, NJ 07054
(800) 521-7300

New York Zone Office
5 Corporate Park Dr.
White Plains, NY 10604
(800) 521-7300

Oklahoma City Zone Office
Northwest Office Center
4334 N.W. Expressway
Suite 222
Oklahoma City, OK 73126
(800) 521-7300

Philadelphia Zone Office
851 Duportail Rd.
P.O. Box 9005
Wayne, PA 19087
(800) 521-7300

Pittsburgh Zone Office
Cliff Mine Rd.
Suite 450
P.O. Box 2892
Pittsburgh, PA 15230
(800) 521-7300

Portland Zone Office
10700 S.W. Beaverton Hwy.
Suite 545
Beaverton, OR 97005
Mail: P.O. Box 1930
Portland, OR 97075
(800) 521-7300

St. Louis Zone Office
727 Craig Rd.
P.O. Box 27303
St. Louis, MO 63141
(800) 521-7300

San Francisco Zone Office
39465 Paseo Padre Pkwy.
GM Bldg.
Suite 2900
Fremont, CA 94538
Mail: P.O. Box 23500
Oakland, CA 94623
(800) 521-7300

Washington Zone Office
1395 Piccard Dr.
P.O. Box 6040
Rockville, MD 20850
(800) 521-7300

Cadillac Division

Home Office

Cadillac Motor Car Division
Consumer Relations
2860 Clark St.
Detroit, MI 48232
(313) 544-5536

Cadillac Division Zone Offices

Atlanta Zone Office
5730 Glenridge Dr.
Atlanta, GA 30328
Mail: P.O. Box 50256
Atlanta, GA 30302
(404) 257-3600

Boston Zone Office
Wellesley Office Park
45 William St.
Wellesley, MA 02181
(617) 237-9000

Chicago Zone Office
475 Alexis R. Shuman Blvd.
Naperville, IL 60566
Mail: P.O. Box 3002
Naperville, IL 60566
(312) 961-6858

Cincinnati Zone Office
155 Trip-County Pkwy.
Cincinnati, OH 45246
Mail: P.O. Box 46530
Cincinnati, OH 45246
(513) 841-5837

Cleveland Zone Office
Two Commerce Park Square
23200 Chagrin Blvd.
Suite 2-108
Beachwood, OH 44112
(216) 265-5124

Dallas Zone Office
130 E. Carpenter Freeway
Irving, TX 75062
Mail: P.O. Box 660118
Dallas, TX 75266-0118
(214) 659-5125

Denver Zone Office
1780 S. Bellaire St.
Suite 401
Denver, CO 80222
(303) 398-7065

Detroit Zone Office
3031 W. Grand Blvd.
New Center One, Suite 425
Detroit, MI 48202
Mail: P.O. Box 33109
Detroit, MI 48232
(313) 556-2410

Jacksonville Zone Office
Deerwood Center
7901 Baymeadows Way
Jacksonville, FL 32216
(904) 737-4000

Kansas City Zone Office
10800 Farley
Overland Park, KS 66210
Mail: P.O. Box 23343
Kansas City, MO 64141
(913) 383-4070

Los Angeles Zone Office
2659 Townsgate Rd.
Suite 132
Westlake Village, CA 91361
Mail: P.O. Box 5018
Westlake Village, CA 91359
(213) 991-3130

Memphis Zone Office
1755 Lynnfield Rd.
Suite 207
Memphis, TN 38119
Mail: P.O. Box 171803
Memphis, TN 38117
(901) 682-7893

Minneapolis Zone Office
7701 Normandale Road-Edina
Minneapolis, MN 55435
(612) 830-4141

New York Zone Office
9 Sylvan Way
Parsippany, NJ 07054
Mail: P.O. Box 3003
Parsippany, NJ 07054
(201) 993-4090

Philadelphia Zone Office
851 Duportail Rd.
Wayne, PA
Mail: P.O. Box 9010
Wayne, PA 19087
(215) 296-6691 or 296-6692

Portland Zone Office
Park Plaza West
Bldg. 3, Suite 595
10700 S.W. Beaverton-Hillsdale Hwy.
Beaverton, OR 97005
Mail: P.O. Box 14667
Portland, OR 97214
(503) 641-8373

San Francisco Zone Office
39465 Paseo Padre Pkwy.
Suite 2300
Freemont, CA 94538
Mail: P.O. Box 23850
Oakland, CA 94623
(415) 498-5252

Washington Zone Office
1395 Piccard Dr.
Suite 260
Rockville, MD 20850
Mail: P.O. Box 6050
Rockville, MD 20850
(301) 258-1424

Chevrolet Division

Central Office

Chevrolet Motor Division
Customer Assistance Division
Chevrolet Central Office
Warren, MI 48090
(313) 492-5500

Chevrolet Division Zone Offices

Atlanta Zone Office
GM Bldg.
5730 Glenridge Dr., N.E.
Atlanta, GA 30328
Mail: P.O. Box 50282
Atlanta, GA 30302
(404) 257-3962

Birmingham Zone Office
3490 Independence Dr.
Homewood, AL 35259
Mail: P.O. Box 59000
Birmingham, AL 35259-9000
(205) 870-5320

Boston Zone Office
505 Blue Hill Dr.
Westwood, MA 02090
(800) 222-1020

Charlotte Zone Office
6000 Monroe Rd.
Charlotte, NC 28212
Mail: P.O. Box 30548
Charlotte, NC 28230
(704) 336-5116

Chicago Zone Office
475 Alexis R. Shuman Blvd.
Naperville, IL 60566
Mail: P.O. Box 3005
Naperville, IL 60566
(312) 961-6380

Cincinnati Zone Office
144 Tri-County Pkwy.
Cincinnati, OH 45246-5615
Mail: P.O. Box 465615
Cincinnati, OH 45246-5615
(513) 841-5871

Dallas Zone Office
130 E. Carpenter Freeway
Irving, TX 75062
Mail: P.O. Box 660115
Dallas, TX 75266-0115
(214) 659-5400

Denver Zone Office
5460 S. Quebec St.
Suite 330
Englewood, CO 80111
Mail: P.O. Box 5520
Denver, CO 80217-5520
(303) 930-5710

Detroit Zone Office
3031 W. Grand Blvd.
Detroit, MI 48202
Mail: P.O. Box 33108
Detroit, MI 48232
(313) 974-0550

Houston Zone Office
13101 N.W. Freeway
Suite 101
Houston, TX 77040
Mail: P.O. Box 40911
Houston, TX 77240
(713) 460-7300

Jacksonville Zone Office
6622 Southpoint Dr., S.
Suite 200
Jacksonville, FL 32216
Mail: P.O. Box 10027
Jacksonville, FL 32207
(904) 739-7739

Kansas City Zone Office
10800 Farley
Suite 100
Overland Park, KS 66210
Mail: P.O. Box 419348
Kansas City, MO 64141
(913) 451-4300

Los Angeles Zone Office
515 Marin St.
Suite 101
Thousand Oaks, CA 91360
Mail: P.O. Box 5053
Thousand Oaks, CA 91359-5053
(213) 393-9356

Memphis Zone Office
866 Ridgewood Loop Rd.
Memphis, TN 38119
Mail: P.O. Box 171802
Memphis, TN 38117
(901) 756-3370

Minneapolis Zone Office
7600 Metro Blvd.
Edina, MN 55435
Mail: P.O. Box 509
Minneapolis, MN 55440
(612) 830-4000

New Orleans Zone Office
3545 I-10 Service Rd.
Metairie, LA 70002
Mail: P.O. Box 53346
New Orleans, LA 70153
(504) 456-3900

Oakland Zone Office
39465 Paseo Padre Pkwy.
Fremont, CA 94538
Mail: P.O. Box 23550
Oakland, CA 94623
(415) 498-5060

Philadelphia Zone Office
851 Duportail Rd.
Wayne, PA 19087
Mail: P.O. Box 9015
Wayne, PA 19087
(215) 296-6610

Pittsburgh Zone Office
Two Penn Center-West
Suite 200
Pittsburgh, PA 15276
Mail: P.O. Box 2000
Carnegie, PA 15106-2000
(412) 928-5100

Portland Zone Office
10300 S.W. Greenburg Rd., Suite 500
Portland, OR 97223
Mail: P.O. Box 5818
Portland, OR 97228-5818
(503) 293-5000

St. Louis Zone Office
83 Progress Pkwy.
Maryland Heights, MO 63043
(314) 469-8600

Syracuse Zone Office
Salina Meadows Pkwy., Suite 100
Syracuse, NY 13212
Mail: P.O. Box 4907
Syracuse, NY 13221
(315) 477-1600

Tarrytown Zone Office
2500 Westchester Ave.
Purchase, NY 10577
Mail: P.O. Box 892
Purchase, NY 10577-0892
(914) 251-5100

Washington Zone Office
1395 Piccard Dr.
Rockville, MD 20859
Mail: P.O. Box 6070
Rockville, MD 20850
(301) 258-1430

Oldsmobile Division

Central Office

Oldsmobile Division
Customer Service Dept.
920 Townsend St.
Lansing, MI 48921
Mail: P.O. Box 30095
Lansing, MI 48909
(517) 377-5546

Oldsmobile Division Zone Offices

Atlanta Zone Office
5730 Glenridge Dr.
Atlanta, GA 30328
Mail: P.O. Box 50335
Atlanta, GA 30302
(404) 257-3880

Boston Zone Office
Point West Office Center
3 Speen St., Suite 250
Framingham, MA 01701
(617) 872-8553

Buffalo Zone Office
5820 Main St.
Williamsville, NY 14221
(716) 633-2900

Charlotte Zone Office
2101 E. Rexford Rd.
The Esplanade
Suite 123
Charlotte, NC 28211
(704) 336-5126

Chicago Zone Office
475 Alexis R. Shuman Blvd.
Naperville, IL 60566
Mail: P.O. Box 3008
Naperville, IL 60566
(312) 961-6815

Cincinnati Zone Office
155 Tri-County Pkwy.
Cincinnati, OH 45246
Mail: P.O. Box 465614
Cincinnati, OH 45246
(513) 841-5790

Cleveland Zone Office
Three King James S.
24600 Center Ridge Rd.
Westlake, OH 44145
(216) 835-1700

Dallas Zone Office
130 E. Carpenter Freeway
Irving, TX 75062
Mail: P.O. Box 660119
Dallas, TX 75266-0119
(214) 659-5100

Denver Zone Office
1450 South Havana St.
Suite 720
Aurora, CO 80012
(303) 398-7135

Detroit Zone Office
3031 W. Grand Blvd.
New Center One
Suite 401
Detroit, MI 48202
Mail: P.O. Box 33111
Detroit, MI 48232
(313) 556-2389

Houston Zone Office
521 North Belt
Suite 540
Houston, TX 77060
(713) 931-6053

Indianapolis Zone Office
9011 N. Meridian
Suite 210
Waterplace Park
Indianapolis, IN 46240
Mail: P.O. Box 40369
Indianapolis, IN 46240
(317) 269-5890

Jacksonville Zone Office
Gulf Life Tower, Suite 1742
Jacksonville, FL 322076
(904) 398-6401

Kansas City Zone Office
10800 Farley, Suite 370
Overland Park, KS 66210
Mail: P.O. Box 23345
Kansas City, MO 64141
(913) 383-4213

Los Angeles Zone Office
2277 Townsgate Rd.
Suite 205
Westlake Village, CA 91361
Mail: P.O. Box 5070
Thousand Oaks, CA 91359
(818) 706-1122
(805) 496-4888

Memphis Zone Office
Clark Tower Bldg.
5100 Poplar Ave., Suite 1210
Memphis, TN 38137
(901) 767-4143

Milwaukee Zone Office
Mayfair Plaza
2421 N. Mayfair Rd.
Milwaukee, WI 53226
(414) 258-8898

Minneapolis Zone Office
Northland Executive Office Center
3500 W. 80th St.
Suite 540
Minneapolis, MN 55431
(612) 830-4232

Oklahoma City Zone Office
Oklahoma Mortgage Bldg.
5100 North Brookline
Suite 200
Oklahoma City, OK 73112
Mail: P.O. Box 26748
Oklahoma City, OK 73126
(405) 943-9566

Omaha Zone Office
7171 Mercy Rd., Suite 150
Omaha, NE 68106
(402) 399-5488

Philadelphia Zone Office
851 Duportail Rd.
Wayne, PA 19087
Mail: P.O. Box 9020
Wayne, PA 19087
(215) 296-6555

Pittsburgh Zone Office
One Penn Center, W.
Suite 310
Pittsburgh, PA 15276
(412) 928-5200

Portland Zone Office
Park Plaza W.
Bldg. 3, Suite 650
10700 S.W. Beaverton-Hillsdale Hwy.
Beaverton, OR 97005
(503) 641-8370

St. Louis Zone Office
Mark Twain Bank Bldg.
Suite 300
16100 Chesterfield Village Pkwy.
Chesterfield, MO 63017
Mail: P.O. Box 1005
Chesterfield, MO 63017
(314) 532-7040

San Francisco Zone Office
General Motors Bldg.
Suite 3500
39465 Paseo Padre Pkwy.
Fremont, CA 94538
Mail: P.O. Box 24470
Oakland, CA 94623
(415) 498-5111

Tarrytown Zone Office
555 White Plains Rd.
Tarrytown, NY 10591
(914) 631-6336

Washington D.C. Zone Office
1395 Piccard Dr.
P.O. Box 6090
Rockville, MD 20850
(301) 258-1640

Pontiac Motor Division

Central Office

Pontiac Motor Division
Customer Service Department
One Pontiac Plaza
Pontiac, MI 48053
(313) 857-1316

Pontiac Zone Offices

Atlanta Zone Office
5730 Glenridge Dr.
Atlanta, GA 30328
Mail: P.O. Box 50303
Atlanta, GA 30302
(404) 257-3841

Boston Zone Office
45 William St.
Wellesley Office Park
Wellesley, MA 02181
(617) 237-6910

Buffalo Zone Office
150 Essjay Rd.
Williamsville, NY 14221
(716) 634-7870

Charlotte Zone Office
6525 Morrison Blvd., Suite 210
Charlotte, NC 28211
(704) 371-5220

Chicago Zone Office
475 Alexis R. Shuman Blvd.
Naperville, IL 60566
Mail: P.O. Box 3009
Naperville, IL 60566
(312) 961-6452

Cincinnati Zone Office
155 Tri-County Pkwy.
Cincinnati, OH 45246
Mail: P.O. Box 465616
Cincinnati, OH 45246
(513) 841-5805

Cleveland Zone Office
25000 Great Northern Corporate Ctr.
North Olmstead, OH 44070
(216) 265-5800

Dallas Zone Office
130 E. Carpenter Freeway
Irving, TX 75062
Mail: P.O. Box 660122
Dallas, TX 75266-0122
(214) 659-5024

Denver Zone Office
1st National Bank of Englewood
Suite 810
333 W. Hampden Ave.
Englewood, CO 80110
(303) 398-7160

Detroit Zone Office
3031 W. Grand Blvd.
New Center One
Suite 490
Detroit, MI 48202
Mail: P.O. Box 33110
Detroit, MI 48232
(313) 556-5340

Houston Zone Office
16630 Imperial Valley Dr.
Suite 115
P.O. Box 60745, AMF
Houston, TX 77205
(713) 931-7250

Jacksonville Zone Office
800 Barnett Regency Tower
9550 Regency Square Blvd.
Jacksonville, FL 32211
(904) 724-2842

Kansas City-Midwest Zone Office
10800 Farley
Overland Park, KS 66210
Mail: P.O. Box 23347
Kansas City, MO 64141
(913) 451-4310

Los Angeles Zone Office
Townsgate Executive Bldg., Ltd.
2659 Townsgate Rd., Suite 211
Westlake Village, CA 91361
Mail: P.O. Box 5015
Thousand Oaks, CA 91359
(213) 991-4310

Memphis Zone Office
5350 Poplar Ave.
Suite 220
Memphis, TN 38119
(901) 761-4720

Milwaukee Zone Office
165 Bishop's Way
Suite 142
Brookfield, WI 53005
(414) 784-0410

Minneapolis Zone Office
7600 Parklawn Ave.
Suite 300
Minneapolis, MN 55435
(612) 830-4258

Newark Zone Office
9 Sylvan Way
Parsippany, NJ 07054
Mail: P.O. Box 3005
Parsippany, NJ 07054
(201) 993-4022

New York Zone Office
555 White Plains Rd.
Tarrytown, NY 10591
(914) 332-0770

Oklahoma City Zone Office
Grand Centre Bldg.
5400 Grand Blvd.
Suite 265
Oklahoma City, OK 73112
(405) 843-2804

Philadelphia Zone Office
851 Duportail Rd.
Wayne, PA 19087
Mail: P.O. Box 9025
Wayne, PA 19087
(215) 296-6564

Pittsburgh Zone Office
Cliff Mine Rd.
Bldg. 1
Suite 350
Pittsburgh, PA 15275
Mail: P.O. Box 1012
Pittsburgh, PA 15230
(412) 928-5075

Portland-Northwest Zone Office
1 Lincoln Center
Suite 460
10300 S.W. Greenburg Rd.
Portland, OR 97223
(503) 238-7911

St. Louis Zone Office
The Plaza Tower
111 West Port Plaza
Suite 1101
St. Louis, MO 63141
(314) 895-8650

San Francisco Zone Office
39465 Paseo Padre Pkwy.
Fremont, CA 94538
Mail: P.O. Box 23090
Oakland, CA 94623
(415) 498-5157

Washington Zone Office
1395 Piccard Dr.
Rockville, MD 20850
Mail: P.O. Box 6060
Rockville, MD 20850
(301) 258-1518

GMC Truck & Coach Operation

Central Office

GMC Truck and Coach Operation
Customer Service Dept.
31 Judson St.
Pontiac, MI 48058
(313) 456-4547

GMC Truck & Coach Zone Offices

Atlanta Zone Office
5730 Glenridge Dr.
Atlanta, GA 30302
Mail: P.O. Box 50267
Atlanta, GA 30302
(404) 257-3666

Chicago Zone Office
475 Alexis R. Shuman Blvd.
Naperville, IL 60566
Mail: P.O. Box 3006
Naperville, IL 60566
(312) 961-6476

Dallas Zone Office
130 E. Carpenter Freeway
Irving, TX 75062
Mail: P.O. Box 660123
Dallas, TX 75266-0123
(214) 659-5154

Denver Zone Office
5680 S. Syracuse Circle
Suite 500
Englewood, CO 80111
(303) 398-7083

Detroit Zone Office
140 S. Saginaw
P.O. Box 456
Pontiac, MI 48056
(313) 456-3553

Houston Zone Office
363 N. Belt Bldg.
Suite 800
Houston, TX 77060
(713) 591-0804

Kansas City Zone Office
10800 Farley
Overland Park, KS 66210
Mail: P.O. Box 23346
Kansas City, MO 64141
(913) 383-4173

Los Angeles Zone Office
875 Westlake Blvd., Suite 223
Westlake Village, CA 91361
(213) 991-9234

Memphis Zone Office
3495 Lamar Ave.
Memphis, TN 38118
Mail: P.O. Box 18467
Memphis, TN 38118-0467
(901) 346-5253

Minneapolis Zone Office
3001 Broadway, N.E.
Minneapolis, MN 55413
(612) 378-3470

New York Zone Office
9 Sylvan Way
Parsippany, NY 07054
(201) 993-4065

Oakland Zone Office
39465 Paseo Padre Pkwy.
Fremont, CA 94538
Mail: P.O. Box 23510
Oakland, CA 94623
(415) 498-5236

Washington Zone Office
1395 Piccard Dr.
Rockville, MD 20850
Mail: P.O. Box 6080
Rockville, MD 20850
(301) 258-1480

appendix B

Foreign Automotive Manufacturers: U.S. Locations

Audi Division

888 W. Big Beaver
Troy, MI 48078
(313) 362-7300

Audi Northwest
Alaska, Idaho, Montana, Oregon,
Washington
5 Oaks Industrial Park, Rt. 1
Box 220 VW
(503) 645-5511

Audi Mid-America
Arkansas, Kansas, Missouri,
Nebraska
8825 Page Blvd.
St. Louis, MO 63114
(314) 429-8100

Audi Atlantic
Delaware, Maine, Maryland,
Massachusetts, New Hampshire,
North Carolina, Pennsylvania,
Rhode Island, Vermont, Virginia,
Washington, D.C., W. Virginia
9300 Georgia Palmer Hwy.
Lanham, MD 20801
(301) 459-7000

Audi Southern Region
Alabama, Florida, Georgia,
Louisiana, Mississippi,
Oklahoma, South Carolina,
Tennessee, Texas (excluding El
Paso)
1940 The Exchange
Atlanta, GA 30339
(404) 955-9000

Audi Central Region
Illinois, Indiana, Iowa, Kentucky,
Michigan, North Dakota, Ohio,
South Dakota (excluding Rapid
City), Wisconsin
420 Barclay
Lincolnshire, IL 60069
(312) 634-6000

Audi Pacific Region
Arizona, California, Colorado,
  Hawaii, Nevada, New Mexico,
  South Dakota (Rapid City),
  Texas (El Paso), Utah, Wyoming
11300 Playa
St. Culver City, CA 90230
(213) 390-8011

Audi Eastern
Connecticut, New Jersey, New
  York
Greenbush Rd.
Orangeburg, NY 10962
(914) 578-5000

Alfa Romeo, Inc.

National Office

Customer Relations Coordinator
250 Sylvan Ave.
Englewood Cliffs, NJ 07632
(201) 871-1234

BMW of North America, Inc.

National Office

Customer Relations Manager
BMW of North America, BMW Plaza
Montvale, NJ 07645
(201) 573-2091

BMW Regional Offices

Eastern Regional Office
Connecticut, Maine,
  Massachusetts, New Hampshire,
  New Jersey, New York, Rhode
  Island, Vermont
Walnut & Hudson Sts.
Norwood, NJ 07648
(201) 784-0145

Central Regional Office
Illinois, Indiana, Iowa, Kentucky,
  Michigan, Minnesota, North
  Dakota, Ohio, South Dakota,
  Wisconsin
1002 East Algonquin Rd.
Schaumburg, IL 60195
(312) 397-5700

Western Regional Office
Arizona, California, Hawaii, Nevada
12541 Beatrice St.
P.O. Box 66916
Los Angeles, CA 90066
(213) 305-2913

Southwest Regional Office
Arkansas, Colorado, Kansas,
 Louisiana, Missouri, Nebraska,
 New Mexico, Oklahoma, Texas,
 Wyoming
2300 Valley View Lane
Suite 300
P.O. Box 819003
Dallas, TX 75381
(214) 484-4840

Northwest Regional Office
Alaska, California, Idaho,
 Montana, Nevada, Oregon,
 Utah, Washington
6606 Owens Dr.
Pleasanton, CA 94566
(414) 463-0725

Southeast Regional Office
Alabama, Florida, Georgia, North
 Carolina, South Carolina,
 Tennessee
6160 Peachtree-Dunwoody Rd.
Suite A-100
Atlanta, GA 30328
(404) 399-5979

Mid-Atlantic Regional Office
Delaware, Maryland, New Jersey,
 New York, North Carolina,
 Pennsylvania, Virginia,
 Washington, D.C., West Virginia
1861 Wiehle Ave.
Suite 300
Reston, VA 22090
(703) 478-2800

Fiat Motors of North America, Inc.

National Office

National Customer Relations Manager
Fiat Auto USA, Inc.
777 Terrace Ave.
Hasbrouck Heights, NJ 07604
(201) 393-4000

American Honda Motor Co., Inc.

National Office

National Customer Affairs Representative
American Honda Motor Co., Inc.
P.O. Box 50
100 W. Alondra Blvd.
Gardena, CA 90247
(213) 327-8280

Honda Zone Offices

Central Zone Office
Indiana, Kentucky, Michigan,
Ohio
6400 Sand Lake Rd.
Dayton, OH 45414
(513) 890-1717

Northeast Zone Office
Connecticut, Massachusetts,
Maine, New Hampshire, New
Jersey, New York, Rhode
Island, Vermont
115 Gaither Dr.
Moorestown, NJ 08057
(609) 235-5333

Mid-Atlantic Zone Office
Delaware, Maryland, North
Carolina, Pennsylvania, Virginia,
Washington, D.C., West Virginia
209 Perry Pkwy.
Suite 10
P.O. Box 610
Gaithersburg, MD 20877
(301) 860-8982

Southeast Zone Office
Alabama, Florida, Georgia, South
Carolina, Tennessee
1500 Morrison Pkwy.
Alpharetta, GA 30201
(404) 587-3096

Southwest Zone Office
Arkansas, Kansas (except
Topeka), Louisiana, Mississippi,
Oklahoma, Texas (except El
Paso)
4525 Royal Lane
Irving, TX 75016-5408
(214) 258-8080

Western Zone Office
Arizona, California, Hawaii,
Nevada, New Mexico, Texas
(except El Paso)
100 West Artesia Blvd.
Compton, CA 90220
(213) 604-2518

Northwest Zone Office
Alaska, Colorado, Idaho,
Montana, Nebraska, North
Dakota, Oregon, South Dakota,
Utah, Washington, Wyoming
12439 N.E. Airport Way
Portland, OR 97220
(503) 256-0943

North Central Zone Office
Illinois, Iowa, Minnesota,
Missouri, Wisconsin
139 W. Central Rd.
Schaumberg, IL 60195
(312) 991-9787

American Isuzu Motors, Inc.

National Office

National Customer Relations Manager
American Isuzu Motors, Inc.
2300 Pellissier Place
Whittier, CA 90601
Mail: P.O. Box 2280
City of Industry, CA 91746
(213) 949-0611

Isuzu Regional Offices

Central Region
Illinois, Indiana, Iowa, Kansas,
  Michigan, Minnesota, Missouri,
  Nebraska, North Dakota, Ohio,
  South Dakota, Wisconsin
898 Cambridge Dr.
Elk Grove Village, IL 60007
(312) 952-8111

Northeast Region
Connecticut, Delaware, Maine,
  Massachusetts, New Hampshire,
  New Jersey, New York,
  Pennsylvania, Rhode Island,
  Vermont
One Bredfe Plaza
Suite 400
Fort Lee, NJ 07024
(201) 934-0755

Southeast Region
Alabama, Arkansas, Florida,
  Georgia, Kentucky, Louisiana,
  Maryland, Mississippi, North
  Carolina, South Carolina,
  Tennessee, Virginia, West
  Virginia
4258 Communications Dr.
P.O. Box 6250
Norcross, GA 30093
(404) 923-6700

Western Region
Arizona, California, Colorado,
  Idaho, Montana, Nevada, New
  Mexico, Oklahoma, Oregon,
  Texas, Utah, Washington,
  Wyoming
2300 Pellissier Pl.
Whittier, CA 90601
Mail: P.O. Box 2310
City of Industry, CA 91746
(213) 695-7411

Jaguar Cars, Inc.

National Office

National Service Manager
Jaguar Cars, Inc.
600 Willow Tree Rd.
Leonia, NJ 07605
(201) 592-5200

Jaguar Zone Offices

Eastern Zone
Alabama, Arkansas, Connecticut,
  Delaware, Florida, Georgia,
  Iowa, Illinois, Indiana, Kansas,
  Kentucky, Louisiana, Maine,
  Maryland, Massachusetts,
  Michigan, Minnesota,
  Mississippi, Missouri, Nebraska,
  New Hampshire, New Jersey,
New York, North Carolina,
North Dakota, Tennessee,
Texas, Vermont, Virginia,
Washington, D.C., West
Virginia, Wisconsin
600 Willow Tree Rd.
Leonia, NJ 07605
(201) 592-5200

Western Zone
Alaska, Arizona, California,
  Colorado, Hawaii, Idaho,
  Montana, New Mexico, Nevada,
  Oregon, Utah, Washington,
  Wyoming
422 Valley Dr.
Brisbane, CA 94005
(415) 467-9402

Lotus Performance Cars, Inc.

National Office

530 Walnut St.
Norwood, NJ 07648
(201) 784-0726

Mazda Motors of America

Eastern Regional Distributor

Customer Relations Manager
Mazda Motors of America (East), Inc.
8313 Baycenter Rd.
Jacksonville, FL 32216
(904) 731-4010

Western Regional Distributor

Manager, Office of Consumer Communications
Mazda Motors of America (Central), Inc.
3040 East Ana St.
Rancho Dominguez, CA 90221
(213) 537-2332

Mazda Zone Offices

Mazda Distributors Pacific
Arizona, California, Colorado,
  Nevada, New Mexico, Utah,
  Wyoming
9451 Toledo Way
Irvine, CA 92714
(714) 380-7705

Mazda Distributors Gulf
Arkansas, Iowa, Kansas,
  Kentucky, Louisiana,
  Mississippi, Missouri, Nebraska,
  Oklahoma, Tennessee, Texas
10445 Corporate Dr.
Sugar Land, TX 77478
(713) 240-5800

Mazda Distributors Northwest
Alaska, Idaho, Minnesota,
  Montana, North Dakota,
  Oregon, South Dakota,
  Washington
8621 South 180th St.
P.O. C-8010
Kent, WA 98031
(206) 251-5920

Mazda Distributors Great Lakes
Illinois, Indiana, Michigan, Ohio,
  Wisconsin
618 Kenmoor Ave., S.E.
Grand Rapids, MI 49506
(616) 949-7570

Mazda Motors of America (East),
Inc.
Alabama, Connecticut, Delaware,
  Florida, Georgia, Maine,
  Maryland, Massachusetts, New
  Hampshire, New Jersey, New
  York, North Carolina,
  Pennsylvania, Rhode Island,
  South Carolina, Virginia,
  Vermont, Washington, D.C.,
  West Virginia
8313 Baycenter Rd.
Jacksonville, FL 32216
Mail: P.O. Box 16305
Jacksonville, FL 32245-6305
(904) 731-4010

Mercedes-Benz of North America, Inc.

National Office

Manager, Owner Service
Mercedes Benz of North America, Inc.
One Mercedes Dr.
Montvale, NJ 07645
(201) 573-0600

Mercedes-Benz Zone Offices

New York Zone
Attention: Service Dept.
One Glenview Rd.
P.O. Box 277
Montvale, NJ 07645
(201) 573-2501

Washington Zone
Attention: Service Dept.
5530 Wisconsin Ave.
Chevy Chase, MD 20815
(301) 654-1676

Jacksonville Zone
Attention: Service Dept.
8813 Western Way
P.O. Box 17604
Jacksonville, FL 32245
(904) 731-4040

Chicago Zone
Attention: Service Dept.
3333 Charles St.
Franklin Park, IL 60131
(312) 455-9131

Houston Zone
Attention: Service Dept.
9550 North Loop East
P.O. Box 24396
Houston, TX 77229
(713) 675-6126

San Francisco Zone
Attention: Service Dept.
513 Eccles Ave.
South San Francisco, CA 94080
(415) 871-5125

Los Angeles Zone
Attention: Service Dept.
851 East Watsoncenter

P.O. Box 4625
Los Angeles, CA 90745
(213) 835-8315

Mitsubishi Motor Sales of America

National Office

National Consumer Relations Manager
Mitsubishi Motor Sales of America, Inc.
West Office Tower
10540 Talbert Ave.
Fountain Valley, CA 92708
(714) 963-7677

Mitsubishi Regional Offices

Western Regional Office
6450 W. Katella
Cypress, CA 90630
(800) 521-0749
(800) 621-0185 (within California)

Eastern Regional Office
Pureland Industrial Complex
516 Heron Dr.
Bridgeport, NJ 08014
(609) 467-1772
(800) 222-0037
(800) 222-0268 (within New Jersey)

Nissan Motor Corporation

National Office

National Consumer Affairs Manager
Nissan Motor Corp., U.S.A.
18501 S. Figueroa St.
Carson, CA 90248-4504
P.O. Box 191
Gardena, CA 90247-7638
(213) 532-3111

Nissan Regional Offices

Boston Regional Office
777 West St.
P.O. Box 198
Mansfield, MA 02048-0198
(617) 339-3721

Chicago Regional Office
51 Shore Dr.
P.O. Box 510
Hinsdale, IL 60521-0510
(312) 325-9050

Columbus Regional Office
150 E. Wilson Bridge Rd.
Suite 100
P.O. Box 6
Worthington, OH 43085
(614) 846-6900

Dallas Regional Office
13405 N. Stemmons Freeway
Farmers Branch, TX 75234-5767
P.O. Box 814450
Dallas, TX 75381-4450

Denver Regional Office
11000 E. 45th Ave.
P.O. Box 39729
Denver, CO 80239-0729
(303) 371-4230

Jacksonville Regional Office
8743 Western Way
P.O. Box 2279
Jacksonville, FL 32203-2279
(904) 737-7100

Los Angeles Regional Office
1683 Sunflower Ave.
P.O. Box 5555
Costa Mesa, CA 92628-5555
(714) 549-1277

Memphis Regional Office
5775 Summer Trees Dr.
P.O. Box 34848
Memphis, TN 38184-0848
(901) 372-5700

New York Regional Office
Number 4 Corporate Pl.
P.O. Box 242
Pascataway, NJ 08854-0242
(201) 981-0220

Norfolk Regional Office
151 Harbor Dr.
P.O. Box 1057
Portsmouth, VA 23705-1057
(804) 399-4011

Portland Regional Office
17853 N.W. Cornell Rd.
Beaverton, OR 97006-3273
P.O. Box 4729
Portland, OR 97208-4729
(503) 629-9029

San Francisco Regional Office
355 Wiget Lane
P.O. Box 8028
Walnut Creek, CA 94596-1065
(415) 932-0550

Peugeot Motors of America, Inc.

National Office

National Consumer Affairs Manager
Peugeot Motors of America, Inc.
One Peugeot Plaza
Lyndhurst, NJ 07071
(201) 935-8400

Peugeot Zone Offices

Eastern Zone Office
Connecticut, Delaware, Indiana,
 Maine, Massachusetts, Michigan,
 New Hampshire, New Jersey,
 New York, Ohio, Pennsylvania,
 Rhode Island, Vermont

40 Van Nostrand Ave.
Englewood, NJ 07631
(201) 894-0210

Central Zone Office
Alabama, Arkansas, Colorado,
  Florida, Illinois, Iowa, Kansas,
  Louisiana, Minnesota,
  Mississippi, Nebraska, New
  Mexico, North Dakota,
  Oklahoma, Puerto Rico, South
  Dakota, Southern Georgia,
  Texas, Wisconsin, Wyoming
94444 Old Katy Rd., Suite 108
Houston, TX 77055
(713) 461-9700

Western Zone Office
Alaska, Arizona, California,
  Hawaii, Idaho, Montana,
  Nevada, Oregon, Utah,
  Washington
1020 E. 230th St.
Carson, CA 90745
(213) 549-9880

Eastern Auto Distributors, Inc.
Kentucky, Maryland, Northern
  Georgia, North Carolina, South
  Carolina, Tennessee, Virginia,
  Washington, D.C., West Virginia
933 E. Little Creek Rd.
P.O. Box 14219
Norfolk, VA 23518
(804) 588-1334

Chicago Zone Office
Illinois, Indiana, Iowa, Kansas,
  Michigan, Minnesota, Missouri,
  Nebraska, North Dakota, Ohio,
  South Dakota, Wisconsin
870 Cambridge Dr.
Elkgrove Village, IL 60007
(312) 952-9046

Porsche Cars North America, Inc.

National Office

Customer Relations Manager
Porsche Cars North America, Inc.
200 S. Virginia St.
Reno, NV 89501

Rolls-Royce Motors, Inc.

National Office

Field Service Manager
Rolls-Royce Motors, Inc.
P.O. Box 476
Lyndhurst, NJ 07071
(201) 469-9600

Saab-Scania of America, Inc.

National Office

National Consumer Relations Coordinator
Saab-Scania of America, Inc.
P.O. Box 697
Orange, CT 06477
(203) 795-5671

Saab-Scania Regional Offices

Eastern Region
Connecticut, Delaware, Maine,
  Maryland, Massachusetts, New
  Hampshire, New York,
  Pennsylvania, Rhode Island,
  Vermont, Virginia
P.O. Box 697, Saab Dr.
Orange, CT 06477
(203) 795-1326

Western Region
Arizona, California, Idaho,
  Montana, Nevada, Oregon,
  Utah, Washington
1225 E. Artesia Blvd.
P.O. Box 6202
Carson, CA 90746
(213) 537-3901

Central Region
Arkansas, Colorado, Illinois,
  Indiana, Iowa, Kansas,
  Kentucky, Louisiana, Michigan,
  Mississippi, Missouri, New
  Mexico, Nebraska, North
  Dakota, Ohio, Oklahoma, South
  Dakota, Texas, West Virginia,
  Wisconsin, Wyoming
10415 United Pkwy.
Schiller Park, IL 60176
(312) 671-4920

Subaru of America, Inc.

National Office

National Customer Relations Manager
Subaru of America, Inc.
7040 Central Hwy.
Pennsauken, NJ 08109
(609) 488-8500

Subaru Regional Offices

Subaru of New England
Connecticut, Maine,
  Massachusetts, New Hampshire,
  Rhode Island, Vermont
95 Morse St.
Norwood, MA 02062
(617) 769-5100
(617) 769-4636

Subaru Distributors Corp.
New York, Northern New Jersey
6 Ramland Rd.
Orangeburg, NY 10962
(914) 359-2500

Penn Jersey Subaru, Inc.
Delaware, Southern New Jersey,
  Pennsylvania
Glen Ave. and Foster Rd.
P.O. Box P
Moorestown, NJ 08057
(609) 234-7600

Subaru Atlantic, Inc.
Maryland, North Carolina,
  Virginia, Washington, D.C.,
  West Virginia
8611 Larkin Rd.
P.O. Box 427
Savage, MD 20763
(301) 498-1700

Subaru South, Inc.
Alabama, Arkansas, Louisiana,
  Mississippi, Tennessee
8923 Fourche Dam Pike
Little Rock, AR 72206
(501) 490-2770

Great Lake Subaru, Inc.
Indiana, Kentucky, Michigan,
  Ohio
401 N. Hamilton Rd.
P.O. Box 16513
Columbus, OH 43216
(614) 864-6650

Subaru Mid-America, Inc.
Illinois, Iowa, Minnesota,
  Missouri, North Dakota, South
  Dakota, Wisconsin
301 Mitchell Ct.
Addison, IL 60101
(312) 953-1188

Southeast Subaru, Inc.
Florida, Georgia, South Carolina
P.O. Box 3007
West Palm Beach, FL 33402
(305) 683-3066

Southwest Subaru, Inc.
Oklahoma, Texas
12615 San Pedro
P.O. Box 32906
San Antonio, TX 78216
(512) 496-1441

Subaru Inter-Mountain
Arizona, Colorado, Kansas,
  Missouri, Nebraska, New
  Mexico
15000 East 39th Ave.
Aurora, CO 80011
(303) 371-3820

Subaru of Northern California
Northern California, Northern
  Nevada, Utah
2505 Port St.
P.O. Box 985
West Sacramento, CA 95691

Subaru of Southern California
Southern California, Southern
  Nevada
12 Whatney Dr.
Irvine, CA 92714
(714) 951-6592

Subaru Northwest, Inc.

Alaska, Idaho, Montana, Oregon,
  Washington, Wyoming
8040 East 33rd Dr.

P.O. Box 11293
Portland, OR 97211
(503) 287-4171

Toyota Motor Sales, U.S.A., Inc.

National Office

National Customer Relations
  Administrator
Toyota Motor Sales, U.S.A., Inc.
19001 S. Western Ave.
Torrance, CA 90509
(213) 618-4000

Toyota Regional Offices

Boston Regional Office
Vermont, New Hampshire,
  Massachusetts, Rhode Island
440 Forbes Blvd.
Mansfield, MA 02048
(617) 339-5701

Chicago Regional Office
Minnesota, Wisconsin, Illinois,
  Indiana
500 Kehoe Blvd.
Carol Stream, IL 60187
(312) 260-6249

Cincinnati Regional Office
Michigan, Ohio, Kentucky,
  Tennessee
4550 Creek Rd.
Cincinnati, OH 45242
(513) 745-7500

Denver Regional Office
Nevada, Utah, Vermont,
  Wyoming, Colorado, New
  Mexico, Arizona
9033 E. Easter Pl.
Suite 200
Englewood, CO 80112
(303) 773-1404

Gulf States Regional Office
Texas, Oklahoma, Arkansas,
  Mississippi, Louisiana
10310 Harwin Ave.
Houston, TX 77036
(713) 776-6700

Kansas Regional Office
North Dakota, South Dakota,
  Nebraska, Kansas, Iowa,
  Missouri
11111 N.W. Airworld Dr.
Kansas City, MO 64195
(816) 891-1000

Los Angeles Regional Office
2800 Jamboree Rd.
Newport Beach, CA 92660
(714) 833-8123

Mid-Atlantic Regional Office
Pennsylvania, West Virginia,
  Virginia, Maryland, Delaware,
  Washington, D.C.
6710 Baymeadow Dr.
P.O. Box 1030
Glen Burnie, MD 21061
(301) 760-1500

New York Regional Office
Connecticut, New York
16 Henderson Dr.
West Caldwell, NJ 07006
(201) 575-7600
(201) 575-9044 (Customers Only)

Portland Regional Office
Alaska, Washington, Oregon,
  Idaho, Montana
6111 Northeast 87th Ave.
Portland, OR 97220
(503) 255-6440

San Francisco Regional Office
2451 Bishop Dr.
San Ramon, CA 94583
(415) 829-6000
(415) 829-8010 (Customers Only)

Southeast Regional Office
North Carolina, South Carolina,
  Alabama, Georgia, Florida
1751 Tallyrand Ave.
Jacksonville, FL 32201
(904) 358-3634

Volvo of America Corporation

National Office

National Customer Affairs Manager
Volvo of America Corp.
1 Volvo Dr.
Rockleigh, NJ 07647
(201) 767-4737

Volkswagen of America, Inc.

National Office

Customer Assistance Manager
888 W. Big Beaver
P. O. Box 3951
Troy, MI 48007-3951
(313) 362-6000

Volkswagen of America Regional Offices

Boston Regional Office
Maine, Massachusetts, New
  Hampshire, Rhode Island,
  Vermont
100 Fordham Rd.
Wilmington, MA 01887
(617) 658-6700

World-Wide Volkswagen
Connecticut, New Jersey, New
  York
Greenbush Rd.
Orangeburg, NY 10962
(914) 578-5000

Valley Forge Regional Office
Pennsylvania, Delaware
P.O. Box 830
1001 South Trooper Rd.
Valley Forge, PA 19482
(215) 666-7500

Columbus Regional Office
Indiana, Kentucky, Michigan,
Ohio
1840 MacKenzie Dr.
Columbus, OH 43221
(614) 457-2411

Chicago Regional Office
Illinois, Iowa, Minnesota, North
Dakota, South Dakota
(excluding Rapid City),
Wisconsin
420 Barclay
Lincolnshire, IL 60069
(312) 634-600

Washington, D.C., Regional Office
Maryland, North Carolina,
Virginia, District of Columbia,
West Virginia
9300 George Palmer Hwy.
Lanham, MD 20801
(301) 459-7000

Southeast Regional Office
Alabama, Florida, Georgia, South
Carolina, Tennessee
1940 The Exchange
Atlanta, GA 30339
(404) 955-9000

San Francisco Regional Office
Nevada (Reno), Northern
California
7106 Johnson Industrial Dr.
Pleasanton, CA 94566
(415) 462-8000

Denver Regional Office
Arizona (excluding Yuma),
Colorado, Nevada (excluding
Reno), New Mexico, South
Dakota (Rapid City), Texas (El
Paso), Utah, Wyoming
Greenwood Plaza
7503 Marin Dr. (3-C)
Englewood, CO 80111
(303) 773-6374

Volkswagen Mid-America, Inc.
Arkansas, Kansas, Missouri,
Nebraska
8825 Page Blvd.
St. Louis, MO 63114
(314) 429-8100

San Antonio Region
Louisiana, Mississippi, Oklahoma,
Texas (excluding El Paso)
10515 Gulfdale Dr.
Suite 100
San Antonio, TX 78216
(512) 341-8881

Riveria Motors, Inc.
Alaska, Idaho, Montana, Oregon,
Washington
5 Oaks Industrial Park
Rte. 1
Box 220 VW
Hillsboro, OR 97123
(503) 645-5511

Los Angeles Region
Arizona (Yuma), Southern
California
11300 Playa St.
Culver, CA 90230
(213) 390-8011

Hawaii Operation
2865 Pukolo St.
P.O. Box 3799
Honolulu, HI 96812
(808) 537-4338

appendix C

Better Business Bureau Locations

Where listed, the following toll-free numbers to the Better Business Bureau (BBB) are for *automotive complaints only*. Branch offices are listed only for those states with less than three BBB locations.

Main Office

Council of Better Business Bureaus
1515 Wilson Blvd., 3d Floor
Arlington, VA 22209
(703) 276-0100

Alabama (205) 933-2999 (Call Collect)

Alaska
429 D St.
Suite 213
Anchorage, AK 85014
(907) 276-5901

Arizona (800) 352-3038
4428 North 12th St.
Phoenix, AZ 85014
(602) 264-1721

100 E. Alameda St.
Suite 403
Tucson, AZ 85701
(602) 622-7651

Arkansas (800) 482-8448
1216 South University
Little Rock, AR 72204
(501) 664-7274

California
North (800) 772-2599
South (800) 252-0410

Colorado (800) 332-6446

Connecticut (800) 221-3555

Delaware (800) 368-5638
20 S. Walnut St.
P.O. Box 300
Milford, DE 16663
(302) 856-6969

1901-B West 11th St.
P.O. Box 4085
Wilmington, DE 19807
(302) 652-3833

District of Columbia
1012 14th Street, N.W.
Washington, D.C. 20005
(202) 393-8000

Florida (800) 432-7159

Georgia (800) 282-7765

Hawaii
677 Ala Moana Blvd.
Suite 509
Honolulu, HI 96813
(808) 531-4964 (Call Collect)

Idaho (800) 632-7182
409 West Jefferson
Boise, ID 83702
(208) 342-4649

Illinois (800) 572-6072
35 East Wacker Dr.
Chicago, IL 60601
(312) 444-1188

109 S.W. Jefferson St.
Suite 3050
Peoria, IL 61602
(309) 673-5194

Indiana (800) 622-4800

Iowa (800) 622-8227

Kansas (800) 362-0178
501 Jefferson
Suite 24
Topeka, KS 66607
(913) 232-0454 or 232-0455

300 Kaufman Bldg.
Wichita, KS 67202
(316) 263-3146

Kentucky (800) 722-5080
629 North Broadway
Lexington, KY 40508
(606) 252-4492

844 S. 4th St.
Louisville, KY 40203
(502) 583-6546

Louisiana (800) 392-9468

Maine (800) 322-3236

Maryland (800) 368-5638

Massachusetts (800) 322-3236

Michigan (800) 482-3144
150 Michigan Ave.
Detroit, MI 48226
(313) 962-7566

1 Peoples Bldg.
60 Monroe St., N.W.
Grand Rapids, MI 49503
(616) 774-8236

Mississippi (601) 948-2322 (Call Collect)

Missouri (800) 392-7309

Montana (303) 691-0979 (Call Collect)

Nebraska (800) 642-9332
719 North 48th St.
Lincoln, NE 68504
(402) 467-5261

1613 Farnam St.
Omaha, NE 68102
(402) 346-3033

Nevada (800) 992-3094
1829 East Charleston Blvd.
Suite 103
Las Vegas, NV 89104
(702) 382-7141, 42

372-A Casazza Dr.
P.O. Box 2932
Reno, NV 89505
(702) 322-0657

New Hampshire (800) 852-3757
One Pillsbury St.
Concord, NH 03301
(603) 224-1991

New Jersey (800) 221-3555

New Mexico (800) 432-5196

New York
Downstate (800) 522-3800
Upstate (800) 252-2522

North Carolina (800) 532-0477

**North Dakota (612) 646-4638 (Call
Collect)**

Ohio (800) 545-0209

Oklahoma (800) 522-3654
606 N. Dewey
Oklahoma City, OK 73102
(405) 239-6081, 82, 83

4833 South Sheridan
Suite 412
Tulsa, OK 74145
(918) 664-1266

Oregon (800) 452-6321
520 S.W. Sixth Ave.
Suite 600
Portland, OR 97204
(503) 226-3981

Pennsylvania (800) 462-0425

Puerto Rico
P.O. Box 70212
San Juan, PR 00936
(809) 756-5400
Cable BEBUSBU

Rhode Island (800) 273-2880
248 Weybosset St.
Providence, RI 02903
(401) 272-9800

**South Carolina (704) 375-8305 (Call
Collect)**
1388 Main St.
No. 500
Columbia, SC 29201
(803) 254-2525

608 E. Washington St.
Greenville, SC 29601
(803) 242-5052

**South Dakota (612) 646-4638 (Call
Collect)**

**Tennessee (901) 278-4653 (Call
Collect)**

Texas
North (800) 442-1456
South (800) 392-6911

Utah (800) 662-7182
1588 South Main
Salt Lake City, UT 84115
(801) 487-4656
(801) 377-2611 (Provo)
(801) 399-4701 (Ogden)

Vermont (800) 343-3437

Virginia (800) 368-5638

Washington State (800) 542-1304

West Virginia (800) 368-5638

Wisconsin (800) 242-1555
740 North Plankinton Ave.
Milwaukee, WI 53203
(414) 273-1600

**Wyoming (303) 691-0979 (Call
Collect)**

appendix D

AUTOCAP Locations

Arizona
Arizona Automobile Dealers
  Association
P.O. Box 5438
Phoenix, AZ 85010
(602) 252-2386

California
Northern California Motor Car
  Dealers Association
1244 Larkin St.
San Francisco, CA 94109
(415) 673-2151, 52, or 53

Motor Car Dealers Association of
  Southern California
5757 West Century Blvd.
Los Angeles, CA 90045
(800) 262-1482 (In-State)
(213) 776-0054 (Out-of-State)

San Diego Motor Car Dealers
  Association
2727 Camino del Rio South
Suite 233
San Diego, CA 92108
(619) 296-2265

Colorado
Colorado Automobile Dealers
  Association
517 E. 16th Ave.
Denver, CO 80203
(303) 831-1722

Connecticut
Connecticut Automotive Trades
  Association, Inc.
18 North Main St.
Hartford, CT 06107
(203) 521-8970

Florida
Jacksonville Better Business
  Council
P.O. Box 329
Jacksonville, FL 32201
(904) 725-7366
(Duval County only)

South Florida Automotive Dealers
  Association
9620 N.E. Second Ave.
Miami, FL 33138

(305) 522-2886 (Dade and Monroe
  Counties)
(305) 758-2886 (Broward County)

3015 Exchange Ct.
West Palm Beach, FL 33409
(305) 686-6168 (West Palm Beach)
(305) 272-4445 (Boca Raton and
  Delray)

Georgia
Georgia Automobile Dealers
  Association
1380 West Paces Ferry Rd.
Suite 230
Atlanta, GA 30327
(404) 237-1483

Hawaii
Hawaii Automobile Dealers
  Association
P.O. Box 560
Kailua, HI 96734
(808) 526-0159

Idaho
Idaho Automobile Dealers
  Association
2230 Main St.
Boise, ID 83702
(208) 342-7779

Illinois
Illinois New Car & Truck Dealers
  Association
828 South Second St.
P.O. Box 3045
Springfield, IL 62708
(217) 753-4513

Iowa
Iowa Automobile Dealers
  Association
405 E. First St.
Des Moines, IA 50309
(515) 244-2245

Kansas
Kansas Motor Car Dealers
  Association
Merchants National Bank Bldg.
8th and Jackson
Suite 717
Topeka, KS 66612-1264
(913) 354-4366

Kentucky
Kentucky Automobile Dealers
  Association
123 Walnut St.
P.O. Box 498
Frankfort, KY 40601
(502) 695-3310

Maine
Maine Automobile Dealers
  Association Inc.
P.O. Box 2667
Augusta, ME 04330
(207) 623-3882

Maryland
See Washington, D.C.

Massachusetts
Massachusetts State Automobile
  Dealers Association
59 Temple Place
Room 505
Boston, MA 02111

Michigan
Michigan Automobile Dealers
  Association
1500 Kendale Blvd.
P.O. Box 2525
East Lansing, MI 48823
(800) 292-1923 (In-State)
(517) 351-7800 (Out-of-State)
(Does not cover Macomb,
  Oakland, or Wayne Counties)

Montana
Montana Automobile Dealers
  Association
501 N. Sanders
Helena, MT 59601
(406) 224-2369

New Hampshire
New Hampshire Automobile
  Dealers Association
Rural Rt. 3, Box 12
Concord, NH 13301
(603) 224-2369

New Mexico
New Mexico Automobile Dealers
  Association
510 Second St., N.W.
Suite 202
Albuquerque, NM 87102
(505) 243-1002

New York
Broome County Chamber of
  Commerce
P.O. Box 995
Binghampton, NY 13902
(607) 723-7127
(Broome County only)

Capital District Automobile
  Dealers Association
815 Central Ave.
Albany, NY 12206
(518) 438-0645
(Albany, Saratoga, Schenectady,
  and Troy Counties only)

Niagara Frontier Automobile
  Dealers Association
1144 Wehrle Dr.
Williamsville, NY 14221
(716) 631-8510
(Erie County only)

Rochester Automobile Dealers
  Association
179 Lake Ave.
Rochester, NY 14221
(716) 458-7150

Greater New York Automobile
  Dealers Association
One Hanson Pl.
Room 1212
Brooklyn, NY 11243
(800) 522-3881 (In-State)
(212) 783-2900 (Out-of-State)
(NYC, LI, and Westchester
  County)

New York State Automobile
  Dealers Association
37 Elk St.
Box 7287
Albany, NY 12224
(800) 342-9208 (In-State)
(518) 463-1148 (Out-of-State)
(Serves balance of state)

North Carolina
North Carolina Automobile
  Dealers Association
1029 Wade Ave.
Raleigh, NC 27605
(919) 828-4421

North Dakota
Automobile Dealers Association of
  North Dakota
1325 23rd St. S.
P.O. Box 2524
Fargo, ND 58108
(701) 293-6822

Ohio
Ohio Automobile Dealers
  Association
30 South Young St.
Columbus, OH 43215
(614) 228-6893

Cleveland Automobile Dealers
  Association
1367 E. 6th St.
Suite 300
Cleveland OH 44114
(216) 241-2880
(Metropolitan Cleveland only)

Oklahoma
Tulsa Automobile Dealers
  Association
525 South Main
Suite 210
Tulsa, OK 74103
(918) 587-0141

Oregon
Oregon Automobile Dealers
  Association
P.O. Box 14460
Portland, OR 97214
(503) 233-5044

South Carolina
South Carolina Automobile &
  Truck Dealers Association
1517 Laurel St.
Columbia, SC 29201
(803) 254-4040

South Dakota
South Dakota Automobile Dealers
  Association
3801 S. Kiwanis Ave.
Sioux Falls, SD 57105
(605) 336-2616

Tennessee
Chattanooga Automotive Trade
  Association
P.O. Box 791
Hixson, TN 37343
(615) 842-7636
(Chattanooga area only)

Texas
Texas Automobile Dealers
  Association
1108 Lavaca
P.O. Box 1028
Austin, TX 78767
(512) 476-2686

Utah
Utah Automobile Dealers
  Association
1588 South Main
Salt Lake City, UT 84115
(801) 484-8845

Vermont
Vermont Automotive Trade
  Association
148 State St.
P.O. Box 561
Montpelier, VT 05602
(800) 642-5149 (In-State)
(803) 223-6635 (Out-of-State)

Virginia
Northern Virginia: *See*
  Washington, D.C.

Virginia Automobile Dealers
  Association
1800 W. Grace St.
P.O. Box 5407
Richmond, VA 23220
(804) 359-3578
(Serves balance of state)

Washington State
Puget Sound Automobile Dealers
  Association
805 Lenora St.
Seattle, WA 98121
(800) 552-0746 (In-State)
(206) 623-2423 (Out-of-State)

Washington, D.C.
Automotive Trade Association of
  the National Capital Area
15873 Crabbs Branch Way
Rockville, MD 20855
(301) 670-1110
(Washington, D.C., Northern
  Virginia, Montgomery, and
  Prince Georges counties, MD
  only)

West Virginia
West Virginia Automobile & Truck
  Dealers Association
2101 Washington St., E.
P.O. Box 2028
Charleston, WV 25327
(304) 343-4160

Wisconsin
Wisconsin Automobile & Truck
  Dealers Association
P.O. Box 5345
Madison, WI 53705
(608) 251-3023

Wyoming
Wyoming Automobile Dealers
  Association
523 W. 27th St.
Suite A
Cheyenne, WY 82001
(307) 638-4455

appendix E

Consumer Automotive Manufacturers and Suppliers, Agencies, and Organizations

When calling or writing, contact Customer Assistance or Public Affairs unless otherwise indicated.

Oil Companies

Amoco Oil Company
200 E. Randolph
Chicago, IL 60601
(312) 852-0984

Atlantic Richfield Co.
A.P. 715
515 So. Flower St.
Los Angeles, CA 90071
(213) 486-2165

Chevron, U.S.A., Inc.
P.O. Box 5010
Concord, CA 94524
(800) 243-8766

Conoco, Inc.
Box 2197
Houston, TX 77252
(713) 293-1000

Exxon Oil Company
P.O. Box 2180
Houston, TX 77001
(713) 656-4845

Mobil Oil Corporation
3225 Gallows Rd.
Fairfax, VA 22037
(703) 849-3986

Phillips Petroleum Company
16 A3 Phillips Bldg.
Bartlesville, OK 74004
(918) 661-6172

Shell Oil Company
P.O. Box 2463
Houston, TX 77001
(713) 241-5711

Sohio, B.P. Gulf, Boron
550 Midland Bldg.
Cleveland, OH 44115
(216) 575-1567

Sun Oil Co. (Sunoco)
Customer Relations
1801 Market St.
Philadelphia, PA 19103
(215) 977-3000
(800) 331-3350 (Credit card
  problems only)

Tenneco, Inc.
P.O. Box 2511
Market Dept.
Houston, TX 77001
(713) 757-4018

Texaco, Inc.
2000 Westchester Ave.
White Plains, NY 10650
(914) 253-4145

Tires

Dunlop Tire Corp.
P.O. Box 1109
10 Sheridan Dr.
Buffalo, NY 14240
(716) 879-8300

Firestone Tire & Rubber Company
P. O. Box 81120
Cleveland, OH 44181
(800) 321-1252 (Outside Ohio)
(216) 379-7085

General Tire & Rubber Company
One General St.
Akron, OH 44329
(216) 798-2036

The BF Goodrich Company
500 South Main St.
Akron, OH 44318
(216) 794-4941

Goodyear Tire & Rubber Company
Akron, OH 44316
(216) 794-4941

Michelin Tire Corporation
P.O. Box 19001
Greenville, SC 29602
(803) 234-5000

Uniroyal Tires
1230 Avenue of the Americas
New York, NY 10020
(212) 841-9200

Independent Automotive Organizations

Automobile Protection Association
  (Canadian Consumer Group)
292 St. Joseph Blvd., W.
Montreal, Quebec, Canada H2V
  2N7
(514) 273-1733

Automatic Transmission Rebuilders
  Association
National Business Office
2472 Eastman Ave., Suite 23
Ventura, CA 93003
(805) 654-1700

Center for Auto Safety (Consumer Group)
2001 S. Street, N.W.
Washington, D.C. 20009
(292) 328-7700

National Automobile Dealers Association (New Cars)
8400 Westpark Dr.
McLean, VA 22102
(703) 821-7000

National Automotive Radiator Service Association
1744 Sumneytown Pike
Kulpsville, PA 19943
(215) 368-6766

National Independent Automobile Dealers Association (Used Cars)
600 E. Los Colinas Blvd., Suite 314
Irving, TX 75039
(214) 556-0044

National Institute for Automotive Service Excellence (Mechanic Certif.)
1825 K St., N.W.
Washington, D.C. 20006
(202) 833-9646

National Rehabilitation Information Center (For Handicapped Drivers)
4407 Eighth St., N.E.
Washington, D.C. 20017
(202) 635-5822

National Tire Dealers and Retreaders Association, Inc.
1250 I St., N.W.
Suite 400
Washington, D.C. 20005
(202) 789-2300

Service Station Dealers of America
2021 K St., N.W.
Suite 303
Washington, D.C. 20006
(202) 293-6868

Tire Industry Safety Council
National Press Bldg.
Suite 766
Washington, D.C. 20045
(202) 783-1022

Aftermarket Service Outlets

AAMCO Transmissions, Inc.
One Presidential Blvd.
Bala Cynwyd, PA 19004
(800) 523-0401

K-Mart Corporation
3100 W. Big Beaver
Troy, MI 48084
(313) 643-1000

MAACO Enterprises, Inc.
381 Brooks Rd.
King of Prussia, PA 19406
(215) 265-6606

Midas Muffler International Corp.
225 North Michigan Ave.
Chicago, IL 60601
(800) 621-0144

Montgomery Ward & Co.
One Montgomery Ward Plaza
Chicago, IL 60671
(312) 467-2000

Poly-Guard Rustproofing
Poly-Oleum Corp.
16135 Harper Ave.
Detroit, MI 48224
(313) 882-4600

Precision Tune
3229 W. Mockingbird Lane
Dallas, TX 75235
(317) 649-9283

Sears, Roebuck and Co.
Sears Tower
Chicago, IL 60684
(312) 875-2500

Tuffy Service Center, Inc.
5462 State St.
Saginaw, MI 48603
(517) 792-4040

Zayre Corp.
235 Old Connecticut Path
Framingham, MA 01701
(617) 620-5000

Ziebart Rustproofing Co.
P.O. Box 1290
1290 E. Maple
Troy, MI 48077
(313) 588-4100

Recreational Vehicles

**Recreation Vehicle Dealers
  Association of North America**
3251 Old Lee Hwy.
Suite 500
Fairfax, VA 22030
(703) 591-7130

Mobile Homes

Manufactured Housing Institute
1745 Jefferson Davis Hwy.
Suite 511
Arlington, VA 22202
(703) 979-6620

Motorcycles

Motorcycle Industry Council, Inc.
3151 Airway Ave.
Bldg. P1
Costa Mesa, CA 92626
(714) 241-9251

appendix F

Federal Government Automotive Agencies

For information on, or to report problems with, automotive emissions tests and warranties:

Warranty Complaint
Field Operations and Support Division (EN-397F)
U. S. Environmental Protection Agency
Washington, D.C. 20460
(202) 382-2633

For information on automotive recalls:

Office of Defects Investigation (NEF-10)
National Highway Traffic Safety Administration
Department of Transportation
400 Seventh St., S.W.
Room 5326
Washington, D.C. 20590
(800) 424-9393; from within the 202 area code, 426-0123
Hearing impaired: (800) 424-9153; Washington, D.C. (202) 755-8919
Spanish-speaking operators are also on duty.

To report problems with automotive arbitration programs:

The Bureau of Consumer Protection
U.S. Federal Trade Commission
The Division of Marketing Practices
Warranties Program
Room 238
6th and Pennsylvania, N.W.
Washington, D.C. 20580
(202) 523-1642

For information on manufacturer service bulletins that apply to your vehicle, write:

The National Highway Traffic Safety Administration
Technical Reference Division/NAD-52
400 7th St.
Washington, D.C. 20590

Be sure to include the year, make, model of your vehicle and the vehicle identification number (VIN).

To obtain or report information pertaining to federal highways:

National Highway Institute
Federal Highway Administration
Department of Transportation
400 7th St., S.W.
Room 6404
Washington, D.C. 20590
(202) 426-1153

To obtain or report information pertaining to federal trade practice violations:

U.S. Department of Justice
Consumers Affairs Section
Tenth St., N.W.
Washington, D.C. 20530
(202) 724-6786

Federal Trade Commission Headquarters:

Sixth and Pennsylvania Ave., N.W.
Washington, D.C. 20580
(202) 523-3598

Federal Trade Commission Regional Offices:

1718 Peachtree St., N.W.
Atlanta, GA 30367
(404) 881-4836

55 E. Monroe St.
Chicago, IL 60603
(312) 353-8156

8303 Elmbrook Dr.
Dallas, TX 75247
(214) 767-7050

11000 Wilshire Blvd.
Los Angeles, CA 90024
(213) 209-7575

450 Golden Gate Ave.
San Francisco, CA 94102
(415) 556-1270

150 Causeway St.
Boston, MA 02114
(617) 223-6621

118 St. Clair Ave.
Cleveland, Ohio 44114
(216) 522-4207

26 Federal Plaza
New York, New York 10278
(212) 264-1207

1405 Curtis St.
Denver, CO 80202
(303) 837-2271

915 Second Ave.
Seattle, WA 98174
(206) 442-4655

For general information on vehicle insurance:

Office of Economics
Department of Transportation
400 Seventh St., S.W.
Room 10301
Washington, D.C. 20590
(202) 426-4416

To report odometer tampering, or for information on odometer laws:

Office of Chief Counsel
National Highway Traffic Safety Administration
Department of Transportation
400 7th St., S.W.
Room 5219
Washington, D.C. 20590
(202) 426-1835

For free pamphlets dealing with used-car buying, warranties, and service contracts, write:

The Federal Trade Commission
Department P
Box 37041
Washington, D.C. 20580

For a listing of U.S. Poison Control Centers:

Division of Poison Control
5600 Fishers Lane
Room 1345
HDF 240
Rockville, MD 20857
(301) 443-6260

BIBLIOGRAPHY

CHAPTER 1

Benedetto, Annette C. Assistant Attorney General of the Commonwealth of Massachusetts. Letter to the author, May 23, 1985.

Better Business Bureau. *Tips on Buying A New Car*. Arlington, VA: Council of Better Business Bureaus, Inc., 1982; reprint edition, 1985.

Consumer Reports. *1985 Buying Guide Issue*. Mount Vernon, NY: Consumers Union of the United States Inc., 1984.

Crowther, Sam, and Winehouse, Irwin. *Highway Robbery*. New York: Stein and Day, 1966.

Ditlow, Clarence, Kinnard, Joyce, and Nader, Ralph. *The Lemon Book*. Ottawa, IL: Caroline House Publishing, 1980.

Edmund Publications Corp. *Edmund's 1985 Used Car Prices*. West Hempstead, NY: Edmund Publications Corp., 1985.

Federal Reserve System. The Board of Governors. *Regulation M, Consumer Leasing*. Washington: U.S. Government Printing Office, April 1, 1981.

Federal Trade Commission. *Truth in Leasing*. Washington: U.S. Government Printing Office, February, 1978.

Ford Motor Company. *What Every Woman Should Know Before Buying a Car*. Detroit: Ford Motor Company, 1985.

Gillis, Jack. *The Car Book*. New York: Harper & Row, 1985.

Hertz Corporation. "Hertz Data Helps Explain How to Calculate Car Ownership & Operating Costs." New York: Press release, February, 1985.

Miller, Moss. *Choosing the Right Car for the 1980s*. Blue Ridge Summit, PA: Tab Books, 1984.

Motor Vehicle Manufacturers Association. *MVMA Motor Vehicle Facts & Figures '84*. Detroit: MVMA, 1984.

Pace Publications. *1985 New Car Prices*. Milwaukee, WI: Pace Publications, Inc., 1985.

Risen, James. "The Games That Automakers Play (with Prices)" *Detroit Free Press,* October 10, 1983, 6F.

Simmons, Bill. "Buyers Should Get What They Want from New Cars." *The Detroit Free Press,* July 22, 1985, 1E.

Sutton, Remar M., Jr. *The Insider's Guide to Buying Your Next Car*. New York: Penguin Books, 1982; reprint edition, 1984.

Wheeler, Dennis W. Garrett Corporation, Turbocharger Training Coordinator. Letter to the author, September 7, 1985.

CHAPTER 2

Andrews, Chris. Open letter to the U.S. Federal Trade Commission: Chicago, IL, January 6, 1984.

Better Business Bureau. *Auto Line; Modified Rules for the Arbitration of Automotive Disputes*. Arlington, VA: Council of Better Business Bureaus, Inc., 1984.

Consumer Arbitrator. Arlington, VA: Council of Better Business Bureaus, Inc., Winter/Spring, 1985.

Billings, Roger D., Jr. "Lemon Laws: A Further Word." *Case and Comment* (May–June 1985): 38–40.

_____. *Handling Automobile Warranty and Repossession Cases*. Rochester, NY: The Lawyers Co-Operative Publishing Company, 1984.

_____. *Handling Automobile Warranty and Repossession Cases,* Cumulative Supplement. Rochester, NY: The Lawyers Co-Operative Publishing Company, September, 1985.

_____. Professor, Salmon P. Chase College of Law, Northern Kentucky University. Letter to the author, October 17, 1985.

Brambilla, R.T. Chrysler Corporation, National Coordinator, Third Party Arbitration. Phone interviews, August 28, 1985, and September 5, 1985.

Danielson, Caroline. FTC Research Analyst: Washington, D.C. Telephone interview, August 28, 1985.

Determan, Dean. Vice President of the Council of Better Business Bureaus: Arlington, VA. Telephone interviews, July 17 and 18, 1985.

Ditlow, Clarence. Director of the Center for Auto Safety, Washington, D.C. Telephone interview, July 23, 1984.

_____. Kinnard, Joyce, and Nader, Ralph. *The Lemon Book*. Ottawa, IL: Caroline House Publishing, 1980.

Dowdy, Lemuel. FTC Assistant Director of the Division of Enforcement, Washington, D.C. Phone interview, August 28, 1985.

Federal Trade Commission. *1984 Audit of Chrysler Corporation's Customer Arbitration Board,* Detroit: R.K. McCreight & Associates, December, 1984.

————. *1984 Audit of the Ford Consumers Appeal Board.* Detroit: R.K. McCreight & Associates, December, 1984.

Gillis, Jack. *The Car Book.* New York: Harper & Row, 1985.

Kattan, Joseph. Attorney, Division of Marketing Practices, Federal Trade Commission, Washington, D.C. Telephone interview, July 11, 1985.

————. Attorney, Division of Marketing Practices, Federal Trade Commission, Washington, D.C. Letter to the author, July 12, 1985.

Kilkka, Carl. Ford Motor Company Owner Relations and Service Spokesman. Telephone interview, August 28, 1985.

Slawnik, E. Ann. Detroit BBB Public Relations Coordinator. Telephone interview, July 11, 1985.

————. Detroit BBB Public Relations Coordinator. Letters to the author, July 17, 1985, and October 17, 1985.

Stepanek, Marcia. "GM's Consumer Arbitration Plan Under Fire." *The Detroit Free Press.* July 25, 1985, 5B.

CHAPTER 3

Bazzarone, A.D. *The Car Fix-Up Book.* Shell Answer Book series, No. 10. Houston: Shell Oil Company, 1977.

Billings, Roger D., Jr. *Handling Automobile Warranty and Repossession Cases.* Rochester, NY: The Lawyers Co-Operative Publishing Company, 1984.

————. *Handling Automobile Warranty and Repossession Cases,* Cumulative Supplement. Rochester, NY: The Lawyers Co-Operative Publishing Company, September, 1985.

Bowman, David. Technical Communications Manager, Fram Division: Providence, RI. Phone interview, August 28, 1985; letter to the author, September 11, 1985.

Consumer Reports. *1985 Buying Guide Issue.* Mount Vernon, NY: Consumers Union of the United States Inc., 1984.

Ditlow, Clarence, Kinnard, Joyce, and Nader, Ralph. *The Lemon Book.* Ottawa, IL: Caroline House Publishing, 1980.

Dowdy, Lemuel. Federal Trade Commission, Assistant Director of the Division of Enforcement, Washington, D.C. Telephone interview, August 28, 1985.

Edmund Publications Corp. *Edmund's 1985 Used Car Prices*. West Hempstead, NY: Edmund Publications Corp., 1985.

Fuller, Don. "Used Rentals" *Motor Trend* (June 1985): 37(6) p. 82.

Hertz Corporation. "New Car Ownership & Operating Costs Climb 2.4-Cents to 45.67-Cents a Mile in 1984." February, 1985.

Jaskoske, Jim. *The Longer Car Life Book*. Shell Answer Book series, No. 31. Houston: Shell Oil Company, 1982.

Maynard, Micheline. "Used Car Sales Reported at High." *The Detroit Free Press*. June 18, 1984, 6D.

Morse, Richard. Chief Odometer Fraud Staff, National Highway Traffic Safety Administration, Washington, D.C. Telephone interview, September 24, 1985.

Nerad, Jack R. "America's Top 40," "The 10 Worst," *Motor Trend* (June 1985) (37; 6) 64,72.

Orme, Ted. "Cheap Buys" *Motor Trend* (June 1985): 37(6) p. 78.

Plave, Lee J. Attorney, Federal Trade Commission, Bureau of Consumer Protection, Washington, D.C. Letter to the author, September 19, 1985.

Shulman, Nat. "A Pro Talks" *Motor Trend* (June 1985): 37(6) p. 88.

Toyota Motor Sales, USA. "Consumer Reports Rates Toyota Quality Tops." *Toyota Today:* Torrance, CA, 1985.

U.S. Federal Trade Commission. *Used Car Buying: A Checklist*. Washington, D.C.: Bureau of Consumer Protection, August, 1983.

————. *Federal Register,* volume 49, number 224. November 19, 1984.

————. *Buying a Used Car*. Washington, D.C.: Bureau of Consumer Protection, May, 1985.

————. *Warranties: Making Business Sense Out of Warranty Law, An FTC Manual for Businesses*. Washington, D.C.: Bureau of Consumer Protection.

CHAPTER 4

The American Automobile Association. *AAA 1985 Towing Manual*. Falls Church, VA: American Automobile Association, 1985.

Brooks, Al. *The Car Crime Prevention Book*. Shell Answer Book series, No. 9. Houston, TX: Shell Oil Company, 1977.

Edmund Publications Corp. *Edmund's Auto-Pedia*. West Hempstead, NY: Edmund Publications Corp., 1984.

Farina, Alfred J. Research Psychologist, National Highway Traffic Safety Administration. Phone interview, September 15, 1985.

Galbraith, Bruce. *The Foul Weather Driving Book*. Shell Answer Book series, No. 11. Houston, TX: Shell Oil Company, 1977.

Gillespie, Paul, and Kippler, Miriam. *No-Fault*. New York: Praeger Publishers, 1972.

Hall, Dick. *The Emergency Repair Book*. Shell Answer Book series, no. 13. Houston, TX: Shell Oil Company, 1978.

Insurance Information Institute. "How to File an Insurance Claim." New York: Insurance Information Institute, November, 1984.

_____. "Insurance for the Car." New York: Insurance Information Institute, March, 1985.

_____. "Auto Insurance Basics." New York: Insurance Information Institute, March, 1985.

_____. *Sharing the Risk*, rev. ed. New York: Colortone Press, March, 1985.

_____. *Property and Casualty Fact Book*. New York: Colortone Press, in press.

Jensen, Chris. "Save That Corvette." *Corvette Fever*. Fort Washington, MD: Prospect Publishing Co., December, 1982.

Laitner, Bill. "Fall Car Care Saves Time, Money, Your Hands." *The Detroit Free Press*, September 30, 1985, 2E.

Lauer, A. R. *The Psychology of Driving: Factors of Traffic Enforcement*. Springfield, IL: Thomas Publishing, 1960; rev. ed., 1972.

Myers, Kenneth. Ford Motor Company Parts and Service Division, Dearborn, MI. Phone interview, December 19, 1985.

Rosenau, Andrews. "Assembling An Emergency Tool Kit." *Fram/Autolite Car Care*. Shrewsbury, NJ: Aqua-Field Publications, Inc., 1985.

U.S. Department of Transportation. *Compensating Auto Accident Victims: A Follow-up Report on No-Fault Auto Insurance Experiences*. Washington, D.C.: U.S. Government Printing Office, May 1985.

Utz, Fred. *Collision Course*. Moore Haven, FL: Rainbow Books, 1984.

Walsh, Richard F. Director of the Office of Economics, Department of Transportation, Washington, D.C. Telephone interview, September 20, 1985.

Wiggers, Charles. Statistician, Office of Economics, Department of Transportation, Washington, D.C. Telephone interview, October 18, 1985.

Zavada, Mary. Director of Press Relations, Insurance Information Institute. Letter to the author, August 30, 1985.

CHAPTERS 5 and 6

Bame, John. *The Gasoline Book*. Shell Answer Book series, No. 19. Houston, TX: Shell Oil Company, 1979.

Chaikin, Don. "Keep Spark Plugs Firing." *Home Mechanix* (March 1985): 80 (683) p. 29.

Ditlow, Clarence, Kinnard, Joyce, and Nader, Ralph. *The Lemon Book*. Ottawa, IL: Caroline House Publishing, 1980.

Dodge, Russell. "What's New Under the Hood." *Fram/Autolite Car Care*. Shrewsbury, NJ: Aqua-Field Publications, Inc., 1985.

Duca, Frank A., Jr. "Sizing Up Your Chevy's Shoes." *Friends Magazine* (May, 1985): 42(5) p. 28. Warren, MI: Ceco Communications, 1985.

Dunphy, John. "Before You Fill 'er Up, Check for Gasoline Blend." *The Detroit Free Press*. February 26, 1984, C3.

Edmund Publications Corp. *Edmund's Auto-Pedia*. West Hempstead, NY: Edmund Publications Corp., 1984.

Emanuel, Dave. "Performance Tuning the Chevy Small Block." *Corvette Fever* (November/December, 1983): 5(6) pp. 48–51.

English, James H., and Rowley, Alan B. Interview on the evolution of batteries and applications, Anderson, IN: Delco-Remy Plant (May 29, 1985).

Fremon, George, and Fremon, Suzanne. *Why Trade It In?* Cockeysville, MD: Liberty Publishing Company, 1983.

Gillis, Jack. *The Car Book*. New York: Harper & Row, 1985.

Glickman, Arthur P. *Mr. Badwrench*. New York: Wideview Books, 1981.

Hansen, Mark L. Product Specialist. Detroit, MI: AC Spark Plugs. Letter to the author, August 8, 1985.

Jelker, Donald. "Filtering Out Major Problems." *Fram/Autolite Car Care*. Shrewsbury, NJ: Aqua-Field Publications, Inc., 1985.

Jones, Harry. *The On-the-Spot Repair Book*. Shell Answer Book series, no. 29. Houston, TX: Shell Oil Company, 1982.

Judson, Howard. *The Car Repair Shopping Book*. Shell Answer Book series, no. 8. Houston, TX: Shell Oil Company, 1977.

Kacev, Les. Inventor of Beep 'n' Keep. Telephone interview, February 16, 1985.

Koblenz, Jay. "Tires and Wheels . . . A Delicate Balance. *"Fram/Autolite Car Care*. Shrewsbury, NJ: Aqua-Field Publications, Inc., 1985.

Laidlaw, Angus. "How to Choose a Mechanic." *Fram/Autolite Car Care*. Shrewsbury, NJ: Aqua-Field Publications, Inc., 1985.

Laitner, Bill. "When It Comes to Tires, Inflation Can Be a Good Thing." *The Detroit Free Press*. February 20, 1984, E3.

————. "Dump Car Wastes Wisely." *The Detroit Free Press*. November 26, 1984, C3.

————. "Unibodies Multiply Fix-Up Concerns." *The Detroit Free Press*. July 30, 1984, E3.

————. "Great Gifts for Drivers." *The Detroit Free Press*. December 3, 1984, C2.

Lankard, Tom. "The Leaded Fuel Controversy," *AutoWeek* (April 22, 1985): 22.

"Mechanics Advisory Panel." *Motor Service* (June 1985): 28–31.

Miller, John R. "Oil . . . A Change for the Better." *Fram/Autolite Car Care.* Shrewsbury, NJ: Aqua-Field Publications, Inc., 1985

Motorcraft Service News Bulletin. "Battery Care." April 22, 1977, Number 77-7.

_____. "Cooling System Operation and Maintenance." April 1979, Number 79-16.

Murphy, Janet. Environmental Protection Agency Attorney/Advisor. Letter to the author, September 25, 1985.

"New Products That Lend Class to Any Car." *Popular Mechanics* (May 1985): 162(5) pp. 192–196.

Prendergast, Matt. "Plugging for Performance." *Popular Hot Rodding* (August 1984): 30–32, 103.

Ross, James R. *How to Get 50,000 More Miles Out of Your Car.* New York: St. Martin's Press, 1982.

Sandberg, Cal. "Premium Leaded Fuel, Going . . . Going . . . ." *Corvette News.* Warren, MI: Chevrolet Motor Division, 1983.

Schultz, Mort. "Car Clinic" *Popular Mechanics* (October 1985): 162(10) p. 29.

Sikorsky, Robert. *Drive It Forever.* New York: McGraw-Hill, 1983.

Taylor, Richard. "Fluids . . . The Lifeblood of Your Car. *Fram/Autolite Car Care.* Shrewsbury, NJ: Aqua-Field Publications, Inc., 1985.

Tire Industry Safety Council. "Questions & Answers on Voluntary Tire Registration." Washington, D.C. Press release, April 15, 1985.

Visser, Ben. *The Tune-Up Book.* Shell Answer Book series, No. 18. Houston, TX: Shell Oil Company, 1979.

CHAPTER 7

Antonius, Kurt. American Honda Assistant Manager Corporate Public Relations, Gardena, CA. Phone interview, July, 1984.

Ditlow, Clarence. Center for Auto Safety Director, Washington, D.C. Phone interview, July, 1984.

_____. Kinnard, Joyce, and Nader, Ralph. *The Lemon Book.* Ottawa, IL: Caroline House Publishing, 1980.

Fawcett, Carl. Nissan National Warranty Manager. Carson, CA. Phone interview, September 13, 1985.

Foley, Tina. National Highway Traffic Safety Administration, Public Affairs Specialist, Technical Reference Division. Phone interview, September 12, 1985.

Franklin, Stephen, and Stepanek, Marcia. "Unanswered Recalls: Who Gets the Blame?" *The Detroit Free Press.* Washington, D.C.: May 22, 1983, 13A.

Hudgens, J. David. General Motors Customer Relations and Service Staff Spokesman, Detroit. Phone interview, September 6, 1985.

Lesko, Matthew. *Information U.S.A.* New York: Penguin Books, 1983.

Morales, Matthew. Toyota National Customer Relations Analyst, Torrance, CA. Phone interview, July, 1984.

Murphy, Gerard N. President, Automotive Consumer Action Program, the National Automobile Dealers Association, McLean, VA. Phone interview, July, 1984.

O'Neill, Thomas. Chrysler Manager Warranty Administration, Highland Park, MI. Phone interview, July, 1984.

Rhoades, Thomas. Ford Motor Company, Parts and Service Public Affairs Manager, Dearborn, MI. Phone interview, July, 1984.

Simmons, Bill. "Carmaker's Suggestion Is Makeshift Protection," *The Detroit Free Press.* September 9, 1985, 1C.

Tomlinson, Phillip. Volkswagen of America, warranty section. Phone interview, September 12, 1985.

Zinger, Donald E. "Emission Performance of Properly Maintained Vehicles." Warrendale, PA: SAE Technical Paper series, May 20, 1985.

Index

About the Author

Michael Spaniola is a Detroit native experienced in automotive mechanics and in automotive diagnostic, technical, and new-car review writing. His background includes work in production assembly, new-car dealership, custom conversions, and stock car racing.

He is a member of the National Panel of Consumer Arbitrators for the Council of Better Business Bureaus, Detroit Automotive Editor for Hunter Publishing Co. of Chicago, and has been a contributing writer to a number of national magazines, including *Home Mechanix, Best Reports, Car Review, Family Handyman,* and *Motor Magazine.*

Catalog

If you are interested in a list of fine Paperback
books, covering a wide range of subjects
and interests, send your name and address,
requesting your free catalog, to:

McGraw-Hill Paperbacks
1221 Avenue of Americas
New York, N.Y. 10020